Affective Labor and Alt-Ac Careers

RETHINKING CAREERS, RETHINKING ACADEMIA

Joseph Fruscione and Erin Bartram, *Series Editors*

Affective Labor and Alt-Ac Careers

Edited by
Lee Skallerup Bessette

University Press of Kansas

Published by the University Press of Kansas (Lawrence, Kansas 66045), which was organized by the Kansas Board of Regents and is operated and funded by Emporia State University, Fort Hays State University, Kansas State University, Pittsburg State University, the University of Kansas, and Wichita State University.

Library of Congress Cataloging-in-Publication Data

Names: Bessette, Lee Skallerup, 1977– editor.
Title: Affective labor and alt-ac careers / Lee Skallerup Bessette, editor.
Other titles: Affective labor and alternative academic careers
Description: Lawrence, Kansas : University Press of Kansas, 2022 | Series: Rethinking Careers, Rethinking Academia | Includes bibliographical references and index.
Identifiers: LCCN 2021027387
ISBN 9780700632985 (Paperback)
ISBN 9780700632992 (eBook)
Subjects: LCSH: College administrators—Psychology—United States. | Teacher-administrator relationships—United States. | Emotions—Social aspects. | Work—Psychological aspects. | Motivation in education. | Affective education.
Classification: LCC LB2341 .A34 2022 | DDC 378.1/01—dc23/eng/20211213
LC record available at https://lccn.loc.gov/2021027387.

British Library Cataloguing-in-Publication Data is available.

Printed in the United States of America

10 9 8 7 6 5 4 3 2 1

The paper used in this publication is acid free and meets the minimum requirements of the American National Standard for Permanence of Paper for Printed Library Materials Z39.48-1992.

To my mentors, thank you for believing in me,
even when I didn't believe in myself.

Contents

Series Editors' Foreword

❖ ❖ ❖ ❖ ❖ ❖ ❖

Let's go back for a moment to the summer of 2018.

We'd just announced on Twitter that we were collaborating on the Rethinking Careers, Rethinking Academia series. Almost immediately, Joe got a message from Lee Skallerup Bessette expressing her interest in something related to a project about alt-ac work and affect. "THIS IS WHAT I WANT TO DO," she said from the get-go. She was clearly ready.

A little after lunch, she wrote again: "So apparently I've been thinking A LOT about this." She included a call for submissions she'd drafted, already showing her signature energy and enthusiasm for the nascent project. Given her tweeting and blogging about the emotional elements of her work in academia, Lee seemed the ideal person to lead such a project, so it's no surprise that she was poised to do so when the series wasn't even a day old.

And now, almost four years later, we give you Lee's fantastic collection, *Affective Labor and Alt-Ac Careers*. Its fourteen chapters and editorial introduction and conclusion give readers a multifaceted look at the intellectual and emotional labor involved in the work its contributors do. "I wanted a space," she writes in her emotionally resonant introduction, "where disparate 'alt-ac' roles within the university could come together to share our profession's knowledge and experiences with affective labor, to share our stories, and hopefully to find solidarity." *Affective Labor and Alt-Ac Careers* is this necessary space—and more.

The contributors share the labor and emotional through-lines of their work in educational development, the writing center, librarianship, and other parts integral to the twenty-first century college or university. Lee's shepherding of this collection from inception to publication was the affective labor crucial to helping others understand the *work*—not just daily tasks and action items a senior administrator might look for—that academic support staff do. What does it mean to "act like staff" and "act like faculty" in modern academia? More pointedly, what does it take—affectively—to navigate these questions while working with students, faculty, fellow staff members, and others? *Affective Labor and Alt-Ac Careers* advances these and other questions as we continue to rethink the careers offered, enabled, and complicated by academia.

Joseph Fruscione and Erin Bartram
Series Editors

Affective Labor and Alt-Ac Careers

Introduction

LEE SKALLERUP BESSETTE

❖ ❖ ❖ ❖ ❖ ❖ ❖

"You need to learn how to behave like staff."

This was the moment that the idea of this book was born. I was sitting in my supervisor's office, a few months after having received a generally positive annual review for my work as a faculty developer, my new alt-ac career, completely blindsided by the comment, which was followed by an hour lecture outlining every single one of my failings and weaknesses. I had designed and delivered a dozen successful workshops, worked effectively and collaboratively with another unit in the service of a large internal grant, developed and maintained an internal communication plan, and did the usual activities associated with being in faculty development and technology. I was led to believe that I was doing a good job.

Wait, I *was* doing a good job.

But my behavior still carried too many holdovers from when I was faculty—contingent faculty, but faculty nonetheless. Despite the disrespect from so-called colleagues, I still carried myself like faculty. I wasn't prepared to be rebuked for carrying myself that way in my new role as a faculty developer, as *staff* who were there to offer services and support to faculty, as my supervisor (a woman tenured faculty member) liked reminding us. I knew I had skills I had to work on—like active listening, for instance—and I was beginning to understand the affective labor I had to engage in in my interactions with faculty and administrators.

But I wasn't prepared for just how much affective labor was going to be required of me. Heck, I didn't even know what affective labor *was*, let alone have the language to describe and understand what was being asked of me. I didn't expect to be rebuffed in such a direct and, honestly, condescending way. I had in fact misstepped in an interaction, but the result of that misstep seemed outsized to the infraction. And if my "behavior" had been such a problem, why did I not hear about it during my recent evaluation? But of course I didn't, couldn't, say any of this, as that would not have been very staff-life behavior.

My infraction boiled down to having an informed opinion based on experience and expertise that didn't agree with the opinion of a tenured (male) faculty administrator that I insisted on a little too forcefully. There was an offer for me to be mentored by a much younger woman who also had a PhD and was thriving as said tenured (male) faculty administrator's assistant. All I could hear in my head were all of the gendered messages implicit in this rebuke: be seen, not heard; quiet competence; be gentle; remain placid; don't show off.

This interaction, and the misstep, along with my reaction and the aftermath, were held against me as not behaving like staff. Furthermore, my tendency to blurt things out, my loudness, my disorganized desk, my inability to stay focused in large meetings, while also sometimes being too intense in one-on-one consultations, my chronic inability to remember people's names—these weren't very "staff"-like behaviors; more often than not, I could cover them up and spent a lot of energy coping, trying to behave like staff, even if it didn't seem like it. I would come home exhausted not from the explicit work itself but from managing my emotions and reactions to fulfill a certain expectation of my behavior. These were behaviors that were largely overlooked, ignored, or even celebrated as an instructor but made me look un-staff-like.

There were other elements at my job that I was excellent at and that ultimately sustained and fulfilled me: being able to juggle multiple projects, having wide and varied interests, learning quickly and effectively about new things, as well as being able to write quickly and well and to improvise in a variety of situations. My work, my deliverables, were outstanding, as my recent evaluation had shown. But it was product versus process—the product was good, but the process was faulty. I was faulty. So the work, I was basically being told, didn't matter. What mattered was how *I* was perceived.[1]

I saw my alt-ac position as a long-awaited and well-earned opportunity to continue doing work that I enjoyed and was good at in an academic setting with a commensurate salary, benefits, job title, stability, and respect—all things that I didn't have as a contingent faculty member. I had on rose-colored glasses, and to be honest, anything looked better than what I had been doing before. Why didn't anyone warn me that with this new role came with a whole new set of gendered, ableist, classist, and racialized expectations?

As we say in the South: *bless my heart.*

Well, people *had* warned me, but again, the way out of contingency blinded me to anything but getting out. You wouldn't be the first person, as you read this, to shake your head at how naive I was. But my drawn-out period as a contingent faculty member shifted my perspective, causing a distorted view of the alt-ac job as *the* way out. As described in Sendhil Mullainathan and Eldar Shafir's book *Scarcity*,[2] I had fallen into a scarcity trap, with not enough bandwidth to process and understand the various consequences of the alt-ac role I had long coveted. Contingency has its own way of demanding affective labor, and the transition out of contingency was another layer of emotional work to unpack and process. I just didn't know it yet.

Like a good academic facing a problem that was ill-defined and thus impossible to solve, I started to research and read. I searched for the language I needed, the frameworks necessary to articulate and process what I was experiencing. I had long written about "feelings" on my blog (and was resoundingly called out for it, repeatedly, in the comments), but was finally starting to explore affective studies. While there was a growing body of literature and writing about teaching and emotions/emotional labor, I hadn't found anything that specifically addressed *staff*.

And then my friend and colleague Paige Morgan wrote and published "Not Your DH Teddy Bear"[3] in *DH+Lib*. This is where I will forever be grateful for Twitter in particular, because I don't know if I ever would have found this piece had I not known Paige via Twitter and began following her work and the work of other digital humanities (DH) librarians. I read about affective labor and *The Managed Heart* for the first time, and something clicked—I wasn't crazy and I wasn't alone. I read Bethany Nowviski writing about an ethics of care in DH and libraries,[4] while Alexis Logsdon, Amy Mars, and Heather Thompson wrote about the emotional labor of being "betwixt and between" as digital librarians.[5] When I shared the latter article with one of my colleagues, she almost burst into tears, as what the authors described exactly matched her own experience.

These texts gave me the language to articulate what the difference is between acting like faculty and acting like staff; I approached my interactions with faculty like I was their peer, their colleague, rather than someone who was in a lower-status position. I had to do a better job of managing my emotions and reactions, and instead prioritize the emotions of the faculty. This is the very definition of emotional labor, as first defined by Hochschild in *The Managed Heart:* to "induce or suppress feeling in order to sustain the outward countenance that produces the proper state of mind in others."[6]

Certainly, I thought, I wasn't alone in feeling this way as a faculty developer. I began searching for similar writing and theorizations in faculty development literature. I crowdsourced a relatively sparse list, and it was lacking. One article used clearly racist colonial theories of "passing" to describe the positionality of faculty developers, while others talked around the issue of emotional labor, instead focusing on empirical data and structural tensions.[7] Certainly, there were a number of articles concerning the gendered nature of faculty development work, but, again, they talked around the issue of emotional labor. Adrien Kelly, who was also looking at intimacy and faculty development,[8] and Catherine Manathunga, who was applying postcolonial theories to better theorize faculty development,[9] were the only two who really didn't shy away from discussing and theorizing the affective and emotional labor involved in faculty development.

So what *is* affective and emotional labor? The phenomenon has long been studied within various professions, but primarily within service professions. The aforementioned book, *The Managed Heart: Commercialization of Human Feeling,* by sociologist Arlie Russell Hochschild, was the first to identify and define emotional labor. As for affective labor, Michael Hardt and Antonio Negri differentiate it from other kinds of emotional labor as follows:

> Unlike emotions, which are mental phenomena, affects refer equally to body and mind. In fact, affects, such as joy and sadness, reveal the present state of life in the entire organism, expressing a certain state of the body along with a certain mode of thinking. Affective labor, then, is labor that produces or manipulates affects. . . . One can recognize affective labor, for example, in the work of legal assistants, flight attendants, and fast-food workers (service with a smile). One indication of the rising importance of affective labor, at least in the dominant countries, is the tendency for employers to highlight education, attitude, character, and "prosocial" behavior as the primary skills employees need. A worker with a good attitude and social skills is another way of saying a worker is adept at affective labor.[10]

Sarah Ahmed, in her book *The Cultural Politics of Emotion,* takes the concept of affect one step further in staking the claim that affect is "what sticks" and goes on to show how affect shapes societies, norms, and our worklife.[11] In other words, *emotional labor* is what we are asked to manage within ourselves, while *affective labor* involves managing other people's emotions. What we are being asked to do, in our roles and in the affective labor that comes with it, is to work to ensure that the university continues to function smoothly; that we shape the way our faculty approach the upcoming semesters in order for students to have well-designed learning experiences. As put by Alicia Grandley, "Emotional labor, then, is the process of regulating both feelings and expressions for the organizational goals."[12] As the two concepts have evolved in parallel and with much overlap in definitions, the two terms will be used interchangeably throughout.

Emotional labor is very much still undertheorized within higher education more generally[13] and in faculty development more specifically.[14] Lisa Sloniowski explores affective labor in the library profession, and her mission to explore this undertheorized and under-discussed issue mirrors our own. Substitute "academic librarian" for "alt-ac staff" when reading her article and we can understand why this kind of examination is important because it "acknowledges dependence on the often invisible pink collar labor of academic librarians in [knowledge and education] production processes."[15] This collection, then, is an attempt to expand the scholarly conversation on the issues of emotional and affective labor in academia specifically as it relates to alt-ac staff positions.

When I initially sent out the call for submissions for this collection, I was purposefully vague as to what I meant by "alt-ac" (alternative academic careers) in order to solicit a wider variety of chapters from people working across the institution. Part of the challenge is that different institutions have different designations for various types of staff, and the various roles that staff can undertake; a staff member may also be a part of the administration in their role as a director, but also not in a position of relative power because they are not also tenured faculty. Some alt-ac staff are former faculty, and some staff moved through the staff ranks to administrative positions. Others, like librarians, depending on the institution, are a part of the faculty. How we view or understand our roles within our institutions can differ greatly from what the organizational chart says about our role, and while the contributors all have different skill sets, reporting lines, responsibilities, job titles, and terminal degrees, we all share the experience of being caught "betwixt and between" in our roles in higher education.

One cannot read these chapters and consider these approaches without acknowledging the role that *power* plays in these affective interactions, both perceived and actual. In my own anecdote, the power differential was made clear to me by my supervisor insofar as I was understood to be less-than and beneath the faculty. At the same time, when I first announced to friends and colleagues that I was moving into an alt-ac role, I was accused of going over to the proverbial "dark side" or joining with the enemy, illustrating the perceived power *over* faculty I was to have in an "administrative" role. Manathunga acknowledges that tension, leading her to practice faculty development "ambivalently" insofar as she was not interested in participating in the administration's potentially colonial dictates on what constitutes "good" teaching and learning. While there is power in these liminal, marginal spaces within academia, there is still also a real affective component of being okay with said "marginal" status.

Personally, as I began my own research, I was particularly interested in the concepts of intimacy and love—not romantic love, but love as bell hooks defines it, "a combination of care, commitment, knowledge, responsibility, respect, and trust" in relation to my work as a faculty developer.[16] I was particularly interested in how faculty developers could do their jobs effectively when the "love" we felt for the person sitting in front of us during a consultation or workshop or meeting was unidirectional, where what was returned back to us was resentment, superiority, disrespect, and dismissiveness. How could we cultivate this feeling of love that hooks describes toward members of the academy whom we know are openly hostile to adjuncts, lower-level staff members, and even our peers within the same unit who don't have the "proper" educational attainment?

But really, I realized recently, I was finding an acceptably gendered way to talk about rage. What do I do with these real feelings of anger, not to be explained away as frustration or exasperation or weariness or some other more gender-appropriate emotion, but anger and even rage that I feel toward the institution, toward some of my (who I would see as, in any case) peers and my superiors. I couldn't *appear* angry, because of gendered but also professional expectations, the very definition of emotional labor.

This is a perfect illustration of what Karen Rosenberg in her chapter in this volume titled "toxic emotional labor"—emotional labor that is not inauthentic, but instead deeply felt and destructive. There are realms of affective labor I enjoy in my position: forging relationships with faculty, collaborating with disparate parts of the institution, mentoring junior colleagues, supervising and mentoring students. But these are ultimately *productive* relationships for the most part; the results of the affective labor are clear, tangible deliverables of some kind for both parties. Toxic emotional labor is not productive, nor is it collaborative; the results are one-sided, with the work ultimately turning unproductive and even destructive. Certainly, as the chapters in this collection illustrate, there are gray areas: Where does placating the ego of an administrator in order to get the support necessary to move forward on a project fall on this spectrum? What about dealing with daily microaggressions (and outright aggressions) based on our perceived status within the university's hierarchy?

Communication scholars Katherine I. Miller, Jennifer Considine, and Johny Garner tease out some of these distinctions through naming the different kinds of emotions in the workplace. They differentiate five different and distinct (but intersecting) types: emotional labor ("the display of emotion that is some way defined and controlled by management"), emotional work ("emotion that . . . is a part of the job itself but which is a natural outgrowth of job-related communications"), emotion with work ("emotion that emerges through relationships and interactions with other employees"), emotion at work ("emotion that has its genesis outside of the workplace"), and emotion toward work ("emotional experience in which the work or job is the target of the emotion").[17] While their study does not focus on academia, it does provide a framework for thinking about the various forms of affect we engage with in our day-to-day engagements. Any of these can be positive or negative, depending on the situation, and not all of these are emotional labor—they are emotions we experience at work and have to deal with in order to do our jobs.

I also don't want to fall into the trap of turning *everything* into affective labor, particularly negative or burdensome emotional labor. Some of this is work we enjoy doing, that we are good at, that we thrive at. As some of the chapter titles suggest, love, desire, allyship, and mentorship are all positive outcomes; they are emotional work that we enjoy engaging in, for better or for worse. There is also the rage that comes from the work not being recognized and compensated or celebrated as work when it is successful, and some of these chapters are a reclamation of this space, of these roles, and of this work as ultimately valuable and deserving to be valued.

This collection sprang from a place in me that wanted to do something productive with that anger, that rage I was feeling, to try to answer these lingering questions. And, as is my M.O., I wanted to do so by building a community around the topic, by bringing voices together to be heard, and to be in conversation with one another. As I grew into my own staff role, I began to better understand the affective labor required of other staff members, from student services and student affairs/student life to the bursar's office to writing centers and other tutoring centers to administrative assistants. I wanted a space where disparate "alt-ac" roles within the university could come together and share our profession's knowledge and experience with affective labor, to share our stories, and hopefully to find solidarity while advancing the conversation on affective labor, staff, and higher education.

And this collection largely fulfills that goal. The response to my call was overwhelming, and the assembled group of alt-ac scholars you'll find in this volume help us to better understand, conceptualize, and theorize the intersections of race, class, gender, and disability on the affective labor we perform in our varied roles, all in the name of supporting students. This is probably *the* aspect that unifies these chapters—the work we do for our students outside of the classroom. Even if students aren't our direct responsibility, the *care* that all of these chapter authors show for the institution and the students therein is clear.

In editing this volume, I also wanted to preserve the very real emotions that fueled the writing: the impetus for exploring the concepts of emotional labor, and the *passion* that drove the authors to respond, to write, to share. To talk about emotional and affective labor in the abstract depersonalizes it, removing the impact that it has on individuals who are doing the work. Our experiences have heavily informed our understanding of affective and emotional labor; to remove those experiences would be to ask the authors, and myself, to remain "neutral" as so much academic research and writing demands of us, akin to asking ourselves to perform another layer of emotional labor in order to earn the approval of academia, to have academia validate our experiences through their negation. I refuse to participate in such forms of coerced affective labor; if we must suppress our anger and frustrations—keep offering service with a smile in our day-to-day jobs—then this is the space to be honest and confront academia with the reality of the labor we perform.

The first chapters of the book clearly lay out the general landscape of affective labor and alt-ac roles, complementing and enhancing my own introduction here. Traci Freeman opens with a sweeping overview of the evolution of alt-ac as a profession, as well as its intersections with affective labor, all while interrogating the idea of managing desire; in this case, desire for alt-ac or administrative work. This work, she notes, is often misunderstood, demeaned, and marginalized. What is it to want a job like *that?* Melissa Dalgleish traces her own journey into an alt-ac role, examining love (and despair) as a driving force toward alt-ac work, embodying the internal conflict that we face within the neoliberal institutions we love. Grace Pollock looks at the possibilities of affective allyship in and through the various alt-ac roles on campus. Alt-ac work is often marginalized within our institutions, limiting our voices, with all of the affective impact that has on a person, but also creates spaces for allyship with those other marginalized voices on campus. Next, Nicole Papaioannou asks about the role and impact of those working as an alt-ac outside of academia. Challenging the very definition of alt-ac and who "gets" to be an academic or produce scholarship, Papaioannou claims her space as an academic outside the academy and outlines ways "insiders" can help our colleagues working on "the outside." All four chapters are linked very powerfully in their analysis of identity formation for alt-acs and the affective consequences.

The next five chapters are loosely based on with whom the persons in the alt-ac role primarily interact. The chapters regard different spaces on campus (writing center, faculty development, and the library) that speak to the pressure to "always-already be okay," borrowing a term from Martha Diede's contribution. As I noted earlier, Karen Rosenberg, in her aptly titled chapter, "Plays Well with Others," differentiates between the types of emotional labor she is called upon to perform, deeming certain kinds "toxic emotional labor" that can flourish in alt-ac situations. Lindsay Bernhagen and Emily O. Gravett provide a follow-up to their important 2017 article, "Educational Development as Pink Collar Labor," in a more personal and probing account of how what they wrote about in 2017 impacts and was informed by their day-to-day work and affective state. If studies on affective labor and faculty development work is still in its infancy, then it is still waiting to be developed at all in the field of academic technology; Celeste Tường Vy Sharpe and Carly J. Born begin this important work by exploring the complicated affective and relational dynamics of working in academic technology. How do you navigate both the complex hierarchies of academia alongside the complex and gendered expectations of information technology? Finally, Jennifer Solomon and Rebekah Kati explore the affective labor that is required of them as open-access (OA) librarians charged with promoting OA across campus.

I am particularly appreciative of those who wrote from student-facing alt-ac roles: advisors, program coordinators, and directors of support units staffed exclusively by students. Alt-acs who work with students are in a different position, in terms of their power-differential; at once they are in positions viewed as "lesser than" traditional academic positions, and yet they have a tremendous amount of influence and power over students. Starting off the third set of chapters, Elizabeth Lundberg outlines the tensions that exist as an alt-ac academic advisor, facing her own questions about "what are you going to do with that" alongside the students she advises and advocates for new, better narratives about success. Daniel Dale examines the affective labor that goes into supervising students—labor that is still underappreciated and undertheorized within the profession. Matthew J. Trybus with Emily O. Gravett explore the affective aspects at the intersection of disability, alt-ac, and gender norms when advising and supervising students, and trying to find, among it all, joy.

So what do we *do*; how do we move forward productively? Leeann Hunter provides a framework for honoring others by honoring ourselves in relation to mentorship programs, but the lessons here can be expanded into all forms of alt-ac work. And finally, Deborah Maron explores and theorizes the very real, very difficult, but ultimately necessary affective labor of working toward antiracist practices—in this context, in the library; but, the strategies and concepts she brings forward are relevant in all our work within the institution. I conclude with my own affective theorizing and reflections based on the editing of this collection, from the initial call for submissions to turning in the final manuscript, with the hope of providing another framework for thinking and feeling about the affective work we do.

I am grateful for the time and care each contributor put into their chapter. The result is at once intimate and critically engaged, expanding and exploring what scholarships in our fields could and should be. My one disappointment was that there wasn't more diversity (more on that in my conclusion). A special issue of *New Directions in Teaching and Learning* in summer 2019 was devoted entirely to the issue of diversity in the field of educational development, with articles on masculinity, friendship, microaggressions, implicit bias, gendered roles, and racial exclusion, all from an affective perspective. I would recommend it as a companion to this book—while this book reflects a diversity of staff roles, the issue of *New Directions* contains a more racially and ethnically diverse set of authors.

I invite you, as a reader, to approach this collection with the kind of generous thinking that Kathleen Fitzpatrick describes, where the default mode isn't to be critical but instead to be open and curious; to think *with* contributors, to place them in conversation with one another, to treat the book and your experience reading it as being one long *yes, and*.[18] Read it together with colleagues, listen to each other's stories and experiences, write, and respond. I am grateful that each contributor, whether they meant to or not, approached the topic generously, and I hope that you, as a reader, will do the same.

Every academic hopes that their work will be read, discussed, critically engaged with, cited, assigned, and eventually create change. This book is a beginning, building on the work of others, in the hope that yet others will continue the conversations. And while I hold that hope, too, in no small part because I believe in the quality of these chapters, my deepest and more modest hope is that this book finds its way into the hands of someone who needs to know that they are not alone.

NOTES

Special thanks to Traci Freeman, Martha Diede, Joshua Eyler, and Kevin Gannon for reading a draft of this introduction and providing invaluable feedback.

1. I would later learn that I had undiagnosed ADHD, which contributed to my difficulty at being able to behave "like staff." This disclosure is not to discount the very real affective labor that is expected of staff in terms of our reactions and behavior with faculty and administrators, as many of the chapters in this volume also attest to. I instead chose to disclose because of the intersectional challenges that a disability such as ADHD brings to the discussion, to be taken up later in my conclusion.

2. Sendhil Mullainathan and Eldar Shafir, *Scarcity* (New York: Times Publishing, 2013).

3. Paige Morgan, "Not Your DH Teddy-Bear," *DH+Lib*, July 29, 2016, https://acrl.ala.org/dh/2016/07/29/not-your-dh-teddy-bear/

4. Bethany Nowviskie, "On Capacity and Care," *Bethany Nowviskie Personal Blog*, October 4, 2015, http://nowviskie.org/2015/on-capacity-and-care/.

5. Alexis Logsdon, Amy Mars, and Heather Tompkins, "Claiming Expertise from Betwixt and Between: Digital Humanities Librarians, Emotional Labor, and Genre Theory," *College & Undergraduate Libraries* 24, no. 2–4 (2016): 155–170.

6. Arlie Russell Hochschild, *The Managed Heart: Commercialization of Human Feeling* (Berkeley: University of California Press, 2012), 7.

7. Deandra Little and David A. Green, "Betwixt and Between: Academic Developers in the Margins," *International Journal for Academic Development* 17, no. 3 (September 2012): 203–215. See also Deandre Little and David A. Green, "Academic Development in the Margins," *Studies in Higher Education* 38, no. 4

(2013): 523–537, where they uncritically liken doing academic development as being like building the Suez or Panama Canals.

8. Adrian Kelly, "Intimacy and Emotional Labour in Academic Development," *International Journal for Academic Development* 20, no. 1 (2015): 93–104.

9. Catherine Manathunga, "Doing Academic Development Ambivalently: Applying Post-Colonial Metaphors to Educational Development?," *International Journal for Academic Development* 11, no. 1 (May 2006): 19–29; Catherine Manathunga, "'Unhomely' Academic Developer Identities: More Post-Colonial Explorations," *International Journal for Academic Development* 12, no. 1 (May 2007): 25–34.

10. Michael Hardt and Antonio Negri, *Multitude: War and Democracy in the Age of Empire* (New York: Penguin, 2004), 108.

11. Sara Ahmed, *The Cultural Politics of Emotion* (New York: Routledge, 2010).

12. Alicia A. Granley, "Emotion Regulation in the Workplace: A New Way to Conceptualize Emotional Labor," *Journal of Occupational Health Psychology* 5, no. 1 (2000): 97.

13. Brandi Lawless, "Documenting a Labor of Love: Emotional Labor as Academic Labor," *Review of Communication* 18, no. 2 (2018): 85–97.

14. Kelly, "Intimacy and Emotional Labour in Academic Development."

15. Lisa Sloniowski, "Affective Labor, Resistance, and the Academic Librarian," *Library Trends* 64, no. 2 (2016): 647.

16. bell hooks, *Teaching Community: A Pedagogy of Hope* (London: Routledge, 2003), 131.

17. Katherine I. Miller, Jennifer Considine, and Johny Garner, "'Let Me Tell You about My Job': Exploring the Terrain of Emotion in the Workplace," *Management Communications Quarterly* 20, no. 3 (February 2007): 232–233.

18. Kathleen Fitzpatrick, *Generous Thinking: A Radical Approach to Saving the University* (Baltimore: Johns Hopkins University Press, 2019).

BIBLIOGRAPHY

Ahmed, Sara. *The Cultural Politics of Emotion*. New York: Routledge, 2010.

Fitzpatrick, Kathleen. *Generous Thinking: A Radical Approach to Saving the University*. Baltimore: Johns Hopkins University Press, 2019.

Granley, Alicia A. "Emotion Regulation in the Workplace: A New Way to Conceptualize Emotional Labor." *Journal of Occupational Health Psychology* 5, no. 1 (2000): 95–110.

Hardt, Michael, and Antonio Negri. *Multitude: War and Democracy in the Age of Empire*. New York: Penguin, 2004.

Hochschild, Arlie Russell. *The Managed Heart: Commercialization of Human Feeling*. Berkeley: University of California Press, 2012.
hooks, bell. *Teaching Community: A Pedagogy of Hope*. London: Routledge, 2003.
Kelly, Adrian. "Intimacy and Emotional Labour in Academic Development." *International Journal for Academic Development* 20, no. 1 (2015): 93–104.
Lawless, Brandi. "Documenting a Labor of Love: Emotional Labor as Academic Labor." *Review of Communication* 18, no. 2 (2018): 85–97.
Little, Deandre, and David A. Green. "Academic Development in the Margins." *Studies in Higher Education* 38, no. 4 (2013): 523–537.
———. "Betwixt and Between: Academic Developers in the Margins." *International Journal for Academic Development* 17, no. 3 (September 2012): 203–215.
Logsdon, Alexis, Amy Mars, and Heather Tompkins. "Claiming Expertise from Betwixt and Between: Digital Humanities Librarians, Emotional Labor, and Genre Theory." *College & Undergraduate Libraries* 24, no. 2–4 (2016): 155–170.
Manathunga, Catherine. "Doing Academic Development Ambivalently: Applying Post-Colonial Metaphors to Educational Development?" *International Journal for Academic Development* 11, no. 1 (May 2006): 19–29.
———. "'Unhomely' Academic Developer Identities: More Post-Colonial Explorations." *International Journal for Academic Development* 12, no. 1 (May 2007): 25–34.
Miller, Katherine I., Jennifer Considine, and Johny Garner. "'Let Me Tell You about My Job': Exploring the Terrain of Emotion in the Workplace." *Management Communications Quarterly* 20, no. 3 (February 2007): 231–260.
Morgan, Paige. "Not Your DH Teddy-Bear." *DH+Lib*. July 29, 2016. https://acrl.ala.org/dh/2016/07/29/not-your-dh-teddy-bear/.
Mullainathan, Sendhil, and Eldar Shafir. *Scarcity*. New York: Times, 2013.
Nowviskie, Bethany. "On Capacity and Care." Bethany Nowviskie [blog]. October 4, 2015. http://nowviskie.org/2015/on-capacity-and-care/.
Sloniowski, Lisa. "Affective Labor, Resistance, and the Academic Librarian." *Library Trends* 64, no. 2 (2016): 645–666.

1

"Why Would You Want to Do That?"

Managing Desire for Alt-Ac Work

TRACI FREEMAN

In an article published in the 2004 edition of the *Writing Lab Newsletter*, one of the central publications for writing center administrators, Melissa Nicolas describes her experience looking for a position as a writing center director. Although she was initially optimistic that she would find a job at an institution that valued administrative work, she discovered during her campus interviews that many faculty members on search committees were deeply suspicious of her interest in administration. She writes, "The unofficial message I received was that while the institution would love to have me on staff, this or that particular faculty member cannot understand why someone with my talent or credentials would want the position."[1] Jackie Grutsch McKinney describes having a similar experience while she was on the job market. During a campus interview, a senior faculty member asked Grutsch McKinney, "So why do you want to be a writing center director?" And then he added, "Anyone can direct a writing center."[2]

While it might not be surprising that faculty outside of the writing center community question the desire for administrative work and the expertise required to do this work, even those within the community have expressed skepticism. Nathalie Singh-Corcoran, for example, recounts an experience in graduate school when she found herself seated next to a prominent writing center scholar before a conference presentation. When the scholar asked her what she wanted to do once she completed her degree, Singh-Corcoran replied that she wanted to direct a writing center. This scholar turned to her "rather matter-of-factly and asked, 'Why would you want to do that? It's such a low status job."[3] Singh-Corcoran describes receiving a similar response during her comprehensive exams after telling one of her committee members that she wanted to research writing centers for her dissertation work. She writes, "He didn't exactly discourage me from pursuing writing center research, but he did tell me that if I wanted to be considered a scholar and not just an administrator (his words), my future research needed to consider more than writing centers."[4]

As these writing center directors' experiences illustrate, PhDs in writing studies who express a desire for administrative positions learn that we must repress our desires and our enthusiasm for this work when we talk with faculty colleagues, even in the context of job interviews. That even prominent scholars in the field question our desire for these positions speaks to the ways that writing center directors themselves have internalized an academic value system that places service work or administrative labor at the bottom of the academic prestige hierarchy. Underlying many of these comments is the widespread belief, articulated by Singh-Corcoran's advisor, that scholarship focusing on administration is not "real" scholarship and therefore administrators are not "real" academics. As Singh-Corcoran's experiences suggest, the process of socialization into this belief system begins early. In graduate programs, doctoral students are often taught that the roles of "administrator" and "scholar" are mutually exclusive and that research that might focus on program administration is not a serious or worthy scholarly endeavor.

Anecdotes like these are commonplace in the writing center literature. Such stories predate the rise of the alternative academic (alt-ac) class of employees in higher education,[5] but they resonate with the experiences of many alt-ac professionals. Like other PhDs with administrative roles, writing center directors historically have inhabited positions without tenure, departmental affiliations, and research support, and, consequently, we have struggled to access traditional institutional structures of power. Regardless of our backgrounds, credentials, and even our resemblance to faculty, writing center directors have found ourselves cast in subordinate roles in relation to our faculty colleagues.

Although writing centers have emerged out of a particular disciplinary and historical context, writing center directors' experiences illustrate the need, common among alt-ac professionals, to deny, repress, or otherwise manage our desire for administrative work, particularly in the company of faculty.

In this chapter, I argue that alt-ac professionals who express a desire for administrative positions must actively manage our desires (and others' responses to our desires) because such emotions threaten our dominant institutional narratives and unsettle structures of power in higher education. The dominant narrative about alt-ac professionals is that we fell into administrative roles by chance or were forced into these roles because of our lack of options.[6] On our blogs and listserv posts, as well as in our casual conversations, we too often describe our professional lives through expressions of frustration, alienation, and loss. Even among other alt-ac professionals, we rarely express a desire for our work.

Throughout this chapter, I draw upon social theories of emotion to explore what the desire for alt-ac positions tells us about the social context of our institutions. As Sara Ahmed writes, "Rather than seeing emotions as psychological dispositions, we need to consider how they work, in concrete and particular ways, to mediate the relationship between the psychic and the social, and between the individual and the collective."[7] Rather than focusing on *why* alt-acs might desire administrative work, I am concerned about what such desires *do* and what they *mean.* The desire for administrative positions, like other expressions of illicit desire, transgresses deeply held cultural beliefs and values and entails significant personal risk. This risk is apparent in the many posts on alt-ac listservs and message boards asking for advice on how to tell your advisors that you want to pursue an alt-ac position. To mitigate this risk, alt-ac professionals must manage our desires through acts of denial, repression, and self-silencing.

In the pages that follow, I consider how alt-ac professionals who desire administrative positions occupy an interesting vantage point from which to critique institutional power structures. Next, I analyze some of the emotion management strategies that alt-acs employ to negotiate daily interactions in our institutional contexts. Finally, I reflect on this analysis for the insight it provides into the well-established economies of knowledge and power in our institutions.

ALT-ACS AND THE MEANING OF DESIRE

In my analysis, I adopt a fairly narrow definition of alt-ac positions, one exemplified by writing center directors. I want to acknowledge, however, that what constitutes an alt-ac career track or an alt-ac professional is still very much a subject of debate. Brenda Bethman and C. Shaun Longstreet, for example, define as alt-ac those positions in higher education for full-time or administrative staff in which research and teaching are not among the primary duties. Within this broad definition, alt-ac positions can be found across universities, as well as outside of academe in institutes, foundations, museums, and think tanks.[8] I find this definition problematic for what it excludes—the work of research and teaching—as well as for what it includes, which is virtually any job outside of the corporate sector that a person with a PhD might have.

In contrast to Bethman and Longstreet's broad definition, Joshua Kim describes alt-ac careers as "non-faculty *educational* positions" (emphasis mine).[9] By calling attention to the educational aspects of alt-ac work, Kim makes an important distinction between PhDs who work in professional fields and those who work in higher education off the tenure track but in roles that require them to blend teaching with service and scholarship. As Kim argues, the defining feature of an alt-ac position is that it is "liminal," rest[ing] somewhere between non-faculty and faculty." "This matters," he writes, "as even highly productive alt-acs working in high impact roles lack many of the protections and privileges of traditional faculty."[10] Although alt-ac positions often entail much of the same work as tenure-track faculty positions, alt-acs are situated outside of the traditional categories and institutional power structures for professionals who typically engage in this work.

Like Kim, I view alt-ac professionals' resemblance to faculty as critical to the definition of the category. Alt-acs have the same training as faculty. Many of us possess expertise in the areas of teaching, research, and service, and our work requires us to engage our expertise, although perhaps in different ways than faculty. Many of us have stellar academic credentials and are as well-published as our tenure-track and tenured peers. Precisely because of our similarities, as Ji-Young Um notes, "the presence of so many of us in the margins of the academy—the visibility of our bodies, our work, and stories—is unsettling and threatening."[11] We are threatening because we complicate constructions of academic subjectivity, constructions that depend on hierarchical distinctions between faculty and staff.

Kim's narrower definition of alt-ac careers, particularly his emphasis on the liminality of alt-ac positions and their precarious relationship to the university's power structures, helps to highlight the problem I aim to address: within this nonfaculty/faculty space are distinct economic, political, and ideological tensions that require alt-ac workers to enact strategies for emotion management. As Arlie Hochschild explains in *The Managed Heart*, employees in certain work environments are required to "induce or suppress feeling in order to sustain the outward countenance that produces the proper state of mind in others."[12] This work, which she refers to as emotional labor, necessitates the worker engage in a kind of emotion management, whereby an employee, in "attending to inner sensations in a given way, by defining situations in a given way, and by managing in given ways" participates in the creation of a social reality.[13] Within the framework of emotional labor, emotions are not psychological states so much as they are social and cultural practices, not something that we *feel* but rather something that we *do*.[14] Emotions are not merely expressions of individual experiences; they emerge as "patterns of sentiment that are structured by the specific political and cultural organization of everyday life."[15] When we express emotions, we reconcile our individual responses with our social worlds, often reinforcing dominant cultural values.

When an individual's expressions of emotion are normative, these expressions reify our social world, reinforce its values, and align an individual with the dominant culture. Not everyone, however, experiences emotions that are socially appropriate for a given situation. Alison Jaggar calls unconventional or unacceptable emotional responses "outlaw emotions." She writes, "Outlaw emotions are distinguished by their incompatibility with the dominant perceptions and values."[16] If the expression of socially appropriate emotions creates community and affords individuals a sense of belonging, the expression of outlaw emotions involves personal risk and can be socially isolating. As Jaggar observes, people who experience outlaw emotions "often are subordinated individuals who pay a disproportionately high price for maintaining the status quo. The social situation of such people makes them unable to experience the conventionally prescribed emotions. . . . When unconventional emotional responses are experienced by isolated individuals, those concerned may be confused, unable to name their experience; they may even doubt their own sanity."[17] Alt-ac professionals who articulate a desire for administrative work are expressing an outlaw emotion, an illicit desire. Such expressions challenge rather than reinforce the values of our institutions and can have the effect of isolating us from our peers. This desire leaves us without an ability to make meaning out of our experiences and can lead us to fractured relationships with ourselves and with our communities. The consequences of managing outlaw emotions, of repressing, redirecting, or concealing our illicit desires, may be grave for us as individuals, but this form of emotion management is essential for our sense of safety and belonging, as well as for maintaining the integrity of our cultural systems.

While normative expressions of emotion are both influenced by and reify our social world, outlaw emotions, like illicit desire, might also be instrumental in the development of critical consciousness. As Jaggar writes, the experience of outlaw emotions encourages an individual to question existing social scripts and "may provide the first indications that something is wrong with the way alleged facts have been constructed, with accepted understanding of how things are."[18] Outlaw emotions, like the desire for administrative work in higher education, are worth interrogating because they open up a space for us to critique the normative assumptions, practices, and values of our institutional cultures.

The daily interactions of alt-ac professionals afford us considerable opportunities for institutional critique. As Billy Ehn and Orvar Löfgren observe, "many of the fundamental rules and regulations and emotions of university life are embedded in the tools, the aesthetics, and the mundane practices, in lab work, blackboard drawings, the corridor chit-chat or the order in which gratitude is expressed in a preface."[19] Throughout the following section, I analyze examples that are representative of the lived experiences of alt-ac professionals and the ways that we are called upon to manage our desires for administrative work, while we are negotiating our relationships with faculty and with our institutions. Such experiences are significant because they lay bare myths about the meritocratic system of the university and complicate commonplace narratives about the role of faculty in higher education and the privileged nature of intellectual work.

THE STORIES WE TELL: MANAGING DESIRE FOR ADMINISTRATIVE WORK

Conventional narratives about the rise of alt-ac professionals as a category of employee often attribute this phenomenon to a fundamental restructuring of academic labor in universities.[20] Historically, faculty, through their service obligations, contributed to the basic operational and administrative functions of the institution. With the shrinking of the professoriate over the past thirty years, universities have reduced the number of faculty who can engage in service work as part of their academic appointments. The increasing number of alt-ac positions has also coincided with the growing complexity of higher education administration, which is characterized by more federal oversight, high-stakes accreditation processes, compliance, and risk management. Institutions are under mounting pressure to secure grants, boost research productivity, and promote technology transfer. They are also increasingly accountable for the student experience and must meet demands for more robust services in support of teaching and learning. Just as universities have decreased the number of faculty who can contribute to service, they have experienced growing administrative demands and a corresponding need for professionals with specific areas of expertise who can meet these demands.

Critics of neoliberal influences on our universities view the growing number of alt-ac positions as evidence that institutions of higher education are shifting away from models of faculty governance and toward a corporate managerial model for employment. These critics see a causal relationship between the increasing numbers of new alt-ac positions and the decline in the number of tenure-track faculty, as well as the power that faculty command.[21] In fact, many faculty interpret the presence of alt-ac staff on campus as a direct threat to their autonomy and decision-making authority. In response to this threat, those of us with PhDs who inhabit alt-ac positions must manage not only our own affective responses to our work but also the emotions of the faculty with whom we work. Because of our subordinate positions in relation to faculty, the burden of this emotional labor falls to us. Through our expressions and management of emotion, we maintain our own precarious positions within the university power structure while also mitigating the existential threat that our very presence on our campuses poses for faculty and for our institutions as a whole.

Because of the nature of our positions, alt-acs are obliged to participate in discursive practices that diminish our institutional identities and reinscribe academic hierarchies and systems of privilege. Among these practices, as the opening anecdotes suggest, are having to deny or repress our desire for this work in the first place. Taking an alt-ac position, according to Ji-Young Um, often means needing to reconcile a career spent in an environment that is defined at once by one's "belonging and exclusion."[22] It is not sufficient, however, for alt-ac workers to experience such feelings of ambivalence in our nonfaculty/

faculty roles. We must perform our ambivalence for faculty and thus fortify faculty's privileged standing in the institution. For example, alt-acs are often subject to comments like: "I am so sorry that you need to write that report" or "It is such a shame that you are here all summer" or "I have another committee meeting, how do you do this all day?" There is a performative identity at play in these expressions of pity—by voicing their disdain for administrative work and minimizing its value, faculty are reinforcing their positionality in the broader system of academic privilege.

When faculty express their pity, the role of an alt-ac is to mirror back to the faculty their relative privilege, reinforcing institutional values and neutralizing the threat we pose. Regardless of how alt-ac professionals feel about our roles, when we are the recipients of our faculty colleagues' pity because of the work that we do, we have few legitimate options for response. We can display enthusiasm for work that faculty clearly do not value, or we can echo a faculty member's contempt for administrative labor, or we can negate the work involved in these administrative activities through comments like: "No, it's nothing really." All of these possible responses reinforce the notion that administrative work is not intellectually or personally rewarding and that no reasonable person with a PhD would desire to do it. If we respond in any way at all to such comments, we participate in our own subordination by acknowledging that unlike our faculty colleagues, we are unable to opt out of what they perceive to be unbearable obligations. In most instances, the safest response is to smile and remain silent. Although we might actually value administrative labor and desire this kind of work, we must manage our own emotional responses in order to maintain the institutional status quo.

When our faculty colleagues offer us their pity, we must respond with some care. Beyond the gesture itself, such statements are reassertions of faculty's privilege. As Robert Kimball argues, unlike other altruistic or empathetic emotions, pity often includes "a feeling of superiority on the part of the pitier and an element of contempt for the person pitied."[23] Entailed in the emotion of pity is a kind of psychological distancing, whereby the individuals who are expressing pity engage in a comparative exercise and reinforce their differences from those they pity. Pity, Kimball writes, "allows us to feel sorrow at another's plight without the full empathetic engagement or identification of compassion."[24] Moreover, pity does not demand a response from the individual who is expressing the emotion. Unlike compassion, pity does not necessarily motivate a person to act, and therefore pity is not an emotion that is likely to lead a person to work against injustice. When alt-acs mask our emotions and silence ourselves, we further enable our colleagues and institutions to perpetuate the belief that our universities are just systems.

Alt-acs embody the tensions between the ideal of the university and the economic and social realities of our institutions. Because we represent the inconsistencies in our institutional narratives, alt-acs must take care not to be too vocal or too visible. As Um writes of his experience working in an alt-ac position, "Deans and department chairs do not particularly like seeing and talking to me: I make them uncomfortable. I'm an uncomfortable presence because I'm a 'failed' academic and because I expose the fantasy of an egalitarian, meritocratic community of intellectuals as a lie."[25] Although alt-acs may resemble our faculty colleagues, our differences within the institutional hierarchy serve as an unpleasant reminder that hierarchy exists. Thus, faculty rationalize alt-ac professionals' subordinate positions by believing that our positions are a consequence of our own individual failures, rather than a result of inequitable systems. As Um's comments and the introductory stories suggest, the dominant narrative around alt-ac positions—that they are the last refuge for the failed academic—is one that many alt-acs have themselves internalized and normalized. The growing visibility of alt-ac employees serves as a reminder that higher education does not occupy a special place in our society: universities are not apolitical, value-neutral, or fair. Despite universities' articulated institutional values—commitments to reason and social justice—universities are implicated in the very market forces that underlie social inequality. Thus, alt-acs must strive to be invisible so as to manage the anxiety our faculty colleagues might feel about their position within our institutional power structures, a position from which they clearly benefit. We must repress our desire for our work, in part because this desire complicates the story of our failure as academics, a story that justifies the existence of our institutional hierarchies.

The desire for administrative work complicates the narrative that higher education is an equitable, just, and meritocratic system, and, more fundamentally, it challenges the way institutions value individual achievement. Although alt-ac professionals may participate in activities that support our individual aims and build our own reputations, our primary roles are in service to our institutions. Our contributions differentiate us from faculty, who participate in economies of individual advancement. As Donald Hall notes, faculty are "trained and professionalized to operate as solitary agents whose primary responsibility is to and for the self."[26] Processes for evaluating faculty contributions rest on the assumption that faculty bear sole responsibility for their own successes and failures and for their own decisions and priorities. While alt-acs resemble faculty in our training and, to varying degrees, in the work that we do, we represent a different system of values, one that privileges service to the institution over individual achievement. As a result, many faculty struggle to make sense of alt-ac professionals' roles on campus. Such struggles are exemplified by comments like the one directed at me during a meeting, in which a faculty member told me that my job is to "serve" faculty and "to make their lives easier." Such comments rest on the idea that our institutions exist to support faculty members' individual contributions, and, therefore, all of the structures of the university must work toward this goal. To view the institution in this way distorts the role of the university in contemporary society and conflates service to the institution with servitude. Such slippage serves a metonymic function, whereby an individual faculty member represents "the university," in the same way that the "king" might represent "the kingdom." Because faculty often see themselves as the embodiment of the university, when alt-ac professionals respond to such comments we risk challenging not only prevailing institutional values but also our faculty colleagues as individuals. In such situations, the best we can do is suppress our emotional responses and refocus our conversations on shared institutional goals, recognizing that faculty may be perplexed by our investment in such goals.

Alt-ac professionals challenge our institutional cultures when we express a desire for work that is not only misunderstood but also deeply undervalued. As a result of the increasing complexity of our universities, administrative work has become more central in higher education. This work, which traditionally has been defined as "service," remains the least appreciated of the domains of academic labor, valued far less than research and teaching.[27] The institutional reward system does not sufficiently recognize the importance of service, and faculty internalize this system. As Hall remarks, few faculty view service work as a potentially "meaningful" intellectual activity. He writes, "Service is often denigrated as "'busy work,' 'a waste of time,' or simply tedious. . . . It draws us away from that which [faculty] too often define narrowly as [their] 'real work.'"[28] As Williams observes, when faculty are asked, "What do you work on?," they generally respond by discussing their research agenda.[29] In reality, faculty spend much of their time at work engaged with administrative duties related to teaching and service to their disciplines and institutions. What faculty choose to identify as their "work," however, as Williams argues, "designates not only labor but the affective attachment that we have to our jobs and our professions."[30] Faculty crave intellectual engagement with their research and scholarship and interactions with colleagues and with students—administrative responsibilities are "obligations," "duties," or "labor," but not part of a vocation or what faculty would consider their "work."

The distinction between work and labor is critical to understanding the values of academic institutions. This is the very distinction that alt-ac professionals complicate when we express a desire for administrative positions. Quoting from Hannah Arendt, Thomas Discenna argues that universities have defined the work of knowledge production as "the expression of personal and collective freedom," in contrast to labor, which is merely "a response to brute material scarcity.[31] Because of the university's role in producing knowledge, it has been defined as a refuge or sanctum, where faculty are dedicated to "reading, thinking, talking, discussing, while the outside world focuses on production, consumption, labor, and jobs."[32] In aligning the tasks of the professoriate with the values of "work and culture," and in opposition to the idea of "labor," our institutions cast the work of faculty as one of the last remaining forms of what Williams identifies as "unalienated labor." This belief offers faculty the illusion that they are protected from the market forces that have dramatically transformed the academy.[33]

Because alt-ac positions may entail both knowledge creation and service to the institution, alt-ac professionals complicate the distinctions between work and labor. Further, and on a more basic level, we also challenge assumptions that are fundamental to the process of academic inquiry. Administrative work involves the study of the institution's organizational structures, systems, and practices. To desire this work is to transform what most faculty believe to be the context for inquiry into the object of inquiry, to view the institution as worthy of critical analysis rather than cast it in special relation to structures of knowledge and power. Implicit in the devaluation of service work, as Hall argues, is the notion that service does not draw upon the same critical and analytical processes as activities like research and teaching.[34] Hall questions the belief that service does not also require "close reading, interpretation, and the consideration of preceding arguments, and a careful marshalling of evidence . . . critical interaction with the texts of our institutions, disciplines, and professional communities."[35] That faculty maintain and even police the distinction between their academic interests and their service work—that they engage differently with these different activities—points to persistent beliefs about the distinctive nature of academic inquiry, and, further, the tension between those who think and those who do.

Perhaps the greatest threat that alt-acs pose to the university—and that we must manage—is that we trouble distinctions between theoretical knowledge and practical knowledge and the tendency within academic environments to privilege thought over action. Our presence on campus as academics and administrators, scholars and practitioners, thinkers and doers, complicates what Donald Schön identifies as the epistemology of the modern research university. Based on the German model of higher education, whose epistemological foundations lie in what Schön calls "technical rationality," research universities in the United States were designed for the purpose of contributing to "fundamental science and systematic knowledge."[36] In this epistemological framework, such knowledge is defined in opposition to "practitioner knowledge" or the understanding that might come from experience. Such assumptions are evident when a faculty member tells an alt-ac professional that their scholarship is not "real," either because our positions are off the tenure track or because our work has practical implications. Such comments reinforce both the academic hierarchy and the epistemological foundations of our institutions. Though alt-acs might know that our contributions have equal value, we must manage our responses or risk challenging not only the structures of power but also pervasive beliefs about the relative value of different ways of knowing.

FINAL THOUGHTS ON DESIRE

What the experiences of writing center directors and other alt-ac professionals beg us to interrogate is the culture of academic privilege and the practices of valuation and epistemic injustice that are a consequence of higher education's systems and practices. These systems and practices are grounded in beliefs about the prestige or value of certain forms of work over others, but they are also a result of our inclination in institutions of higher education to identify with some, but not all, of the work that we do. The increasing number of administrative positions in higher education held by PhDs may reflect the economic conditions of our institutions and the changing nature of academic labor in higher education. The *desire* for such positions, however, challenges us to reckon with the emotional labor and the high personal cost required to sustain academic cultures in the face of such changes. The burden of this emotional labor falls disproportionately on the shoulders of those of us in alt-ac positions.

If, as Sara Ahmed suggests, emotionality represents "responsive to and openness towards the worlds of others," then emotion has clear social consequences. On the contrary, "to resist this emotion or to deny its possibility is to resist the individual but also the social reality that an individual participates in—denying emotions of others is also denying social reality."[37] When a faculty member denies our desire for administrative positions, we might feel such denials personally, at least in the moment, but these gestures are not so much personal as they reflect a broader and perhaps more troubling denial of the changing nature of higher education.

NOTES

1. Melissa Nicolas, "Where the Women Are: Writing Centers and the Academic Hierarchy," *Writing Lab Newsletter* 29, no. 1 (2004), 11.

2. Nicole Caswell, Jackie Grutsch McKinney, and Rebecca Jackson, *The Working Lives of New Writing Center Directors* (Boulder: University Press of Colorado, 2016), 11–12.

3. Nathalie Usha Singh-Corcoran, "Revising the Writing Center: A Reconsideration of Writing Center Work," 2005, 8, https://repository.arizona.edu/bitstream/handle/ 10150/194766/ azu_etd_1226_sip1_m.pdf?sequence=1.

4. Singh-Corcoran, "Revising the Writing Center," 8.

5. According to Elizabeth Bouquet, writing centers first appeared on college campuses between 1920 and 1940, though the methods of instruction aligned with writing centers have an even longer history. Elizabeth H. Bouquet, "'Our Little Secret': A History of Writing Centers, Pre- to Post-Open Admissions," *College Composition and Communication* 50, no. 3 (1999), 463–482. The profes-sionalization of writing center directors began in the early 1980s with the emergence of scholarship focused on writing centers. In contrast, the rise of alt-ac as a category of employment dates back to 2010, when the term was claimed to denote what had been previously called "nonacademic" careers. Brenda Bethman and C. Shaun Longstreet, "Defining Terms," Inside Higher Education, May 22, 2013, https://www.insidehighered.com/advice/2013/05/22/essay-defining-alt-ac-new-phd-job-searches.

6. For examples, see Gretta Perel, "Getting Ready to Leave Academe," Inside Higher Education, March 8, 2018, https://www.insidehighered.com/advice/2018/03/08/ how-prepare-leave-academe-opinion; Christine Kelly, "Stop Resisting Non-Faculty Careers," Inside Higher Education, July 7, 2016,

https://www.insidehighered.com/advice/2016/07/07/phd-candidates-should-consider-careers-other-faculty-essay; and Ji-Young Um, "On Being a Failed Professor: Lessons from the Margins and the Undercommons," #Alt-Academy. August 11, 2014, http://mediacommons.org/alt-ac/pieces/being-failed-professor-lessons-margins-and-undercommons.

7. Sara Ahmed, "Collective Feelings: Or, the Impressions Left by Others," *Theory, Culture, and Society* 21, no. 2 (2004): 27.

8. Brenda Bethman and C. Shaun Longstreet, "Defining Terms," Inside Higher Education, May 22, 2013, https://www.insidehighered.com/advice / 2013/05/22/essay-defining-alt-ac-new-phd-job-searches.

9. Joshua Kim, "Trying to Understand Alt-Acs," Inside Higher Education, February 2, 2015, https://www.insidehighered.com/blogs/technology-and-learning/trying-understand-alt-acs.

10. Kim, "Trying to Understand Alt-Acs."

11. Ji-Young Um, "On Being a Failed Professor: Lessons from the Margins and the Undercommons," #Alt-Academy, August 11, 2014, http://mediacommons.org/alt-ac/pieces/being-failed-professor-lessons-margins-and-undercommons.

12. Arlie Russell Hochschild, *The Managed Heart: Commercialization of Human Feeling* (Berkeley: University of California Press, 2012), 7.

13. Hochschild, *The Managed Heart*, 27.

14. Sara Ahmed. *The Cultural Politics of Emotion* (New York: Routledge, 2013), 4.

15. Billy Ehn and Orvar Löfgren, "Emotions in Academia," in Helena Wolf, ed., *The Emotions: A Cultural Reader* (Oxford, UK: Berg Publishers, 2007), 115.

16. Alison M. Jaggar, "Love and Knowledge: Emotion in Feminist Epistemology," *Inquiry* 32, no. 2 (1989): 166.

17. Jaggar, "Love and Knowledge," 166.

18. Jaggar, 167.

19. Ehn and Löfgren, "Emotions in Academia," 115.

20. Thomas A. Discenna, *Discourses of Denial: The Rhetoric of American Academic Labor* (New York: Routledge, 2018).

21. For an extended discussion of this topic, see Larry G. Gerber, *The Rise and Decline of Faculty Governance: Professionalization and the Modern American University* (Baltimore: Johns Hopkins University Press, 2014); and Benjamin Ginsberg, *The Fall of the Faculty: The Rise of the All-Administrative University and Why It Matters* (New York: Oxford University Press, 2011).

22. Um, "On Being a Failed Professor."

23. Robert H. Kimball, "A Plea for Pity," *Philosophy and Rhetoric* 37, no. 4 (2004), 304.

24. Kimball, "A Plea for Pity," 305.

25. Um, "On Being a Failed Professor."

26. Donald A. Hall, "The Hermeneutics of Service," in Michelle A. Massé and Katie J. Hogan, eds., *Over Ten Million Served: Gendered Service in Language and Literature Workplaces* (Albany: State University of New York Press, 2010), 220.

27. Hall, "The Hermeneutics of Service," 220.

28. Hall, 225.

29. Jeffrey J. Williams, "Uneasy Work," *Symplok* 18, no. 1–2 (2010): 220.

30. Williams, "Uneasy Work," 220.

31. Discenna, *Discourses of Denial*, 5.

32. Discenna, 59.

33. Williams, "Uneasy Work," 222.

34. Hall, "The Hermeneutics of Service," 225.

35. Hall, 225.

36. Donald A. Schön, "Knowing-in-Action: The New Scholarship Requires a New Epistemology," *Change: The Magazine of Higher Learning* 27, no. 6 (1995): 28.

37. Ahmed, "Collective Feelings," 28.

BIBLIOGRAPHY

Ahmed, Sara. "Collective Feelings: Or, the Impressions Left by Others." *Theory, Culture, and Society* 21, no. 2 (2004): 25–42.

———. *The Cultural Politics of Emotion*. New York: Routledge, 2013.

Bethman, Brenda, and C. Shaun Longstreet. "Defining Terms." Inside Higher Education. May 22, 2013. https://www.insidehighered.com/advice/2013/05/22/essay-defining-alt-ac-new-phd-job-searches.

Caswell, Nicole, Jackie Grutsch McKinney, and Rebecca Jackson. *The Working Lives of New Writing Center Directors*. Boulder: University Press of Colorado, 2016.

Discenna, Thomas A. *Discourses of Denial: The Rhetoric of American Academic Labor.* New York: Routledge, 2018.

Ehn, Billy, and Orvar Löfgren. "Emotions in Academia." In Helena Wolf, ed., *The Emotions: A Cultural Reader* , 101–117. Oxford, UK: Berg Publishers, 2007.

Gerber, Larry G. *The Rise and Decline of Faculty Governance: Professionalization and the Modern American University.* Baltimore: Johns Hopkins University Press, 2014.

Ginsberg, Benjamin. *The Fall of the Faculty: The Rise of the All-Administrative University and Why It Matters.* New York: Oxford University Press, 2011.

Hall, Donald A. "The Hermeneutics of Service." In Michelle A. Massé and Katie J. Hogan, eds., *Over Ten Million Served: Gendered Service in Language and Literature Workplaces*, 219–229. Albany: State University of New York Press, 2010.

Heinert, Jennifer, and Cassandra Phillips. "Special Cluster on Gendered Service in Rhetoric and Writing Studies: Transforming the Value of Gendered Service through Institutional Culture Change." *Peitho: Journal of the Coalition of Feminist Scholars in the History of Rhetoric and Composition* 21, no. 2 (2019): 255–278.

Hochschild, Arlie Russell. *The Managed Heart: Commercialization of Human Feeling.* Berkeley: University of California Press, 2012.

Jaggar, Alison M. "Love and Knowledge: Emotion in Feminist Epistemology." *Inquiry* 32, no. 2 (1989): 151–176.

Kelly, Christine. "Stop Resisting Non-Faculty Careers." Inside Higher Education. July 7, 2016. https://www.insidehighered.com /advice/2016/07/07/phd -candidates-should-consider-careers-other-faculty-essay.

Kim, Joshua. "Trying to Understand Alt-Acs." Inside Higher Education. February 2, 2015. https://www.insidehighered.com/blogs/technology-and-learning/trying-understand-alt-ac.

Kimball, Robert H. "A Plea for Pity." *Philosophy and Rhetoric* 37, no. 4 (2004): 301–316.

Nicolas, Melissa. "Where the Women Are: Writing Centers and the Academic Hierarchy." *Writing Lab Newsletter* 29, no. 1 (2004): 11–13.

Perel, Gretta. "Getting Ready to Leave Academe." How to Prepare to Leave Academe (opinion). March 8, 2018. https://www.insidehighered.com/advice /2018/03/08/how-prepare-leave-academe-opinion.

Schön, Donald A. "Knowing-in-Action: The New Scholarship Requires a New Epistemology." *Change: The Magazine of Higher Learning* 27, no. 6 (1995): 27–34.

Singh-Corcoran, Nathalie Usha. "Revising the Writing Center: A Reconsideration of Writing Center Work." 2005. https://repository.arizona.edu/bitstream /handle/10150/194766/azu_etd_1226_sip1_m.pdf?sequence=1.

Um, Ji-Young. "On Being a Failed Professor: Lessons from the Margins and the Undercommons." #Alt-Academy. August 11, 2014. http://mediacommons.org /alt-ac/pieces/being-failed-professor-lessons-margins-and-undercommons.

Williams, Jeffrey J. "Uneasy Work." *Symplok* 18, no. 1–2 (2010): 219–227.

2

What's Love Got to Do with It?

MELISSA DALGLEISH

LOVE AND DESPAIR ON THE AC TRACK

I fell desperately in love with academia as a master's student. Head over heels, swoony, obsessive, adrenaline-spiked love. I loved it so much I wrote a 130-page thesis in ten weeks. I loved it so much I thought my decrepit, mouse-inhabited campus office was a cozy hideaway. I loved it so much I dreamed about it. I bathed in that love. I lost myself in it. I built a community of other people around it. That love energized and sustained me even as the marriage that would end nine months into my PhD began its downward spiral and my grad student poverty got more dire and I felt ever farther away from my people 1,600 kilometers to the west.

That love fueled my applications to PhD programs, and it heightened my glee when I got accepted. Then, one day, it was gone.

I started my PhD in 2008, in the midst of the Great Recession. Very quickly, the economic and social decline we still haven't recovered from made my specialized research interests—Toronto poets writing about mythology in the 1960s, so pretty damn niche—seem frivolous when compared to the real problems of the world. Three months into my degree, I was walking the picket lines in a protracted strike against unfair and unstable working conditions that ended with graduate students and contingent faculty being legislated back to work and coming away with fewer tenure lines than we'd started with. My mother-in-law, herself a renowned theorist and translator, died very suddenly, and alongside my partner's overwhelming grief I saw how quickly her decades of genius academic work were forgotten. The job market in my field kept shrinking, and there were no jobs near our home and families. A tenured faculty member I'd once considered a friend sexually harassed me, and then did the same to a dear friend. Most of my academic friends were tired and miserable. The reasons I wanted to earn a PhD in the first place were no longer convincing to me. The love was lost, forgotten, made impossible by myriad structural and social and personal forces.

You've heard a version of this story before. My version isn't even a particularly traumatic or extreme one.[1] Like many PhDs, I'd gotten to the point where something had to give. I couldn't keep doing what I was doing—following a career path that didn't seem like it wasn't going to get me anywhere but seemingly stuck walking the tenure track. But I no longer knew where to find that give, how to give myself permission to give less, to give fewer fucks, to give up.

Academia was my third career—I had previously been a primary school teacher, then a marketer for a nonprofit publisher—but I'd seemingly lost all ability and knowledge of how to do anything else, or even imagine how to do anything else. I'd forgotten that I had an identity as anything other than as an academic. The academy made sure that I did. As Rebecca Schuman puts it in her classic quit-lit essay "Thesis Hatement,"

> During graduate school, you will be broken down and reconfigured in the image of the academy. By the time you finish—if you even do—your academic self will be the culmination of your entire self, and thus you will believe, incomprehensibly, that not having a tenure-track job makes you worthless. You will believe this so strongly that when you do not land a job, it will destroy you, and nobody outside of academia will understand why. (Bright side: You will no longer have any friends outside academia.)[2]

This happened to me. The idea of doing something else than being a professor became the idea of becoming someone else, and I had no idea who that person was. It was terrifying.

And then, I don't remember where, I heard the term *alt-ac* and found a way forward. The alt-ac community on Twitter became my lifeline. I learned everything I could about how to do something else, how to be something—someone—else. I figured out what would make me happy at work after being so miserable at work as an academic.

Then I got offered part-time alt-ac work in my last full-time PhD year. That work—taking what I'd learned about what was out there for PhDs like me and using it to build a university-wide graduate professional development program—showed me that an alt-ac career was the right one for me. With some effort and luck, I parlayed that part-time gig into my full-time career supporting graduate students, postdocs, and research staff in their career and professional development. I love what I do.

That love stems from the same Do What You Love (DWYL) mentality that made leaving the professorial career path so hard for me, and for so many. It seems contradictory, but it's that same love—and its cousin, happiness—that give alt-ac careers their radical potential to fulfill and realize the potential of PhDs.

DWYL: THE WORST AND THE BEST

The DWYL ethos, pervasive throughout white Western culture, has been thoroughly co-opted by academia to keep people who aren't those who get most of the tenure-track jobs—the straight, white men from a precious few elite institutions—working in badly paid, precarious conditions.[3] As Miya Tokumitsu argues,

> Nowhere has the DWYL mantra been more devastating to its adherents than in academia. The average PhD student of the mid-2000s forwent the easy money of finance and law (now slightly less easy) to live on a meager stipend in order to pursue his passion for Norse mythology or the history of Afro-Cuban music.
>
> The reward for answering this higher calling is an academic employment marketplace in which about 41 percent of American faculty are adjunct professors—contract instructors who usually receive low pay, no benefits, no office, no job security, and no long-term stake in the schools where they work.
>
> There are many factors that keep PhDs providing such high-skilled labor for such low wages, including path dependency and the sunk costs of earning a PhD, but one of the strongest is how pervasively the DWYL doctrine is embedded in academia. Few other professions fuse the

personal identity of their workers so intimately with the work output. Because academic research should be done out of pure love, the actual conditions of and compensation for this labor become afterthoughts, if they are considered at all.[4]

Academia's version of DWYL tells PhDs that they could not love any other work, and that no other work is going to love them back—keep them engaged, enriched, elite, ensconced within a comfy ivory tower of other intellectuals—the way academia does.[5] Academia tells us that we are special and smart, and that there is no other place full of special, smart people doing work they love, so we stay.

And as Sarah Brouilette writes, "Our faith that our work offers non-material rewards, and is more integral to our identity than a 'regular' job would be, makes us ideal employees when the goal of management is to extract our labor's maximum value at minimum cost."[6] Even when things are bad—when the conditions and compensation for this labor of love are insufficient, unethical, harmful—this conflation of labor, love, and identity keeps many people working for institutions where the conditions of and compensations for their labor are miserable, exploitative, damaging, or all three.

And the flip side of the love at the heart of the academy's DWYL ethos? Fear.

The terror I felt when I thought about life as something other than a professor is a feature, not a bug, of the conditioning graduate school puts most people through. That terror comes of the nothingness that people who have bought into the DWYL face when thinking about doing something other than that which they believe they love. As Tokumitsu argues, "If we believe that working as a Silicon Valley entrepreneur or a museum publicist or a think-tank acolyte is essential to being true to ourselves, what do we believe about the inner lives and hopes of those who clean hotel rooms and stock shelves at big-box stores? The answer is: nothing."[7]

Academia exploits the terror that comes from facing that (demonstrably false, but nonetheless convincing) sense that we will be nothing if we can't be academics. Perhaps more than any other industry, academia trains its members to conflate their professions and their identities, to the point that considering leaving academia can feel like considering the annihilation of your identity. The fear this causes is the dark underbelly of the rhetoric of love that traps so many in underpaid, unstable, unappreciated academic work, right where academia needs them to be to keep its 101 courses taught and its teaching overheads low.

Like you may have, I bought this DWYL line. Academia told me to do what I loved, and that I should only love, and work within, academia. (Even more narrowly, academia told me I should love and invest all my efforts in research. Not in teaching, and certainly not in the administrative and service parts of the academic job, at least below the decanal level and definitely not as alt-ac staff.) But when I had my "something's gotta give" crisis I didn't love research anymore, and I was increasingly convinced that the love I felt during my master's program was unattainable now that I knew more and better what the academic life really entailed—what was in store for me if I decided to pursue the tenure track.

But despite the damage that academia's DWYL ethos had caused me, and so many other people, I still wanted to do what I loved, what made me happy and excited to go to work every day. I wanted what I'd once had, just in some other form.

At the time, my desire to find a new career to love was an instinctual one, along with a healthy dose of shaping by the DWYL culture all around me, inside and outside the academy. But it turns out that a large body of research backs this instinct.

In my quest to better help PhDs like me figure out how to overcome that terror and move on to careers where their skills and knowledge are valued with good pay, stability, options for what they do with their working lives, and happiness, I immersed myself in research coming out of the field of positive psychology, which is the science of human flourishing: how to be happy and how real happiness can transform our lives and the world around us.

Positive psychologists like Sonja Lyubomirsky, Mihaly Csikszentmihalyi, Martin Seligman, Barbara Fredrickson, Daniel Gilbert, and Lori Santos have demonstrated, in numerous contexts, that doing work that we love, with love—that is, work that is in alignment with our character and values, and that allows us to make meaningful connections with others—makes us happy. And being happy makes us healthier, wealthier, more open minded, and better able to do good in the world. If we can figure out what we love—and, as Barbara Fredrickson argues, find moments of human connection (which she argues is the essence of love, and the supreme emotion that drives our well-being and flourishing) in whatever work we're doing—we can find value and fulfillment in all kinds of careers.

It turns out doing what you love is important after all. And, as positive psychology suggests, doing what you love *with* love has the greatest potential of all to help PhDs, and the people they serve in their alt-ac roles, flourish. So let's dig into what positive psychology suggests about the radical potential of alt-ac careers to let PhDs DWYL with L.

WHAT IS LOVE, ANYWAY?

I've been playing fast and loose with how I use the terms *love* and *happiness* thus far, and I want to zero in on a few definitions that will be useful to us as we think through the relationship between affect (love, happiness) and labor on the alt-academic career path. We all have a general idea of what we think happiness means, although Immanuel Kant suggests that this idea is a pretty vague one: "Unfortunately, the notion of happiness is so indeterminate that although every human being wishes to attain it, yet he can never say definitely and consistently what it is that he really wishes and wills."[8]

Given that I'm interested in what positive psychology can tell us about the relationship between affect, alt-ac careers, and helping PhDs flourish off the tenure track, the definition of happiness used by positive psychologists is useful here. As Chris Tkach and Sonja Lyubomirsky (the latter a leading figure in positive psychology) define it, "Happiness is characterized by the experience of more frequent positive affective states than negative ones . . . as well as by the perception that one is progressing toward important life goals."[9] In her later book *The How of Happiness*, Lyubomirsky restates this definition in even simpler terms: happiness is "the experience of joy, contentment, or positive well-being, combined with a sense that one's life is good, meaningful, and worthwhile."[10]

Importantly, positive psychology sees happiness not solely as a hedonic state—a good mood, a general sense of contentment—but also as a eudaemonic one: the by-product of living a meaningful life. Eudaemonic happiness is tied to a number of factors that enhance our sense of social, personal, and psychological well-being. All of these factors are very present, and often most strongly present in our lives, in the realm of work: a sense of control or autonomy, a feeling of meaning and purpose, personal expressiveness, feelings of belongingness, social contribution, competence, personal growth, and self-acceptance.[11] Happiness does not result just from the pursuit of pleasure, or at least not primarily from it, but rather from developing our individual strengths and acting in accordance with our characters and virtues.[12]

I've been spending a lot of time talking about happiness, but to return to the title of this chapter, what does love have to do with it? I'm interested here in the redefinition of love by positive psychologist Barbara Fredrickson, who calls love—not happiness—our supreme emotion. The primacy of love will become clear when we delve into the research that suggests creating lives where we have ample opportunity to experience positive emotional states—love, foremost, but happiness too—can have a transformative effect not only on our own lives, but on our ability to do good in the world.

Fredrickson defines love rather differently from the common conception. It is, she argues, not a grand, sweeping emotion, not the obsessive devotion I used to describe my early experiences of diving deep into research, but rather "the momentary upwelling of three tightly interwoven events: first, a sharing of one or more positive emotions between you and another; second, a synchrony between your and the other person's biochemistry and behaviors; and third, a reflected motive to invest in each other's well-being that brings mutual care."[13] Fredrickson's research suggests that love, so defined, is a biological imperative, that our bodies are designed to live in a world where we regularly have these moments of mirrored connection with other people, and that having lots of these moments makes us both mentally and physically healthier, better, and able to do good in the world.

Given that we spend much of our time at work, finding employment with lots of potential for moments of connection can have a transformative effect on our happiness. Finding that kind of work is, truly, the essence of doing what you love. Doing what you do with love. Work AS love.

I love my alt-ac job. But it is also, far more than my academic career was, one in which I work with love, where I have ample opportunity to share warmth and connection with the people I work with and the people I serve. And I get to do that work in the city where my lifelong friends and my family also live and work, giving me additional opportunities to give and experience love outside of my job.

Alt-ac jobs are by definition service work—academic staff serve the mission of the university and the researchers and teachers who work within it. While there is much to legitimately critique about this service model and its effects on alt-ac staff and the systems in which we work, the research coming out of positive psychology suggests that there is radical potential in this kind of career, that the affective nature of alt-ac work is one of its beautiful strengths. I've certainly found it so. Let's dig into why positive psychologists think that is.

WHY LOVE AND HAPPINESS MATTER AT WORK

I don't want to ignore the fact, however, that the idea of happiness and loving what you do, especially at work, is a fraught one.

Who gets to be happy?

Who gets to do what they love and love what they do?

What makes us happy at work and love our jobs?

What is the use of happiness?

What does it mean to live in a country (or, as I do as a Canadian, in close proximity to one) where life, liberty, and the pursuit of happiness is baked into the social and political fabric? How does emotional labor—playing at happiness for the benefit of those we're serving even when we're not actually happy—factor in?

As Sara Ahmed argues in *The Promise of Happiness*, written in response to and in critique of the "happiness turn" out of which emerges much of the positive psychology research I reference in this chapter, happiness has long been used to ignore or uphold inequity and injustice.[14] Think of the idea of the happy slave, the happy housewife, the happy house elves in the Harry Potter books: why challenge racial, gender, social, or economic injustice when the people being oppressed are apparently happy?[15] Happiness is also, Ahmed argues, antithetical to necessary ways of being and working in our messed-up world: protest, feminist killjoying, complaint, and activism are more likely to make one actively unhappy (or angry, or sad, or nervous, or excited).[16]

And yet, I'd argue, we haven't yet found a more compelling or effective way of guiding our exploration of possible futures and of choosing new careers, at least for those people who have a multitude of possible career paths and need a guiding principle to direct their exploration and development.

All recent graduates from programs other than professional ones are in this boat, absolutely. But PhDs have the additional challenge of going from an environment in which they are trained—more than trained, indoctrinated—to believe that they are qualified for, and should have as their singular goal, one possible career that is better and more worthy than all others. Even worse, that same culture teaches PhDs that their identities are wrapped up in being academics. So PhDs have the double challenge of figuring out what work is going to make them happy, and for which they are qualified, while simultaneously working to shape a new, nonprofessorial identity.

Positive psychology researchers are obsessed with the idea of happiness. Partly that's because white settler patriarchal social norms have so thoroughly screwed with our understanding of what will make us happy that we're prone to make bad decisions in the pursuit of happiness, and positive psychologists are fascinated by the brain structures implicated in our misguided wants and choices. The things society tells us we should want—money (beyond what we need to feel secure),[17] "true love,"[18] a body that meets current norms for beauty[19]—are not actually what will make us happy. Thanks to mechanisms like hedonic adaptation (we get used to good things and go back to our baselines of happiness,[20] which research suggests is at least 40 percent genetic), relative set points (we base our wants on what we already have and what others around us have, not on what we really need), and terrible predictive ability (we far overestimate how much failing at a worthwhile risk will hurt or disappoint us), we are very prone to miswanting. And this miswanting shows up especially forcefully in how we make decisions about our careers—not taking a risk in leaving the tenure-track career path, thinking money or a prestigious academic job will make us happy, wanting the professorial life because that's what everyone around us wants.

But, it turns out, graduate students—at least when they start grad school—are doing a great job of avoiding miswanting, and in ways that can be incredibly useful in figuring out a new alt-ac career path. The old joke from *The Simpsons*—Marge admonishing Bart to not "make fun of graduate students. They just made a terrible life choice"[21]—is funny, at least to me, in part because it's so wrong. Bart mocks a grad student for his age and poverty: "Look at me, I'm a grad student! I'm 30 years old and made $600 last year!"[22] But positive psychology research suggests that in foregoing material gain for the less tangible gains of intellectual challenge,[23] a sense of purpose,[24] and working within a community of like-minded people,[25] graduate students are actually making excellent life choices.

When it comes to REALLY doing what you love, the secret seems to be finding work that (1) aligns with your personal and professional values,[26] (2) challenges you enough, but not too much,[27] (3) allows for a sense of time affluence,[28] (4) pays about US$75,000 per year,[29] and (5) provides ample opportunity for moments of warmth and engagement with others (love).[30] DWYL redefined means that we can see meaning and value in all kinds of work—not just in prestigious jobs like professor.

LOVE AND THE ALT-AC

For many of us coming off the tenure-track career path, that love is easy to find in alt-ac careers—easier, even, I'd argue than in professorial ones. We've all trained inside the academy and had, even if we no longer feel it with quite the same intensity, a belief in the value of research and teaching to make the world a better place. We also understand the norms and structures of academia, which is both useful and comforting in a new professional role. And alt-ac careers have the benefit of providing more opportunities for connection making and working in the service of others while leveraging the skillsets and cultural competencies we developed in the PhD: opportunities not only to do what we love, but to do work with love, to use love to make the academy a better place for the people within and the world outside of it.

Bethany Nowviskie is widely credited with popularizing the term *alt-ac* in the late 2000s, and while its definition has broadened in the decade since, her definition is most useful to us here: "a banner . . . under which to host conversations about the special challenges and opportunities facing . . . scholars who choose to keep their talents within the academy but who work outside the narrow zone for which grad school prepared them."[31] The term *alt-ac* is purposefully capacious, one that encompasses any of the many research- or teaching-supportive careers that exist within universities but outside the professoriate. At my current institution, which focuses entirely on the biomedical sciences and doesn't actually grant degrees (so with a narrower range of alt-ac careers than existed at the university I worked previously), we have PhDs overseeing multi-million-dollar grant portfolios, supporting other PhDs in their career development, managing labs with dozens of researchers, directing research ethics oversight, leading teams of administrative staff, coordinating major system enhancements, teaching researchers how to talk to the public, and working in dozens of other areas too numerous to list. What all of these jobs—and all alt-ac jobs, everywhere—have in common are their shared mission of supporting researchers and research processes in some form so that the organizations in which academics and alt-academics work can generate new knowledge and help that knowledge do good in the world via teaching and other forms of knowledge dissemination.

What most alt-ac jobs also share is their extraordinary potential for work as love, a potential that working in the professoriate has much less of. I'm framing this potential as an extraordinary one and not as a burden of emotional labor for a reason. The latter argument has been made repeatedly about alt-ac jobs—that they are largely feminized, that they require a high amount of caretaking work and emotional labor—and rightly so.[32] As Lee Skallerup Bessette noted in her call for chapters for this collection, "Alt-ac is particularly susceptible to feminization not only because of the nature of the type of alt-ac jobs available, but also because of the gender and racial dynamics of the professoriate: the majority of tenure and tenure-track professors are white men, while women and POC are increasingly forced on to the alt-ac track, or choose to, because of the lack of options."[33]

The closing off of career options to female-identified academics is problematic. But being forced off the tenure track and onto the alt-ac track might be benefiting people in ways we haven't yet identified. Positive psychology research suggests that alt-ac careers have the potential to let us do what we love with love, allowing PhDs to find a broad range of fulfilling, challenging, lucrative careers that make their lives, and the lives of those around them, happy and impactful.

I'd argue that alt-ac careers have an extraordinary potential for doing what you love at work while working with love. And that potential, as Fredrickson argues, can be transformative: love and happiness "can ignite powerful forces of growth in your life. . . . Your outlook literally expands as you come under the influence of any of several positive emotions,"[34] but especially love.

> Put simply, you see more as your vision widens; you see the bigger picture. With this momentarily broadened, more encompassing mindset, you become more flexible, attuned to others, creative and wise. Over time, you also become more resourceful. This is because, little by little, these mind-expanding moments of positive emotions add up to reshape your life for the better, making you more knowledgeable, more resilient, more socially integrated, and healthier. In fact, science documents that positive emotions can set off upward spirals in your life self-sustaining trajectories of growth that life you up to become a better version of yourself.[35]

If we go back to Fredrickson's definition of love as moments of connection, the barriers to working with love from within the professoriate become clearer. Let's start by thinking about research. Most research techniques—with the exception of qualitative data collection methods like interviews and focus groups—actively prevent or discourage us from making regular human connections. When I'm working in the archives, I'm sitting alone with books and boxes of papers, and I will probably get yelled at by another patron or an archivist if I try to have a conversation with the people around me doing their similarly solitary work. When my students are pipetting or at their microscopes or with their mice, they're similarly focused on individual, rather than relational, work. (Lab meetings, journal clubs, and troubleshooting with other members of the lab make biomedical and engineering research less prone to this than other STEAM fields, although lab-based research is generally less collaborative than nonscientists sometimes assume).

Teaching seems like it would provide ample moments of meaningful connection, but that's typically not possible in a large lecture hall, although it is more so in small tutorials and seminars. And I don't know about you, but I was lucky to get even one student a week visiting my office hours, the place where we'd be most likely to be able to make the kind of in-person, eyes-locked connection that Fredrickson defines as love and that leads to the most meaningful, productive connections and work.

Service work, the least prestigious and most maligned part of the professorial workload, is, I'd argue, the area of academic work ripest with potential for DWYL with L. Service work—which encompasses everything from serving on committees to editing journals to taking on chair or decanal roles—has the greatest potential for working with love. Service work is by nature collaborative, engaged with others, and in service of the institution's greater mission—all key elements not only of loving connection, but of doing work that can, in the right contexts, feel like a vocation and not just work.

And guess what? Alt-ac jobs are this service work made career—collaborative, often team-based, practical work done in service of the university and its researchers and teachers. And although alt-ac careers are widely varied, that variety gives you more potential for doing what you love. PhDs are qualified to take on many, many academic staff roles, and that diversity of options means you can find the job that fits your personal values and skills. Too, at least in my experience, alt-ac careers are amenable to flow—they're the right level of challenging while drawing on a deep well of existing knowledge and skill developed during graduate school—generally pay well, are far more available than tenure-track jobs in places near our people, and allow us to work with others who share our values within an environment we're comfortable in and care about. In short, alt-ac careers can and often do have all the ingredients necessary for long-term happiness.

FIGURING OUT WHAT YOU LOVE

Positive psychologists and many others—from time-management specialists to career coaches—have designed tools and techniques to figure out what it is that you love, what you value, and what will make your work feel like a vocation. The range of alt-ac jobs is deep and wide, and there is ample opportunity to find work that closely aligns with your strengths and values, far more closely than the narrow limits of a professorial job allows. Some of the tools I like best for doing this self-assessment work are the exercises in Susan Basalla and Maggie Debelius's classic book *So What Are You Going to Do with That?: A Guide to Career-Changing for M.A.s and PhDs*,[36] Seligman and Peterson's VIA character strengths survey,[37] Laura Vanderkam's time audit (which I've written about adapting for career exploration),[38] and the old classic Strengthsfinder 2.0.[39]

Whatever tool or exercises you choose, the idea is to figure out what you value and what you're good at so that you can start looking for alt-ac roles that, in addition to (generally by default) paying well, existing close to your chosen home and community, and enabling you to create lots of healthful and happiness-generating loving connections, challenge you enough to create flow and align with your values and character. I've been fortunate to do that—I work directly with graduate students, fellows, and faculty on improving the conditions and career outcomes of graduate and postdoctoral training in the biomedical sciences. I get paid well, I walk to work, I get to put my kid to bed every night, and I get to do work rooted in love—connecting with my students and fellows, lovingly guiding them toward the next stage of their lives and watching them go on to do what they love. Find an alt-ac job with these ingredients—connection, challenge, love—and you've set yourself up for a career, and a life, that you love—and that loves you back.

CONCLUSION

Alt-ac jobs are, by their very natures, service work. As academic staff, we serve the institutes and disciplines for and within which we work. More importantly, we serve and connect with the people in those institutions, working to make their lives and work more effective, easier, more humane. The version of the academy that Miya Tokumitsu and Rebecca Schuman denigrate—and rightfully so—more often than not sees this kind of service work as less important, less useful, and less prestigious than research. Those of us who absorbed some or a lot of the academic indoctrination that Tokumitsu and Schuman describe may have also seen service careers—alt-ac careers—as lesser, as Plan B, as a thing to if we couldn't do what we loved (that it, become professors).

But, as the research out of the field of positive psychology suggests, the fact that alt-ac careers are service careers is no bad thing. To move into an alt-ac career is to work in service of the mission of the universities in which we've spent much of our learning and working lives and in service of the people, like and often including ourselves, who are working to generate and share new knowledge that can make the world better. To work in alignment with our values and characters, in jobs that challenge and remunerate us appropriately, doing labor that allows us many moments of human connection at and outside of work, is the true definition of doing what you love, with love.

Love has everything to do with it.

NOTES

1. This is largely due to my intersections of privilege, which I think are important to lay out so that you can place my writing and career trajectory in a context that may be helpful to you. I'm a white settler woman. I'm queer but I'm married to a man, so I pass as straight. My mental health conditions are well controlled with SSRIs. I'm cis and abled and tall. I'm fat, but I'm small enough not to be subject to much weight-related discrimination. I'm a first-generation university student, but I come from a family who would (and have) given me money and a place to stay when I needed it. The sexual harassment I experienced during grad school wasn't violent or traumatic. It was my decision to leave the tenure-track career path, not one that was forced on me, although the structures of the academy—lack of support for parents, expectation of total geographic mobility, disinterest in work-life balance and boundaries, precarious working conditions for all but a privileged few—certainly shaped that decision.

2. Rebecca Schuman, "Thesis Hatement," *Slate*, April 5, 2013, http://www.slate.com/articles/life/culturebox/2013/04/there_are_no_academic_jobs_and_getting_a_ph_d_will_make_you_into_a_horrible.html.

3. Joel Warner and Aaron Clauset, "The Academy's Dirty Secret," *Slate*, February 23, 2015, https://slate.com/human-interest/2015/02/university-hiring-if-you-didn-t-get-your-ph-d-at-an-elite-university-good-luck-finding-an-academic-job.html.

4. Miya Tokumitsu, "In the Name of Love," *Jacobin*, January 12, 2014, https://www.jacobinmag.com/2014/01/in-the-name-of-love/.

5. I seem to be addicted to working in sectors where DWYL is used to undervalue and overwork people—the three other worst job sectors for DWYL exploitation are nonprofits, public education, and motherhood.

6. Sarah Brouilette, "Academic Labor, the Aesthetics of Management, and the Promise of Autonomous Work," Nonsite, May 1, 2013, https://nonsite.org/article/academic-labor-the-aesthetics-of-management-and-the-promise-of-autonomous-work.

7. Tokumitsu, "In the Name of Love."

8. Immanuel Kant, *Groundwork for the Metaphysics of Morals*, ed. Lara Denis (Peterborough, ON: Broadview Press, 2005), 78.

9. Chris Tkach and Sonja Lyubomirsky, "How Do People Pursue Happiness?: Relating Personality, Happiness-Increasing Strategies, and Well-Being," *Journal of Happiness Studies* 7, no. 2 (June 2006): 184.

10. Sonja Lyubomirsky, *The How of Happiness* (New York: Penguin, 2007), 32.

11. See Lyubomirsky, *The How of Happiness*, and Daniel Gilbert, *Stumbling on Happiness* (Toronto: Vintage Canada, 2007).

12. Dianne A. Vella-Brodrick, Nansook Park, and Christopher Peterson, "Three Ways to Be Happy: Pleasure, Engagement, and Meaning-Findings from Australian and US Samples," *Social Indicators Research* 90, no. 2 (January 2009): 165.

13. Barbara Fredrickson, *Love 2.0: Finding Happiness and Health in Moments of Connection* (New York: Plume, 2013), 10.

14. Sara Ahmed, *The Promise of Happiness* (Durham, NC: Duke University Press, 2010), 3.

15. Ahmed, *The Promise of Happiness*, 10.

16. Ahmed, 13.

17. As Sonja Lyubomirsky notes, beyond an annual salary of about US$75,000, money does not make us any happier; in fact, our desire for money rises with our salaries—for every additional dollar per hour we make, we think we need $1.40 per hour more to be happy—so making more can actually make us less happy (because unfulfilled desire tends to lead to unhappiness). See Lyubomirksky, *The How of Happiness*, 44.

18. We adapt to the happiness of marriage after a few years, and our levels return to baseline. See Richard E. Lucas et al., "Reexamining Adaptation and the Set Point Model of Happiness: Reactions to Changes in Marital Status," *Journal of Personality and Social Psychology* 84, no. 3 (2003): 527–539.

19. Research suggests that manipulating our bodies through weight loss or plastic surgery does not make us any happier or alleviate mental health problems. See Sarah E. Jackson et al., "Psychological Changes following Weight Loss in Overweight and Obese Adults: A Prospective Cohort Study," *PLOS One* 9, no. 8 (August 2014): 1–8; and Tilmann von Soest, Ingela Lundin Kvalem,

and Lars Wichstrøm, "Predictors of Cosmetic Surgery and Its Effects on Psychological Factors and Mental Health: A Population-Based Follow-up Study among Norwegian Females," *Psychological Medicine* 42, no. 3 (2012): 617–626.

20. Ahmed, *The Promise of Happiness*, 10.

21. *The Simpsons*, "Home Away from Homer," Season 16, Episode 20, directed by Bob Anderson, written by Joel H. Cohen. Fox Broadcasting, May 15, 2005.

22. *Simpsons*, "Home Away from Homer."

23. Mihalyi Csikszentmihalyi's research tells us that achieving a state of flow makes an experience truly satisfying, as people typically experience deep enjoyment, creativity, and a total involvement with life. His books *Flow: The Psychology of Optimal Experience* (New York: HarperCollins, 2008) and *Optimal Experience: Psychological Studies of Flow in Consciousness* (Cambridge, UK: Cambridge University Press, 1992) offer a comprehensive survey of research on the "flow" experience in various contexts/cultures and how it improves work satisfaction, academic success, and overall quality of life.

24. See Martin Seligman, "Via Character Strengths Survey," Via Institute on Character, accessed September 23, 2019, https://www.viacharacter.org/survey/account/register.

25. Having strong social ties makes you healthier and happier. See David Myers, "The Funds, Friends, and Faith of Happy People," *American Psychologist* 55, no. 1 (January 2000): 56; and Ed Diener and Martin Seligman, "Very Happy People," *Psychological Science* 13, no. 1 (January 2002): 81–84.

26. A large number of studies using the VIA survey demonstrate that working with your signature strengths leads to higher workplace performance, happiness, salary, and sense of living a meaningful life. See "Character Strengths in the Workplace and Organizations," VIA Institute on Character, accessed September 23, 2019, https://www.viacharacter.org/research/findings/character-strengths-in-the-workplace-and-organizations.

27. Csikszentmihalyi, *Flow.*

28. Prioritizing time over money—as your general life ethos—makes you happier. See Ashley V. Whillans, Aaron C. Weidman, and Elizabeth W. Dunn, "Valuing Time over Money Is Associated with Greater Happiness," *Social Psychological and Personality Science* 7, no. 3 (2016): 213–222.

29. Lyubomirsky, *The How of Happiness.*

30. Fredrickson, *Love 2.0.*

31. Bethany Nowviskie, "Two & a Half Cheers for the Lunaticks," *Bethany Nowviskie* (blog), January 8, 2012, http://nowviskie.org/2012/lunaticks/.

32. As Lee Skallerup Bessette notes in her "Call for Submissions," "Librarians are the exception, however, writing eloquently about the affective elements of their role on campus, particularly as they embody both a liminal and feminized space (see Logsdon, Alexis, Amy Mars & Heather Tompkins. "Claiming

expertise from betwixt and between: Digital humanities librarians, emotional labor, and genre theory")."

33. Bessette, "Call for Submissions."

34. Fredrickson, *Love 2.0*, 7.

35. Fredrickson, 8.

36. Susan Basalla and Maggie Debelius, *"So What Are You Going to Do with That?": Finding Careers Outside of Academia*, 3rd ed. (Chicago: University of Chicago Press, 2014).

37. Seligman, "Via Character Strengths Survey."

38. Melissa Dalgleish, "Counting the Hours," Inside Higher Ed, October 29, 2018, https://www.insidehighered.com/advice/2018/10/29/tracking-your-time-can-help-you-determine-what-do-your-life-opinion.

39. "Clifton Strengths," Gallup, accessed September 25, 2019, https://www.gallupstrengthscenter.com/.

BIBLIOGRAPHY

Ahmed, Sara. *The Promise of Happiness.* Durham, NC: Duke University Press, 2010.

Basalla, Susan, and Maggie Debelius. *"So What Are You Going to Do with That?": Finding Careers Outside of Academia*, 3rd ed. Chicago: University of Chicago Press, 2014.

Bessette, Lee Skallerup. "Call for Submissions: Terms of Service: Affective Labor and Alt-Ac Careers." Accessed January 23, 2020. https://docs.google.com/document/d/1TPA1SOhoIOrGqJFG3Kc2GyRk6aCcDZhd4fWajkXANRY/edit.

Brouilette, Sarah. "Academic Labor, the Aesthetics of Management, and the Promise of Autonomous Work." Nonsite, May 1, 2013. https://nonsite.org/article/academic-labor-the-aesthetics-of-management-and-the-promise-of-autonomous-work.

"Character Strengths in the Workplace and Organizations." VIA Institute on Character. Accessed September 23, 2019. https://www.viacharacter.org/research/findings/character-strengths-in-the-workplace-and-organizations.

"Clifton Strengths." Gallup. Accessed September 25, 2019. https://www.gallupstrengthscenter.com/.

Csikszentmihalyi, Mihalyi. *Flow: The Psychology of Optimal Experience.* New York: HarperCollins, 2008.

———. *Optimal Experience: Psychological Studies of Flow in Consciousness.* Cambridge, UK: Cambridge University Press, 1992.

Dalgleish, Melissa. "Counting the Hours." Inside Higher Ed. October 29, 2018.

https://www.insidehighered.com/advice/2018/10/29/tracking-your-time-can-help-you-determine-what-do-your-life-opinion.

Diener, Ed, and Martin Seligman. "Very happy people." *Psychological Science,* 13, no. 1 (January 2002): 81–84.

Fredrickson, Barbara. *Love 2.0: Finding Happiness and Health in Moments of Connection.* New York: Plume, 2013.

Gilbert, Daniel. *Stumbling on Happiness.* Toronto: Vintage Canada, 2007.

Jackson, Sarah E., Andrew Steptoe, Rebecca J Beeken, Mika Kivimaki, and Jane Wardle. "Psychological Changes following Weight Loss in Overweight and Obese Adults: A Prospective Cohort Study." *PLOS One* 9, no. 8 (2014).

Kant, Immanuel. *Groundwork for the Metaphysics of Morals.* Lara Denis, ed. Peterborough, ON: Broadview Press, 2005.

Lucas, Richard E., Andrew E. Clark, Yannis Georgellis, and Ed Diener. "Reexamining Adaptation and the Set Point Model of Happiness: Reactions to Changes in Marital Status." *Journal of Personality and Social Psychology* 84, no. 3 (2003): 527–539.

Lyubomirsky, Sonja. *The How of Happiness.* New York: Penguin, 2007.

Myers, David. "The Funds, Friends, and Faith of Happy People." *American Psychologist* 55, no. 1 (January 2000): 56–67.

Nowviskie, Bethany. "Two & a Half Cheers for the Lunaticks." *Bethany Nowviskie* (blog). January 8, 2012. http://nowviskie.org/2012/lunaticks/.

Schuman, Rebecca. "Thesis Hatement." *Slate.* April 5, 2013. http://www.slate.com/articles/life/culturebox/2013/04/there_are_no_academic_jobs_and_getting_a_ph_d_will_make_you_into_a_horrible.html.

The Simpsons. "Home Away from Homer." Season 16, Episode 20. Directed by Bob Anderson. Written by Joel H. Cohen. Fox Broadcasting. May 15, 2005.

Tkach, Chris, and Sonja Lyubomirsky. "How Do People Pursue Happiness?: Relating Personality, Happiness-Increasing Strategies, and Well-Being." *Journal of Happiness Studies* 7, no. 2 (June 2006): 183–225.

Tokumitsu, Miya. "In the Name of Love." *Jacobin.* January 12, 2014. https://www.jacobinmag.com/2014/01/in-the-name-of-love/.

Vella-Brodrick, Dianne A., Nansook Park, and Christopher Peterson. "Three Ways to Be Happy: Pleasure, Engagement, and Meaning-Findings from Australian and US Samples." *Social Indicators Research* 90, no. 2 (January 2009): 165–179.

von Soest, Tilmann, Ingela Lundin Kvalem, and Lars Wichstrøm. "Predictors of Cosmetic Surgery and Its Effects on Psychological Factors and Mental Health: A Population-Based Follow-up Study among Norwegian Females." *Psychological Medicine* 42, no. 3 (2012): 617–626.

Warner, Joe, and Aaron Clauset. "The Academy's Dirty Secret." *Slate.* February 23, 2015. https://slate.com/human-interest/2015/02/university-hiring-if-you

-didn-t-get-your-ph-d-at-an-elite-university-good-luck-finding-an-aca demic-job.html.

Whillans, Ashley V., Aaron C. Weidman, and Elizabeth W. Dunn. "Valuing Time over Money Is Associated with Greater Happiness." *Social Psychological and Personality Science* 7, no. 3 (2016): 213–222.

3

Affective Allyship

Alt-Ac Identity and Political Work in Higher Education

GRACE POLLOCK

There is a structure of feeling that underlies allyship. At the same time, allyship and its political and moral commitments provide a structure for our feelings. I am interested in how the feelings of being "alt-ac," and the process of exploring "alt-ac" as an identity, might help us *feel our way* to being better allies. Allyship is forged through actions that are grounded in an awareness of our relative privilege or our relative marginalization in relation to others. We arrive at this awareness through relationships, which present us with opportunities for perspective-taking and help us to come closer to understanding what others think and feel. Acknowledging our own social location and how other people are differently located enables us to recognize and ideally to join with them in seeking redress for the inequitable access and distribution of social, material, and cultural resources across our society. As Melinda Epler writes,

> Some people have to work ten times as hard to get to the same place due to many barriers put in front of them by society. . . . Allyship is about understanding that imbalance in opportunity and working to correct it.

> Allyship is really seeing the person next to us. And the person missing, who should be standing next to us. And first, just knowing what they're going through. And then, helping them succeed and thrive with us.[1]

Like Epler, I'm interested in how we approach these "ally" relationships at work, and in trying to understand the institutional context that forms my own identity and practices as an alt-ac worker in the academy. How do our social identities and positions relative to institutional power impact alt-ac workers? What does it mean to perceive others as being "affected" and to be ourselves "affected" by a lack of equity and fairness within society that also manifests across the institution in which we work? Are there ways in which the condition of being "affected" might provide the awareness and motivation needed to challenge and, through our work, to *work against* the inequities and injustice felt by ourselves and others?

Approaching workplace relationships through the lens of allyship, I suggest, can provide a meaningful way to understand our "alt-ac" place, and to rethink our practices within an institution in which we must, awkwardly at times, *feel our way* as "nonacademic" qualified professionals who occupy nontraditional academic roles. Allyship can also provide a model for alt-ac workers to refocus the affective and material labor we are already contributing to the institution to have a positive impact on the people and culture around us in ways that will provide more coherence in terms of who we are as alt-ac professionals and move us closer to establishing a values base that could inform alt-ac community building—ultimately to the benefit of the institutions where we work.

The discussion that unfolds in this chapter represents an effort to better understand how the structure of feeling that underlies allyship might translate in alt-ac work environments, and to explore how allyship enacted by alt-ac staff in the domain of higher education presents the possibility for increased worker agency in terms of how and to what end we contribute our affective labor—whether toward the maintenance or toward the transformation of institutional practices. I draw out connections between two typically distinct lines of thought. The first strand of thought woven throughout the chapter is indebted to a growing body of literature around the politics of emotion, specifically the role of emotion in becoming aware of one's own and others' marginalization and privilege. Ann Cvetkovich's ground-breaking work, *Archive of Feeling*, asserts that we become "marked" by our circulation in communities that bring us close to both our own experience and our witnessing of trauma, as "moments of everyday emotional distress that are often the only sign that trauma's effects are still being felt."[2] I ask, how might we as alt-ac professionals *feel* our way through our work, and how might this increase our self-awareness as actors within an institutional setting?

There are compelling reasons to take issue with the term *alt-ac*, as the label situates the bearer permanently as an outsider with respect to the bona fide academy, and may also signal for some that the academically trained worker never managed to live up to the achievements for which their training was designed.[3] I initially refused to apply the term *alt-ac* to myself, and instead adopted a professional designation, such as "research administrator," that never quite felt like a fit, particularly after spending years dedicated to the cultivation of an academic identity. I now think there is value in reclaiming and asserting the label alt-ac precisely because it names a role that has the capacity, through its distinctiveness or otherness, its alterity, to reconstitute the academy and academic work. There are particular insights regarding the workings of academic institutions that can be gleaned from the experience of being institutionally subordinate, in terms of status, paychecks, and authority, while being privileged, at least educationally, within the overall context of societal forms of marginalization and disempowerment. Connecting the awareness and skills acquired by navigating murky waters of institutional life means asserting the epistemic and ethical value of this experiential learning as a form of *expert knowledge.* Moreover, this "expertise," which, as Eugenia Zuroski argues, "universities have a way of recognizing and extracting without crediting" from socially marginalized workers, is rooted in deeply affective experiences: the condition of "living through, and thinking through, unjust conditions of being."[4] Benefiting from these important reflections on social marginalization, I have come to see my function within the university as "alt-ac staff" as a matter not simply of owning and shaping an otherwise unrecognized professional life and career trajectory; it has become about connecting to my life to work in a way that is, inevitably, deeply personal. The feelings associated with toggling between an awareness, simultaneously, of my privilege, on the one hand, and of my marginalization, on the other, was already familiar to me. Now this exercise has become integral to my work identity as well as my social identity. I have found the bridging of "work" and "life"—rather than the balancing of two realms framed in oppositional terms—reflects the identity formation enabled by my previous and current academic experiences within the specific structure of the university more so than would be possible through selecting from a range of established and strictly professional labels.[5]

This brings me to the second body of literature being engaged in this chapter, which deals with the organizational culture of higher education and the way it manifests, sometimes starkly, uneven degrees of hierarchical and lateral power. Within this structure, alt-ac positions are growing in number. This is unsurprising, given the likewise growing pool of highly skilled, unemployed PhD graduates. Yet the new and varied roles being created for alt-ac professionals do not fit easily within the traditional structure of the university. In what follows, I suggest they serve a distinctive function in acting as boundary roles, navigating within and between traditionally separate and streamlined cultures of the institution.[6] The ambiguous placement and status of alt-ac professional staff make us appear often as ciphers to faculty and administrative staff with more traditional occupations who typically receive specialized training and move into long-standing, well-defined roles. "What do you *do?*" is a question I am asked frequently when people are presented with my official job title "research support facilitator." More often than not, I have different answers for the questioner depending on whether they are faculty, staff, or senior administrators. I would wager that a lack of streamlined responsibilities is common among the proliferating alt-ac roles within higher education. As alt-ac professionals, we are awkwardly located at the edges of a rigid status hierarchy, which is itself situated within the larger corporate bureaucratic enterprise that is the contemporary university.

There is an "abject" quality inherent to being alt-ac staff. The feeling of this abjectness—of never quite belonging while being tied to structural conditions that impose a quasi-permanent sense of shame—intersected with the familiar feelings arising from where I am located, socially, as a disabled queer woman and lone parent. The clichés around achieving work-life balance, and even the idea (let alone the effort), to compartmentalize my work from myself, rang false. The realization of "double" disempowerment, rather than immobilizing me, became a motivator. I stopped trying to disentangle sites of personal oppression with a sense of institutionalized disempowerment. I started searching for communities at work to which I could belong, and this brought me to other people, individuals and groups, who were doing both formal and informal equity, diversity, and inclusion work across the university. Alliances emerged within this community from a sense of urgency, a critique of institutional power and a shared commitment that oppression must be challenged. It was this affective condition of *feeling my work*, and giving myself permission to *feel at work*, that linked what I was doing, as a laborer *and* agent of power, back to my identity—despite the fact my effort would only occasionally be recognized, and even then usually relegated to some nondescript form of "institutional service." My work could be an integral expression of my values. Feeling became the basis for theorizing how my own practices as nonacademic staff either reinforced or challenged inequities and injustice, marginalization and voicelessness, and how my lived experiences could, in turn, be brought to bear on the content, knowledge, and skills required by my work.

The nature of allyship is complex and fluid, because it depends on relationships that intertwine with multiple layers of social identity and variable contextual circumstances. Many people occupy intersecting social locations. I'm white and cis gendered, which means I carry on my body instantly identifiable markers of belonging to two dominant social groups. I also identify as a queer woman and a feminist, and I encounter frequent systemic barriers as a lone mother living with a chronic health condition. But, in almost all circumstances, I enjoy the privilege of self-disclosure when and with whom I feel safe. When I mentioned to a staff colleague who is a woman of color that I had a disability that informed my commitment to equity (an "invisible" one that can be accommodated by my employer), I quickly followed up with the statement that it is "not the same" as her experience working as a racialized person within a predominantly white department of the university. We should always be wary of setting up a hierarchy of oppressions; yet it is important, especially in allyship, to be attentive to the specificity of difference. The growing body of literature that seeks to unpack white privilege is instructive here. Robin DiAngelo's important work on "white fragility" elaborates how white people, in a society organized according to an allegedly "natural" order of white supremacy, are insulated from experiences of racial stress. As a result, asserts DiAngelo, white people have a low tolerance for the affective and cognitive challenges posed to their own "unmarked" racial identity when asked to consider the social impacts of racism and racialization, and particularly their own "racially based privileges they hold that reinforce racist disadvantage for others."[7] I think there are important lessons to learn from this. Two pitfalls, in my experience, will halt allyship in its tracks. The first is claiming innocence ("I am not racist" or "That's how I am with everyone" or "I didn't mean it that way"), which not only fails to grasp the structural effects of racism but, in doing so, reduces the lived social experience of racialized people to a matter of individualized intent and perception. Add-on phrases like,

"Well, that's your view" or "I'm sorry you think that" are not benign. They redouble the negating effect, not only by failing to recognize the courage it takes another to articulate felt experiences of inhabiting a society that discriminates against them but also by, in a manner suggestive of "gaslighting," insinuating that their grasp of reality has somehow faltered. The claim to innocence is therefore a subtle way to reassert the authority of one's own perception. The second pitfall is assuming that all sites of oppression are the same or that all experiences of oppression carry the same affective and material impacts. This leads, in my experience, to either a denial of or overidentification with the oppression of another. The latter is especially egregious when one has not been invited to draw analogies to one's self or to commiserate with community or culturally based grief. Allyship calls on allies to de-center themselves from the narrative, a privilege allies have always enjoyed and taken for granted. It requires being open and humble, to listen and to learn from what others wish to say, and to assume a lack of knowledge that means asking respectful questions to become better informed.

Allyship calls on allies to refuse neutrality as a performance of equality that functions to mask and sustain inequities. It asks us to recognize and appreciate identity as a valid epistemic lens for understanding our individual and collective realities. It calls on allies to take responsibility and to be accountable for the system that permits white, cis gender, heteronormative people the privilege of simply being individuated "selves." At the same time, as George Yancy points out, there is nothing noble in being aware of one's white privilege, or even in being aware that all white people are racist, despite themselves or their liberal views, because each and every white person has reaped the benefits of living in a racist society.[8] Neither does a declaration that one "means well" communicate anything other than a presumptuous entitlement to forgiveness from the other whom our exercise of privilege has harmed. Naming our privilege gives us no more claim to moral "innocence" than does naming shared sites of oppression in a way that conflates other identities and experiences with our own. It's what we do with privilege that matters. It's what I do affectively and cognitively in the wake of a genuine recognition of difference that does not reduce the other to an object within my own narrow frame of selfhood. Having privilege and possessing humility, and demonstrating a willingness to use power by following the lead of others, in order to make processes and practices more transparent, fair, and equal, are what qualify a person to function as an ally.

Being an alt-ac employee is not the same as belonging to an equity-seeking group. This might be an obvious point. Where we work in terms of our job-seeking and employment options is impacted by, but is certainly not equivalent to, the social location into which, for the most part, we were born and which is as significant in terms of our identity as skin is to the body. I became more deeply aware of the different experiences entailed by my identity at work in a conversation with a white, straight male coworker. We had been asked to discuss, as part of a diversity training exercise, the physical symptoms of our "personal triggers." He shared first. He told me that his face would flush deep red when someone pointed out a typographical error in a document he authored. I was a bit stunned that he did not frame such a minor embarrassment, or the subsequent claim to "perfectionism," as luxuries afforded by his privilege. I carried on. Complying with the expectation of reciprocity, I shared that "silencing" was my trigger; whether it was myself or another person being overtly interrupted or talked over, I feel a falling sensation in the pit of my stomach followed by a tightening in my chest, like a fist constricting my heart. I could have gone on, though I did not, to share that for as long as I could remember, whenever I had expressed a critical idea as a "girl" or had advocated for my adult self as a survivor of gender-based violence, even in what I thought was a reasoned cogent manner, a voice in my head would accuse me, mimicking past voices I had heard, of taking a "shrill" or "shrieking" tone. Witnessing another person to whom I'm speaking respond in ways that convey contempt for my voice or for others' speech produces an embodied sensation of becoming alien that paradoxically is like being lifted out of and hovering apart from my body. Language or body language that says "shut up" or otherwise enforces silence triggers brutal and benumbing feelings of dissociation and helplessness, recalling how I felt as a young victim of violence.

I bring this past experience with me to work every day. Having my "irritating" female voice be unheard and the ideas dismissed, sometimes repeatedly, has made it difficult for me now to express emotion or to speak up in public settings. There are probably direct costs in terms of career advancement that could be tied to a perceived and actual lack of assertiveness on my part, or to apparent emotional disengagement. It is not easy to be social, or to network and form work friendships. I consider myself a private person, which sometimes makes discussions of identity that are central to equity work also very difficult. So, in the exchange described above, I did not share why silencing is a trigger. I also did not call out my colleague on his privilege. I admit his lack of self-awareness, however jovial his naiveté, got me down. At the same time, it got my back up. Is it not a luxury to function with the assurance that supervisors and colleagues might justly correct your work because you were mistaken, rather than wondering always if their particular judgment is motivated, unconsciously or consciously, by bias? It seemed impossible not to feel resentment at the example of "marginalization" that he offered as having elicited the worst feelings he could recall at work, despite the fact I could see he was present and engaged in the task assigned. My resentment might have been better directed at the inexplicable ubiquity of trauma language in the present moment in our culture. Trauma—and socially based traumatization—is deeply rooted in people who have experienced it. Being aware of trauma-informed practices if one works with affected individuals or populations is critical. For this reason, I think we should worry when the label "trauma" is coopted and its meaning so diluted that now almost anything can be claimed by anyone to be a trigger, even having a typo one has made being pointed out.

I do not wish for the analogy I am drawing between social identity and institutional position to elide the fact that the path for me to attain the qualifications for an alt-ac job was relatively barrier-free. I come from a white, middle-class, educated family with two working parents. Within the larger society, as a financial advisor at my bank has reminded me, the salary and unionized status of my job affords me more security than most people. Working in higher education at a degree-granting institution and having in my possession a terminal degree means that I am also granted some status and credibility when I communicate ideas as a PhD, if the listeners check their assumptions about staff and are aware I have the degree (I've encountered incredulous faculty members say, "*You* have a *PhD?*" more than a few times). As this demonstrates, I am patently not a faculty "peer" and will never be given tenure, academic freedom, promotion and salary increases at the faculty rate, or one of the many leadership and governance roles that the institution reserves for faculty. As a result, most days I am situationally marginalized and privileged at the same time. In my current position, I work as a white staff member alongside a still predominantly white liberal arts faculty body that forms a stark contrast with the diverse student body as well as increasingly diverse staff. I am also aware of being part of a collective mass of white women who fill the majority of the middle-to-upper professional and management roles within the university. This largely female-composed staff wield a type of power through our everyday actions. We set in motion a multitude of effects, often turning on a self-made decision whether to share or to withhold the cumulative knowledge we have acquired as permanent staff members. But working at the university, even as part of these middle ranks, is by no means uniformly privileged. A number of colleagues who share my "middle" status have taken stress leaves or complained of burnout. When looking around at coworkers, it is difficult to conclude anything other than labor conditions in higher education are rife with disparities and inequities, and as Lee Skallerup Bessette points out, for administrative staff, adjunct faculty, and facilities personnel, among others, working conditions can be outright "dehumanizing."[9]

What is more, women are not typically found among the white male institutional leaders, a fact that appears consistent within higher education in Canada,[10] and neither do women working as front-line staff seem to be elevated through the managerial ranks as often or as quickly as our male counterparts. The stark discrepancy between those whose power is acknowledged, appropriately compensated, and wielded with impunity—between the predominantly white male upper ranks who occupy visible governance roles—and everyone else is mapped onto the chasm between who defines institutional values and sets institutional practices and who actually does the work. My experience as alt-ac in this institutional context is overlaid by the social identities I bring to work, and this has meant ever shifting between privilege and marginalization according to the structural conditions and experiences that impact me as well as others. Epler remarks that as a white cisgender woman working in the tech industry, she can "work hard every day to be an ally for people with less privilege" and, at the same, "needs allies, too."[11]

Allyship in employment contexts, particularly when equity-oriented initiatives are being done "at the side of one's desk," often takes the form of and shares attributes with affective labor. For this reason, it is important to recognize the critiques regarding how affective labor often goes unrecognized and uncompensated (despite being a commodified asset for a service organization like the university). The expectation of affective engagement in service work can function quickly to reinforce stereotypical gender expectations rooted in inequitable labor practices and cultural norms (men are driven producers, women are caring reproducers). Research done on academic service work, for example, has shown that female faculty contribute significantly more uncompensated service work to the university, and the expectation of senior administrators that faculty will engage in service falls disproportionately to women.[12] Although I do not know of any similar research conducted among staff (which makes the publication of this volume all the more important), it would be surprising if the practice of routinely "tapping on" female staff in support roles to perform work outside of their defined job description varied in any significant degree from the experiences of female faculty—though, for the former, compliance is rarely optional. The appropriation of this "sacrificial labor" is enacted in a contradictory fashion, particularly for women, within the culture of the "modern white-collar workplace" in which emotional self-regulation lies at the center of notions of "competence and professionalism."[13] Emotion, but not *too much* emotion, is the demand placed on staff working in the university. And where to draw this line is also complicated by the dominant cultural stereotypes attached to gender, race, and disability, in which emotional expression can become the very grounds for stigmatization and discrimination.[14] Sara Ahmed's work on the politics of emotion and how affect is read in social contexts as "attributes of bodies" is instructive. Who gets to express feeling, and how that feeling is judged as good or bad, is intimately tied to where on the social hierarchy the body expressing the emotion is located.[15] As it is in life, so it is in work.

Controlled affective displays, despite appearances, do not necessarily signal worker control. As Melissa Gregg argues, workers who project emotional control are often "exhibiting somatic and psychic strategies" in response to anxiety, insecurity, and fear that their workload is getting out of control.[16] Worker self-discipline through the management of affect is also more than an individualistic coping mechanism that conceals stress and hyper-attunement to personal risk. It is a political practice and a key way through which the power of the institution becomes enacted by its constituent parts. Following from Michel Foucault's concept of governmentality, power within a complex organization is "not a matter of imposing a sovereign will, but instead a process of enlisting the cooperation of chains of actors who 'translate' power from one locale to another."[17] As workers within higher education, each of us faces extreme pressure to distance ourselves from genuine affective responses—ones that might be elicited, for example, by listening to personal grievances expressed by coworkers or bearing witness to institutional forms of injustice or inequity—and, at the same time, to produce and channel our affect in order to "smooth out" sanctioned institutional processes, particularly the ones that feel most oppressive. Affect is therefore critical to maintaining the institution, and it is also critical to disrupting the default operations of power within the workplace.

As alt-ac workers, we are uniquely and perhaps treacherously positioned within the academy between staff and faculty in a way that typically offers us little comfort in terms of workplace stability.[18] But this placement, and self-awareness of our "alt" condition, presents opportunities for taking a double perspective that can help us to expose the workings of power and unsettle entrenched hierarchies. I suggest that rather than hand over affect as an uncompensated "add on" to our labor, we should mobilize affect as a means to recondition ourselves as agents and to challenge and change working conditions, when necessary, for ourselves and others. Allyship, in this sense, is a deepening of our affective experience at work, and of our roles as cultural workers, rather than the superficial expression of "service with a smile." I spent several years thinking critically about my practices as a scholar, and I bring that critical reflection into the staff role that I now occupy. We may wish to adopt a new professional identity that supplants or complements our alt-ac identity, but I think there is value in sticking with the nomenclature and defining what it means to be an alt-ac practitioner on our own terms. One way to do this, as Lee Skallerup Bessette writes, is "not [to] lose our commitment to justice and equity."[19] I have not been required in my job to relinquish either my scholarly acumen or my engagement with scholarship. Indeed, I was told explicitly that I was hired because of my graduate and postgraduate experience doing research in the humanities and social sciences. I have come to a place now where I view my critique of the institution for the purposes of exposing inequity and promoting inclusion as a vital service I bring to the institution and an integral part of my role. I believe that alt-ac work in higher education, when filtered through a critical lens that is attentive to the politics of affect, will enable us to draw parallels across experiences at the level of the institutional and the social. My alt-ac experience within the university is distinctive, yet the condition I imagine sharing with other alt-acs is the one of feeling myself perpetually toggling between oppression and power within the larger institutional environment. This can produce stress, even burnout, but it can also prepare us to be attuned to the relative power and powerlessness of different locations and points of access to power that are made available to members of equity-seeking groups as well as other staff within the academic workplace.

I am relying on allyship as a model for this new kind of worker identity because alt-acs, for the most part, hover at the boundary between institutional privilege and institutional marginalization, and because institutional sites of oppression all too often mirror those of the larger society. In calling for allyship, I wish to challenge a prevalent notion—ironically, one I have heard expressed by people who in the same breath acknowledge their privilege—that somehow having privilege renders a person unqualified to identify and resist the oppression on which their privilege depends. Having privilege, and being aware of one's own privilege, certainly raises issues in terms of one's credibility as a spokesperson for others with less privilege. But having privilege hardly disqualifies a person from taking action that facilitates awareness of systemic privilege as a problem. To the contrary, in certain moments, I have seen allies figuratively "stick out their elbows" to point out injustice or demand equitable treatment: first making room, and then stepping back so others might enter the space and articulate their experience. At the same time, I have felt myself and witnessed among my white colleagues a creeping tendency to fall prey to a depoliticizing white shame. Being white means that we have benefited from unmerited privilege; this is a given in a settler colonial society organized around white supremacy. But feeling guilt that persists in centering the white self within the larger equation of racist and colonial oppression immobilizes advocacy: who does it serve if white people quietly slouch away from difficult situations without even trying to take a stand? If members of dominant groups constitute themselves as always and only privileged, then others will only ever be constituted through perpetual victimhood and enforced "resilience."

In an ironic twist, citing the "resilience" of marginalized people has become the response of power not only to well-placed criticisms of privileged people's presumptuousness in "speaking for" others, but also to important demands voiced by equity-seeking groups for power's accountability. Resilience, as the fait accompli of traumatic victimization, requires that victims not be viewed as helpless, constituted only as the objects of power. This recognition of agency is important, and critical in allyship, as the basis for building respectful relationships. But when a term like "resilience" is co-opted by power, it can be used to deny responsibility to the ones whom power has oppressed. "Resilience" is a label I have heard time and again applied to disenfranchised individuals and groups by senior leaders at the university to justify their own "hapless" inaction. In these contexts, citing "resilience" works at once to ennoble those in power and to entrench their moral superiority by allegedly paying tribute to the others' "assets" (but notably not the others' expressed demands). Ironically, acknowledging the strength and endurance of the oppressed keeps the less powerful "on the hook" for the labor involved in advocacy and mentorship, while getting the powerful "off the hook" in terms of exercising their authority to intervene against inequitable circumstances. This is a virtue signaling discourse that also normalizes trauma as a fact of existence, rather than expressing a desire to eliminate or reduce it. As scholars have noted, the appeal of "resilience" is that it can function to obscure the myriad forms of violence and oppression inflicted by neoliberalism's structuring of society[20] as well as its dominance in shaping the institutional policies and practices that prevail within contemporary higher education.[21]

The functional organization of most universities is stratified, with different hierarchical levels occupied by senior academic administrators, faculty, students, and staff. Universities are also historical-cultural organizations that respond to internal and external pressures across contexts of uneven institutional power and within a broader society rooted in colonialism and sustained by white supremacy. As state power has contracted under the weight of global neoliberal forces, particularly since the 1980s, state governments have reorganized to serve the interests of financial capital and to function primarily as mechanisms of surveillance and control.[22] The governance of the university, as well as other institutions that rely heavily on state funding, has responded to these external shifts, turning toward "corporate market bureaucracy" and "managerialism" to remodel internal policies and processes in ways that tend to prioritize financial calculus over older, nonutilitarian models of collegial governance and academic oligarchy.[23] The "mixed" approach to governance that characterizes the contemporary university has been elucidated by Ian McNay's matrix model of the organizational culture within higher education.[24] McNay observed that the university manifested the interplay of four distinct yet interdependent approaches to control and strategic goal formation: enterprise, corporate, collegiate, and bureaucratic. Each of these four approaches, represented as quadrants within the whole, exhibit particular "values." McNay's research explores what happens when values from different approaches actively compete with each other, and when the integrity of one approach is corrupted by values from another. What interests me about this work are the implications for staff—particularly for professional staff. Within this framework, staff roles are primarily "bureaucratic," but individuals may move or find themselves pulled within and between areas. In my own role as research support facilitator located within a semi-autonomous and comparatively "resource poor" faculty[25] and not within a central office of the university, I'm tasked with building collegial connections across various units of the university. I find myself interfacing with others as one of many institutional stakeholders, each of whom is similarly navigating a values-laden and resource-competitive terrain. Operating in this role, in the absence of supervisory authority yet without the protections afforded by tenure or academic freedom, comes with reputational and personal risks in terms of representing my employer's interests, which are not always one and the same with the interests of the broader institution, the interests of the faculty members, students or staff with whom I directly work, or my own interests as either an employee or an activist. In addition to the challenges of this lateral movement across organizational cultures, McNay reports that staff who occupy the middle "squeezed" stratus experience greater stress. In contrast, staff at the top reported feeling "confident," while staff on the front lines felt "carefree."[26] In other words, clear role definitions and established practices provide reassurance for many staff, typically through concentrating power at the top and minimizing it at the bottom. The middle rung where I wager most alt-ac staff would find ourselves positioned is not without power, despite often having few guidelines provided to us regarding our mandate. We can eschew the temptation to mirror the elitism embedded in the institutional culture by claiming a closer affinity with the increasing numbers of precariously employed workers in the university. Our neither/nor placement offers us a perspective through which we might respond to Bessette's call to examine the labor conditions of other staff members and to build solidarity across staff lines as we "acutely feel the sting of budgetary cuts, stagnant wages, and the rigid hierarchies of academia."[27]

As alt-ac staff, we have the potential to be conduits or barriers to the sharing of institutional knowledge as well as technical or field expertise. At the same time, we fit awkwardly within, or range between, what are usually starkly differentiated staff and faculty roles, or faculty and administrator roles—for example, being asked to serve on advisory committees or to be collaborators on research projects—and are granted power in some contexts and none in others. Solidarity happens when we form alliances across labor lines to demand better and more equitable working conditions. Allyship is similar in being a relational condition that forges alliances on the basis of recognizing that bigotry and systemic oppression have differential impacts on particular social identities. Allyship emerges from a set of critical practices developed through everyday experience, in which the interrelated tasks of perceiving and feeling are translated into concrete actions that leverage the ally's privilege to benefit others. One can take allyship training, which is increasingly offered by the mainstream corporations as well as universities; training does not confer the title of ally. We are acknowledged as "allies" by those who wish to make an alliance with us, whose identities are different from our own in some way, and whom we have acknowledged, in a reciprocal manner, as equally deserving of the rights, respect, and access to the material, social, and cultural well-being that we enjoy. In other words, our ally-ness is retroactively constituted as such by the people who have agreed to be allied with us, and with whom we have entered a relationship or made a pact, rather than a label to which we can lay claim or apply to ourselves. Allyship emerges from the ways in which other people feel respected and heard by us, as well as through the efforts we have made to improve their access to resources and to address other issues they have articulated to us. Allyship is about forming relationships with a purpose, but it does not begin and end with sentiment, however necessary the role of empathy for developing the relationships and capacities required for allyship. Within higher education, affective labor that intersects with a commitment to allyship works to translate particular feelings and values into concrete practices designed to remove barriers to the inclusion and participation of people from equity-seeking groups. These values-based labor practices are increasingly recognized across private and public workplace cultures to carry "commodifiable" value as well, particularly as the much-cited "business case" for equity, diversity, and inclusion gains traction.[28]

Equity, diversity, and inclusion, or EDI, initiatives are being launched at a fast pace in higher education, particularly in Canadian universities; a colleague of mine who is a diversity officer remarked in a cynical tone how the work to which she tirelessly dedicated her heart and mind for decades has now become "trendy." Although Epler is right to assert that "we make a mistake when we see diversity and inclusion as a side project over there the diversity people are working on," EDI initiatives being rolled out on an institution-wide basis tend to share a common strategic approach. This involves engaging senior leaders and uppermost management through unconscious bias training and policy shifts focused on recruitment and hiring practices. Adopting this surprisingly traditional method to institutional change—one that effectively takes feeling out of the equation—can work further to diminish the role of staff within the institutional culture, not least of all by giving credence to the illusion that values necessarily trickle down through imposing rote procedures. As staff, we are not mindless or utterly obedient to authority; in fact, staff occupy the center of institutional life in higher education. As staff members, our supervisors and workplace cultures inform our choices, but we also have the agency to set the day-to-day tone for the university as we "do the important work of keeping the institution running."[29] EDI initiatives that search for "champions" may obtain buy-in among the leadership ranks, but at the expense of reinforcing historically entrenched hierarchies. In this way, EDI strategic plans that go about instituting change as it has "always been done" end up turning away from a critique of power and hierarchy that should, instead, inform how the values of equity and inclusion become operationalized in terms of wholesale institutional transformation. Ironically, through targeting the upper ranks, EDI can leave behind a large swath of staff, which is also the labor segment typically comprising the greatest diversity and number of equity-seeking members within the university.

In my role, some days I feel that my own identity and sense of control over my work will be subsumed within the building tensions that arise from myriad "competing values" circulating within the university. I struggle to resist the seduction to serve as either a repository for institutional angst or an unthinking, unfeeling automaton. When I have the energy to assert myself as a self-directed knowledge practitioner, I often find myself running headlong into a tangle of ambivalent feelings regarding how to meet institutional objectives while making "good" choices that are informed by my own ethical framework. What are the implications of *not* feeling for one's self and for others in a work environment where relational dynamics are foundational to the communication and knowledge required to do the work? No matter how much effort we put into partitioning our "life" self from our "work" self, do we really have the choice on the job to determine when and where affect will be demanded and extracted from us? When workplace demands tend toward instrumentalizing emotion, our feelings do not need to remain fixed in a permanent state of either numbness or antagonism; they can guide us in crucial ways so that we are not simply working at the institution but also working *on* the institution.[30] Becoming aware of how others feel can hone our capacity to sense injustice and connect our affect to action. Taking measures to remove barriers for ourselves and for others entails effort, does not avoid conflict, and rarely arrives a point of evident closure.

It is always tempting in morally ambiguous situations to let oneself become emotionally "checked out." The institution will dictate what the "right" feelings should be for its employees and reward those employees who self-monitor and manage "their own business" with minimal supervision. This works out well for the institution but does not come without costs for the worker. Arlie Russell Hochschild explains how the stretch and strain of projecting the positive emotions that employers expect from workers in service roles can lead to "emotive dissonance."[31] Beyond the risk of depersonalization, "burnout is an occupational hazard for all performers of emotional labor, but may be most likely to occur among workers strongly identified with their jobs."[32] It would be quite difficult in the kind of institutions where knowledge is the commodity being circulated not to think about one's work as an expression, if not an extension, of the self. Within such contexts, understanding the consequences of affective labor—its uses and abuses—and the impacts on the worker and the workplace is important. But accounts of job-based stress rarely situate feelings within a framework that includes ethical and political values alongside individual and economic considerations. I have argued that the structure of feeling informed by the simultaneous experience of power and powerlessness relative to our multiple locations, both inside and outside of the institution where we work, prepares us to be attuned to moments and sites that are crucial to sustaining or to disrupting hierarchies of power.

Working in higher education for over a decade, I have heard an increasing number of stories, particularly from colleagues with disabilities, Indigenous colleagues, and colleagues of color, about encountering "unresponsiveness" when they voiced a concern about inequitable policies, harmful treatment, or a lack of resources, on the one hand, while being repeatedly "tokenized" through demands always to stand in or speak for their "group," on the other. Besides being thrust into a contradictory role that means vacillating between feeling ghost-like and feeling hyper-visible, I have heard colleagues express that they felt torn about saying no to offers made by their supervisors or others in the university to take on "service" roles—despite the fact that accepting and following through would typically mean subordinating their professional goals and interests to those of the institution. In my experience, members of equity-seeking groups know better than anyone that offers issued by power, despite appearances, do not exist within a kind of structure that permits the right of refusal. What is more, the call for group representation in these roles, when not having been requested by group members themselves, can shift quickly into a form of labor extraction within the very contexts where the stated aim is to be more aware of the unfair burdens and barriers that harm marginalized groups. Once mired in an institutional process, as a matter of pragmatism, people fear putting their jobs at risk based both on what they say and on what they do not say. At the same time, consenting to participate, often as the sole "minority" voice, feels like an ethical duty if otherwise no voices like their own would be heard—a situation further complicated by the need to educate others and to be agreeable "models" throughout the representational process. All the while, there is the overshadowing worry that seizing the chance to speak in response to institutional pressure (and within a preconceived institutional framework) might actually negate future opportunities for themselves or others to advocate for individual or group needs, being now perceived as an institutional "collaborator." Caught in such an inextricable bind, there is an affective toll to be paid to the institution in addition to the distress associated with the personal, professional, and social costs of responding (or not) to the bidding of power: even if one could escape the tainted feeling of complicity, to what extent will all the effort simply work to absolve the institution of its responsibility to initiate actual interventions and supports related to equity concerns, and, more critically, to engage members of marginalized groups to be the recognized advisors and leaders of such initiatives?

The unease and even exhaustion I feel in response to the routine demands of my office job, if not trivial, are of a different intensity and nature than the feelings evoked by witnessing my colleagues' thoughtful complaints rooted in an ethical demand for recognition, equity, and justice. There are ways in which I identify with these demands. But I also recognize that I rarely, if ever, incur a social cost walking through life, or at work, as a white woman whose disability and sexuality are optional disclosures. Still, it is the process of listening to other peoples' stories that awakened feelings and permitted me to feel and to share feeling with others. These feelings, which one colleague described as a "shadow that sits heavily on the heart," will not be alleviated by joining a workplace wellness group or lunchtime yoga class. What I have learned is that feeling is knowledge-laden, and there is value in pausing for reflection when we experience multiple feelings or ideas, sometimes contradictory, at the same time. Ambivalence and the ethical challenges of working in the university will never go away; it's how we choose to understand and act upon our feelings that matters most.

The psychic pain I have heard being articulated by colleagues is both visceral and intellectual, and it has a visceral and not simply vicarious impact on me. Grounded in the strength of generations of refusal to be subjected, their words moved me. Not in the sense that the experience of listening to stories washed over me and cleansed me in some kind of cathartic process that stayed at the level of sentiment. No, it *contaminated* me through its affective demand that called for movement, an ethics of recognition and action. I felt the pain rise around my own acute anger and abject horror at the constant harm and unmitigated insecurity that I could no longer "unsee." This damage being done to people, their communities, and their dignity was being wreaked by an institution that now showcased—quite visibly in the portraiture of its past presidents—white privilege in all its obscene glory. This is the pain, so raw yet eloquently expressed in Claudia Rankine's *Citizen*, emanating from a heightened awareness of racialized peoples' chronic disappointment with white "allies" and African Americans' communal grief for the past and ongoing confrontation with socially sanctioned racist violence.[33] It was the pain of my own self-awareness, that my existence in a society and my work in an institution where whiteness is always granted privilege means that I live comfortably in a world that batters and breaks down other peoples' personhood. It is the pain of being a witness to the persistent colonialism and the reality of intergenerational trauma for Indigenous communities that Billy Ray Belcourt describes as Indigenous peoples' "closeness to sadness and to misery." For Belcourt, this proximity to suffering is not debilitating; rather it permits "a reworking of the codes of bad affect, enabling us to free them from the apoliticized cages of pathology and the private."[34] Belcourt finds inspiration in Ann Cvetkovich's book *Depression: A Public Feeling*, in which Cvetkovich argues that "feeling bad might, in fact, be the ground for transformation."[35] Nobody who identifies with an equity-seeking group needs allies only to "feel bad,"[36] yet unruly feelings can and should be the beginning of political work.

In this chapter I have suggested that being nonacademic staff with academic qualifications and skills presents alt-ac workers with opportunities for multiple perspective-taking and to form relationships and allegiances across the conventional silos. These alliances intersect with, and I believe also have potential to disrupt, the "anonymous" and "unfeeling" operations of institutional power. At the same time, the opportunities for shaping our work are limited. Workflow variability means that we confront daily a branching network of options that invite us to advise and collaborate, to take instruction and give instruction, to inform and to serve, and to establish, adhere to, or alter policy, processes, and practices as needed and in a manner suitable to the particular exigencies that confront us. All the while we face constant pressures to expand what are often unrecognized contributions to special projects and institutional service work within and outside of our particular areas. I have found I must make critical decisions where to invest my time, without actually *having the time* to reflect on these decisions and their implications, and without mentors who can share their own experience and wisdom to help guide the way. If as alt-ac workers we are the only one of our kind within our area, it can be a lonely existence. I have found it is the kind of work that demands an extraordinary commitment of the self to bear the weight of self-questioning, let alone the questions from others that constantly draw on and challenge our expert knowledge. We must endure the frustration of being brought in and being shut out—as the subordinate subjects of whimsical, though not benign, power. We must outlast the exhaustion of being confronted daily with making moral choices without having the protection of academic freedom—as such, we are the anxious agents of power who must constantly tally personal and professional risks. We must sustain our motivation and integrity as knowledge practitioners and cultural workers, and we must constantly demonstrate creativity, discernment, and agility, stationed at the intersection of various roles and duties, rarely being certain of who it might be that commands or deserves our undivided attention, or who it might be that would undermine us or have our back if anything or everything went awry. Those of us who are placed as alt-ac workers awkwardly *feel our way* in relation to our own marginalization and privilege, both within the institution and in our relationships with others. We can do so productively, when we understand the work of affect as a foundation for building alliances across equity-seeking groups that might, one day, dismantle the "ivory tower."

NOTES

1. Melinda Epler, "Three Ways to Be a Better Ally in the Workplace," web video, filmed June 2018 at TED Salon: Brightline Initiative, https://www.ted.com/talks/melinda_epler_3_ways_to_advocate_for_a_more_inclusive_workplace/transcript?language=en.

2. Ann Cvetkovich, *An Archive of Feeling: Trauma, Sexuality, and Lesbian Public Culture* (Durham, NC: Duke University Press, 2003), 3.

3. Suzanne Bowness, "What's Up with Alt-Ac Careers," University Affairs, September 8, 2015, https://www.universityaffairs.ca/features/feature-article/whats-up-with-alt-ac-careers/.

4. Eugenia Zuroski, "Holding Patterns: On Academic Knowledge and Labor," Medium, April 5, 2018, https://medium.com/@zugenia/holding-patterns-on-academic-knowledge-and-labor-3e5a6000ecbf.

5. Susan D. Porter and Jennifer M. Phelps, "Beyond Skills: An Integrative Approach to Doctoral Student Preparation for Diverse Careers," *Canadian Journal of Higher Education* 44, no. 3 (2014): 54–67.

6. Joshua Kim has described this boundary role as "liminal," in "Defining Alt-Ac before We Systemize Alternative Academic Career Guidance," Inside Higher Ed, November 25, 2018, https://www.insidehighered.com/blogs/technology-and-learning/defining-alt-ac-we-systematize-alternative-academic-career-guidance.

7. Robin DiAngelo, "White Fragility," *International Journal of Critical Pedagogy* 3, no. 3 (2011): 64.

8. George Yancy, *Backlash: What Happens When We Talk Honestly about Racism in America* (Lanham, MD: Rowman & Littlefield, 2018).

9. Lee Skallerup Bessette, "Adjuncts, Staff, and Solidarity," *MLA Profession*, Fall 2018, https://profession.mla.org/adjuncts-staff-and-solidarity/.

10. Malinda S. Smith, with Kimberly Gamarro and Mansharn Toor, "A Dirty Dozen: Unconscious Race and Gender Biases in the Academy," in Frances Henry et al., *The Equity Myth: Racialization and Indigeneity at Canadian Universities* (Vancouver: University of British Columbia Press, 2017), 292.

11. Epler, "Three Ways to Be a Better Ally."

12. Cassandra M. Guarino and Victor M. H. Borden, "Faculty Service Loads and Gender: Are Women Taking Care of the Academic Family?" *Research in Higher Education* 58, no. 6 (2017): 672–694.

13. Melissa Gregg, "Working with Affect in the Corporate University," in Marianne Liljeström and Susanna Paasonen, eds., *Working with Affect in Feminist Readings: Disturbing Differences* (London: Routledge, 2011), 186.

14. See, for example, Alise de Bie's discussion of how university faculty and staff are encouraged to identify students' strong emotional expression within a dominant "biomedical/psychological" framework that codes emotion as a sign of "psychological troubles." De Bie, "Finding Ways (and Words) to Move: Mad Student Politics and Practices of Loneliness," *Disability and Society* 34, no. 7–8 (2019): 1161.

15. Sara Ahmed, *The Cultural Politics of Emotion* (Edinburgh: Edinburgh University Press, 2004), 3–4.

16. Gregg, "Working with Affect," 187.

17. David Garland, "'Governmentality' and the Problem of Crime: Foucault, Criminology, Sociology," *Theoretical Criminology* 1, no. 2 (1997): 182.

18. Joshua Kim, "Negotiating Our Alt-Ac Professional Identities," Inside Higher Ed, January 23, 2019, https://www.insidehighered.com/blogs/technology-and-learning/negotiating-our-alt-ac-professional-identities.

19. Bessette, "Adjuncts, Staff, and Solidarity."

20. Brad Evans and Julian Reid, "Dangerously Exposed: The Life and Death of the Resilient Subject," *Resilience* 1, no. 2 (2013): 83–98.

21. Henry Giroux, *The University in Chains: Confronting the Military-Industrial-Academic Complex* (Boulder, CO: Paradigm, 2007).

22. Henry Giroux, *The Terror of Neoliberalism: Authoritarianism and the Eclipse of Democracy* (New York: Routledge, 2004).

23. Ian McNay, "Changing Cultures in UK Higher Education: The State as Corporate Market Bureaucracy and the Emergent Academic Enterprise," in Dietmar Braun and François-Xavier Merrien, eds., *Towards a New Model of Governance for Universities: A Comparative View* (London: Jessica Kingsley, 1999), 34–58; Dietmar Braun, "Changing Governance Models in Higher Education: The Case of the New Managerialism," *Swiss Political Science Review* 5, no. 3 (1999): 1–24.

24. Ian McNay, "Universities Going International: Choices, Cautions, Conditions," in Peter Blok, ed., *Policy and Policy Implementation in Internationalisation of Higher Education*(Amsterdam: European Association of International Education, 1995), 35–40.

25. The term *faculty* in Canada refers to a large administrative unit comprised of departments (each usually with a single disciplinary focus); in the United States, faculties would typically be called *colleges*.

26. Ian McNay, "Research Quality Assessment: Objectives, Approaches, Responses and Consequences," in Angela Brew and Lisa Lucas, eds., *Academic Research and Researchers*(Maidenhead, UK: Open University Press, 2009), 35–53.

27. Bessette, "Adjuncts, Staff, and Solidarity."

28. The "business case" is based on research that asserts more diverse and inclusive workplaces are more productive, innovative, and ultimately lead to increased profitability for the organization. See, for example, Iris Bohnet, *What Works: Gender Equality by Design* (Cambridge, MA: Belknap Press, 2016).

29. Bessette, "Adjuncts, Staff, and Solidarity."

30. This is a paraphrase of Sara Ahmed, *Living a Feminist Life* (Durham, NC: Duke University Press, 2017), 10.

31. Arlie Russell Hochschild, *The Managed Heart: Commercialization of Human Feeling* (Berkeley: University of California Press, 1983), 90.

32. Amy S. Wharton, "Service with a Smile: Understanding the Consequences of Emotional Labor," in Cameron Lynne MacDonald and Carmen Sirianni, eds., *Working in the Service Society*(Philadelphia: Temple University Press, 1996), 93.

33. Claudia Rankine, *Citizen: An American Lyric* (Minneapolis: Graywolf Press, 2014).

34. Billy Ray Belcourt, *This Wound Is a World: Poems* (Calgary: Frontenac House, 2017), 58.

35. Ann Cvetkovich, *Depression: A Public Feeling* (Durham, NC: Duke University Press, 2011), 3.

36. Zuroski, "Holding Patterns."

BIBLIOGRAPHY

Ahmed, Sara. *The Cultural Politics of Emotion*. Edinburgh: Edinburgh University Press, 2004.

———. *Living a Feminist Life*. Durham, NC: Duke University Press, 2017.

Belcourt, Billy Ray. *This Wound Is a World: Poems*. Calgary: Frontenac House, 2017.

Bessette, Lee Skallerup. "Adjuncts, Staff, and Solidarity." *MLA Profession*. Fall 2018. https://profession.mla.org/adjuncts-staff-and-solidarity/.

Bohnet, Iris. *What Works: Gender Equality by Design*. Cambridge, MA: Belknap Press, 2016.

Bowness, Suzanne. "What's Up with Alt-Ac Careers." *University Affairs*. September 8, 2015. https://www.universityaffairs.ca/features/feature-article/whats-up-with-alt-ac-careers/.

Braun, Dietmar. "Changing Governance Models in Higher Education: The Case of the New Managerialism." *Swiss Political Science Review* 5, no. 3 (1999): 1–24.

Cvetkovich, Ann. *An Archive of Feeling: Trauma, Sexuality, and Lesbian Public Culture*. Durham, NC: Duke University Press, 2003.

———. *Depression: A Public Feeling*. Durham, NC: Duke University Press, 2011.

de Bie, Alise. "Finding Ways (and Words) to Move: Mad Student Politics and Practices of Loneliness." *Disability and Society* 34, no. 7–8 (2019): 1154–1179.

DiAngelo, Robin. "White Fragility." *International Journal of Critical Pedagogy* 3, no. 3 (2011): 54–70.

Epler, Melinda. "Three Ways to Be a Better Ally in the Workplace." Web video. Filmed June 2018 at TED Salon: Brightline Initiative. https://www.ted.com/talks/melinda_epler_3_ways_to_advocate_for_a_more_inclusive_workplace/transcript?language=en.

Evans, Brad, and Julian Reid. "Dangerously Exposed: The Life and Death of the Resilient Subject." *Resilience* 1, no. 2 (2013): 83–98.

Garland, David. "'Governmentality' and the Problem of Crime: Foucault, Criminology, Sociology." *Theoretical Criminology* 1, no. 2 (1997): 173–214.

Giroux, Henry. *The Terror of Neoliberalism: Authoritarianism and the Eclipse of Democracy*. New York: Routledge, 2004.

———. *The University in Chains: Confronting the Military-Industrial-Academic Complex*. Boulder, CO: Paradigm, 2007.

Gregg, Melissa. "Working with Affect in the Corporate University." In Marianne Liljeström and Susanna Paasonen, eds., *Working with Affect in Feminist Readings: Disturbing Differences*, 182–192. London: Routledge, 2011.

Guarino, Cassandra M., and Victor M. H. Borden. "Faculty Service Loads and Gender: Are Women Taking Care of the Academic Family?" *Research in Higher Education* 58, no. 6 (2017): 672–694.

Henry, Frances, Enakshi Dua, Carl E. James, Audrey Kobayashi, Peter Li, Howard Ramos, and Malinda S. Smith. *The Equity Myth: Racialization and Indigeneity at Canadian Universities*. Vancouver: University of British Columbia Press, 2017.

Hochschild, Arlie Russell. *The Managed Heart: Commercialization of Human Feeling*. Berkeley: University of California Press, 1983.

Kim, Joshua. "Defining Alt-Ac before We Systemize Alternative Academic Career Guidance." Inside Higher Ed. November 25, 2018. https://www.insidehighered.com/blogs/technology-and-learning/defining-alt-ac-we-systematize-alternative-academic-career-guidance.

———. "Negotiating Our Alt-Ac Professional Identities." Inside Higher Ed. January 23, 2019. https://www.insidehighered.com/blogs/technology-and-learning/negotiating-our-alt-ac-professional-identities.

McNay, Ian. "Changing Cultures in UK Higher Education: The State as Corporate Market Bureaucracy and the Emergent Academic Enterprise." In Dietmar Braun and François-Xavier Merrien, eds., *Towards a New Model of Governance for Universities: A Comparative View*, 34–58. London: Jessica Kingsley, 1999.

———. "Research Quality Assessment: Objectives, Approaches, Responses and Consequences." In Angela Brew and Lisa Lucas, eds., *Academic Research and Researchers*, 35–53. Maidenhead, UK: Open University Press, 2009.

———. "Universities Going International: Choices, Cautions, Conditions." In Peter Blok, ed., *Policy and Policy Implementation in Internationalisation of Higher Education*, 35–40. Amsterdam: European Association of International Education, 1995.

Porter, Susan D., and Jennifer M. Phelps. "Beyond Skills: An Integrative Approach to Doctoral Student Preparation for Diverse Careers." *Canadian Journal of Higher Education* 44, no. 3 (2014): 54–67.

Rankine, Claudia. *Citizen: An American Lyric*. Minneapolis: Graywolf Press, 2014.

Smith, Malinda S., with Kimberly Gamarro and Mansharn Toor. "A Dirty Dozen: Unconscious Race and Gender Biases in the Academy." In Frances Henry et al., *The Equity Myth: Racialization and Indigeneity at Canadian Universities*, 263–296. Vancouver: University of British Columbia Press, 2017.

Wharton, Amy S. "Service with a Smile: Understanding the Consequences of Emotional Labor." In Cameron Lynne MacDonald and Carmen Sirianni, eds., *Working in the Service Society*, 91–112. Philadelphia: Temple University Press, 1996.

Yancy, George. *Backlash: What Happens When We Talk Honestly about Racism in America.* Lanham, MD: Rowman & Littlefield, 2018.

Zuroski, Eugenia. "Holding Patterns: On Academic Knowledge and Labor." Medium. April 5, 2018. https://medium.com/@zugenia/holding-patterns-on-academic-knowledge-and-labor-3e5a6000ecbf.

4

When Is an Academic Not an Academic?

Embracing Nontraditional Academics in Academia

NICOLE PAPAIOANNOU

❖ ❖ ❖ ❖ ❖ ❖ ❖ ❖ ❖ ❖ ❖ ❖ ❖ ❖ ❖

For the sixth-grade yearbook, we were asked where we see ourselves in the future. I said, "A fashion designer with a PhD." It's a story I admittedly tell often because it still captures my nature. I'm a nerd. I love learning new things. I love reading. I love writing. Research and exploration truly excite me. I am fascinated by the field of rhetoric and composition and all things design related. Though at eleven years old I may not have understood the gravity of the decision to pursue a PhD, being highly educated has always been important to me. As I grew old enough to make decisions about my education, I did go on to pursue a doctoral degree, believing that I would someday become a tenured professor and/or a writing program administrator. At my core, I consider myself an academic.

I completed my PhD in English in May 2018. My dissertation, *Momentum: Why Students Move Writing beyond the Classroom*, focuses on student engagement, writing across the curriculum, and transfer of learning. I spent years recruiting, interviewing, and writing about students who decided to use their class writing for something other than class. I wanted to know what compelled students to use what they are learning in class in other contexts. Despite the time I devoted to studying writing pedagogy and teaching writing, I am not a professor or writing program administrator.

Being an academic came with a set of consequences I didn't fully understand when I began. It took much longer to write my dissertation than I'd imagined, and I was not prepared for the financial strain of remaining an adjunct well into my late twenties. I'd saved nothing and spent a great deal on transportation to get to the three universities where I worked and learned. My students had questions that I felt compelled to answer around the clock. Writing finals while grading finals was exhausting. And as I sat in on department meetings and spoke with mentors, I heard things that were disappointing about university politics, workloads, funding, and the ways in which teaching was devalued in relation to research. Academia started to feel stifling.

Four years into my doctoral degree program, I began to realize that I was holding out for an academic job because I wanted people to be impressed. As someone who had always looked young and whose friendliness had often been misaligned with a lack of intelligence, I loved the surprise when I would tell people "I'm a professor." There was also immense internal pressure. I didn't want to quit when I'd publicly stated my end goal so many times. I didn't want to let down my family, my professors, my students, or any of the other people who had supported me on my path. Eventually, I acknowledged that being unhappy because you want others to think you're smart based on a title is a silly way to live your life.

At that point, I chose the alt-ac path, some might even say the "nonacademic" path. In truth, I am not employed by any institution of higher education, nor am I looking for a role within one. I left my career in higher education in 2014. In October of that year, I said goodbye to my wonderful colleagues at the writing center after five and a half years as a consultant and moved to Los Angeles to pursue a full-time instructional design role at an educational technology company. Just two months later, I completed my last online teaching assignment.

Today, I am an instructional design consultant. The majority of my time is spent developing corporate training for clients in a range of industries. I've worked with commercial airlines, mobile tech companies, digital marketing agencies, major entertainment companies, and more. During an average workday, I might collaborate with clients to identify their organizational needs, create learner profiles, design learning experiences, or produce content. I get to work with interesting people with all sorts of job titles. What is truly wonderful about this career path is that it blends so many of the interests that drew me to graduate work in English. Early in the design process, I get to deconstruct the communication conventions of different fields and organizational cultures. I research the subject matter in depth, as well as the ways in which it's already been taught, when applicable. As I create curricula and learning experiences, I'm constantly immersed in the process of considering students' needs and addressing them. I also assess students' learning at multiple levels and evaluate training impact. Because of my research and teaching background, I can identify actionable responses to the shortcomings I find in performance and existing training. I get to be scholarly and creative. I feel like I hit the nerd lottery. People are paying me to empower their employees to succeed through learning.

Of course, I am just one of the 87 percent of PhD recipients from the United States who did not obtain a traditional academic position post-graduation.[1] There are many of us on the nontraditional path, some of whom have taken up corporate roles, as I have. Unsurprisingly, people with PhDs can be highly valuable in the private marketplace. Our skills in research, written communication, presentation, and (sometimes) teaching enable us to interact thoughtfully with clients and lead teams. We're great at making sense of complex issues and managing priorities. Typically, we know how to study and learn quickly. Our titles alone make us attractive to businesses, who, quite frankly, just like to say they have someone with a PhD—a real expert—in house.

SO, AM I STILL AN ACADEMIC?

For those PhDs who pursue nontraditional career paths, a challenge remains: the marketplace and the university function as mostly separate ecosystems. This becomes even more clear in descriptions of the terms used to describe the work done by those who do not pursue traditional academic paths. In their essay "Toward a Trackless Future: Moving Beyond 'Alt-Ac' and 'Post-Ac,'" Meredith Beck Sayre, Marta Brunner, Brian Croxall, and Emily McGinn use Jason Rhody's description of *alt-ac,* which defines career roles that can be described as non-tenure-track academic positions, and the term *post-ac,* which defines roles that fall outside higher education entirely.[2] The term *post-ac* suggests that ties to academia have been broken, that those who pursue post-ac paths are now operating "after" academia. Other descriptions of nontraditional career paths for academics fail to even acknowledge scholars who pursue roles outside of academia. For example, Joshua Kim uses the term *alt-ac* as an identifier for a person rather than a career path. He argues that only those who have terminal degrees, pursue careers in higher education, and blend teaching with service are "alt-ac."[3] By his definition, people like me, who take on corporate positions, are not included. We are not "academics" in any form. In response, reader Wilfred Toboggan offers an alternative set of categories for the careers that people with PhDs choose to pursue. They are:

1. Academic: traditional faculty positions on TT [tenure track] lines, and 1a. Contingent and Adjunct
2. Alt Ac: in the strict sense, consistent with Kim: campus but primarily nonfaculty positions (e.g., in the writing center, development office, office of career services)
3. Peri-Ac: off campus but still campus related (e.g., as a program officer at NSF, NEH, the Department of Education, or a private foundation; in a higher education association; or working as a journalist in a higher education publication such as Inside Higher Ed)
4. The rest of the big, wide world: avoiding the term *non-ac*. Perhaps divided into two sub-groups: 4a. Discipline focused, e.g., the Wells Fargo Bank's history office; and 4b. General skills reliant, e.g., becoming a Wells Fargo banker.[4]

Again, Toboggan omits defining those of us who pursue careers outside of an institution of higher education. He doesn't want to use the term *nonacademic* but offers no suitable alternative. Looking at these definitions, the general consensus in academia seems to be that once you take a career outside the gates of the institution, you are no longer an academic, even if you didn't intend for that to be the case.

The same is largely true for the way you are identified by the marketplace. For example, I have a PhD. I co-founded and spent years co-moderating #FYCchat (the Twitter chat for first-year composition enthusiasts) with Lee Skallerup Bessette. Until 2017, I owned and published content to a moderately read blog (*comPOSITION*) that focused on rhetoric and composition and teaching writing. My dissertation is on ProQuest. I'm writing this chapter for publication by the University Press of Kansas. In my daily interactions, though, this goes largely unacknowledged. I've been called Dr. Papaioannou just once during professional interactions. People don't ask me about my research interests or invite me to work on research projects. Quite frankly, no one in the business world really cares about the extra education. They might show a moment of fascination, but in the grand scheme, it doesn't mean much in my career, especially since my degree isn't in instructional design. The way people address me and interact with me suggests that I am not an academic, or even a scholar, any longer.

So I raise the question: without the title of professor, lecturer, graduate student, or some other title affiliated with a role in higher education, can someone be an academic? The ways in which academia often prevents those outside its boundaries from participating seems to suggest the answer is no. For those of us who devoted years of our lives to research and education, this answer is disheartening to say the least. I still identify as an academic. In fact, the first words of my Twitter profile are "An academic gone rogue." I suspect many others who chose to pursue alt-ac and post-ac careers feel the same way.

One way to understand this phenomenon can be found in Harry Denny's description of "faces" and "centers," as explained in *Facing the Center: Toward an Identity Politics of One-to-One Mentoring*. Those closest to the center are typically the most privileged. Their faces reflect a mainstreamed vision of the imagined identity. The further from the center one goes, the less likely one is recognized as that identity that lies in the center.[5] In this case, I'm thinking about the identity reflected—or the face—of a scholar. Leaving out gender, race, and class—all of which, of course, inform nearness to the center—I describe the traditional face of a scholar as someone who completed a terminal degree, likely a PhD, positioned themselves to enter the academic job market toward the completion of the degree or immediately after, and secured a full-time tenure-track position as an associate professor before successfully completing tenure review, at which point the person is promoted to full professor. For STEM (science, technology, engineering, and mathematics) folks, there may be a postdoctoral fellowship somewhere in there, as well.

Moving away from the center and occupying a different "face" makes it more challenging to be perceived by others as that central identity. This is a challenge faced by those who pursue alt-ac career paths. Of course, alt-ac can mean a lot of different things. One might still work at an institution of higher education but have a nonteaching career path. They might choose to work for a research institution or policy center that does work quite similar to academic research, but again, without teaching. Further still from the center are corporate roles, becoming more distant as roles are less closely tied to areas of study and research requirements involved. Someone who pursued a PhD in biology and chose to become an account manager for a mobile technology

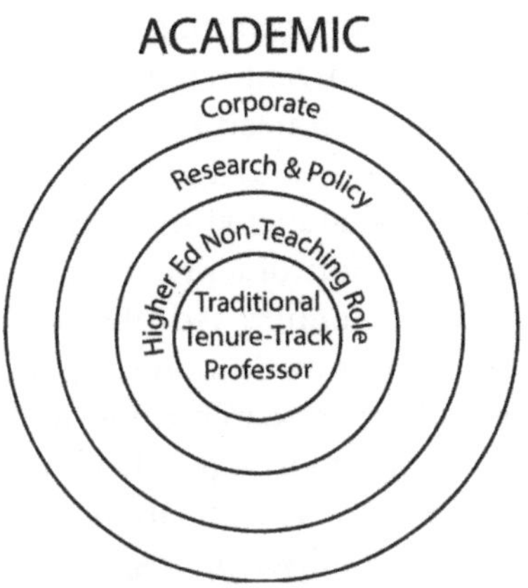

Figure 1

company, for example, would occupy rings much further from the center than someone with a PhD in English who chose to become a university writing center program coordinator (see figure 1).

But while taking on an alt-ac career is no longer frowned upon by the academic community (mostly), it's important to understand that the further away from the center of academia a career path sits, the harder it is to participate as a scholar among colleagues in academia. It takes a significant effort for those completely outside academia to stay connected. That account manager with the PhD in biology will likely find it difficult to get people to acknowledge their identity as an academic. If we're thinking about academic poster children, it's doubtful theirs would ever be presented as *the* face of an academic. As a result, they will find more gatekeepers when they attempt to access the discourse communities and resources available to academics. This is because they are seen as Other. Again, borrowing from Denny's work, the Other is someone who is seen as outside the community.[6] Based on perceived Otherness, neither the marketplace nor the academy acknowledges nontraditional academics in the same way, or possibly at all, as those firmly in the center. While I pursued a career outside of an institution of higher education with enthusiasm, I acknowledge that many hopeful academics are forced onto alt-ac paths after rejection and disappointment has overwhelmed them. That can make this diminishing of identity even more jarring.

Let me give you one funny example of how this Othering impacts scholars who have chosen nontraditional career paths. I submitted my dissertation for publication via ProQuest. My advisor said that was a typical course of action, and it seemed great to have it out there for the world to read. Later, I received notice that my dissertation was published. I went to check it out and was met with a paywall. If I wanted to read the full version of my dissertation online, I would have had to pay ProQuest for access. Yes, I literally would have had to pay to read my own work. Luckily, I have a bound copy of my dissertation, but this is a much broader issue.

In leaving the formal space of academia, I also left behind the privileges of an academic job, which includes access to research, mentors, and certain academic discussions. Of course, if I want to continue claiming expertise in my field, I need to be up to date on current scholarship. If I want to contribute to the body of research, I will need to know the scholarly conversation that's already taking place around that issue. The question becomes, how much can I afford? As I conducted research for this chapter, for example, I came across paywalls for content and had to decide whether or not to pursue those threads of inquiry. Additionally, I no longer have a connection with the university's institutional review board (IRB). Some publications will not publish research done with human participants without IRB approval. Furthermore, there are obstacles that prevent me from fully engaging in conversation with other academics; the cost of journal and database subscriptions, as well as dues for professional organizations and conferences, which are no longer necessary for career success, are prohibitively expensive, and I am not eligible for scholarships or academic grants. I want to contribute to the growing body of research in the field of rhetoric and composition, but without a university to back me, I find it increasingly difficult to do so. There's also the idea that because I'm not in the trenches of the academy (at the center), I don't deserve a voice. I "quit" and should accept that leaving that kind of work behind is part of that decision.

I want to challenge this way of thinking, though. As a significant time investment has been made—both by those pursuing the PhD and those who have prepared them for graduation— in learning about a field in great depth, it's essential that expertise is not excluded from the larger conversation. PhDs with "nonacademic" experience offer a unique critical lens that can only further the work already being done inside institutions.

I AM AN ACADEMIC

For a long time, two parts of me—academic and instructional designer—seemed like two north-facing magnets, repelling each other. I felt like I was being pulled apart. When I took on my first full-time corporate instructional design role in 2014, I had to quit moderating #FYCchat. It was heartbreaking for me to give up the conversation and feelings of connectedness I had to my colleagues across the Twitterverse. I could see what my colleagues had been tweeting when I arrived home from work, but it was never the same as being there with everyone and fostering discussions. As I moved on to managing the instructional design department and then into my role as a solo consultant, I felt myself drifting further and further away from the center of academia. I spent my time thinking about airline operations and automated CPR devices instead of what should be in my next syllabus. In 2019, after nine years of being @comPOSITIONblog, I changed my Twitter handle to @NicolePapaPhD. It reflected a big shift in my identity. At that point I no longer believed there was a place for me in higher education, unless I wanted to return to the traditional path and immerse myself in the things about that space that made me anxious and unhappy. I didn't believe anyone cared about my thoughts on composition or my ability to teach writing anymore. I was, after all, "nonacademic" or "post-ac" in the eyes of my colleagues. Or so I told myself.

The truth is that I was too willing to see the "face" of a traditional academic as *the* face of an academic. I embraced the narratives that told me what an academic should be and decided I was not included in that vision. The longer I operated in the corporate sphere, the more I believed there was no place for me in academia. Yes, dominant narratives partially led me to those conclusions, but it's also evident to me now that I was operating based on fear. At the writing center, I learned not to look at students as "lacking," but to build on their strengths and improve their weaknesses; yet, when I looked at myself in relation to academia, all I saw was "lack." I was lacking the credentials I thought I needed. I was lacking a class of students to talk about. I was lacking a university affiliation. I decided that because I wasn't centered on the traditional academic path, I didn't have anything to offer to academia anymore. I wasn't really an academic. I can't remember anyone telling me that explicitly. It was just something I felt. Deep down, I think I was simply afraid of what it meant to claim myself as an academic. Admittedly, this battle with my own identity left me feeling depressed and confused

It took a lot of introspection and reflective writing to help me realize that I was causing a lot of my own pain. I spent time trying to reframe my inner narrative and work on listing strengths. I had to remind myself that I had expertise in teaching writing, but also expertise in designing learning. I knew cognitive theories of composition and neuroscience related to memory. I could build a class for face-to-face delivery or digital delivery in ways that most educators couldn't. I knew how to navigate the classroom and the boardroom. Slowly, I started to see positive patterns, and that translated into new ideas. I decided that even though I never published as a graduate student, I wanted to do so now. This chapter is the product of that reclamation. I also decided that I wanted to merge my areas of expertise. That became the driving force behind Navigated Teaching & Learning, an online professional development platform dedicated to improving the teaching of writing in higher education. While I'd had the idea for over a year, the "lack" narrative I was telling myself made me feel that I wasn't experienced enough to teach others about teaching writing, despite writing a dissertation dedicated to the subject. Quite frankly, it's new, and I have no idea what will come of it, but I know that working on it has reconfirmed that I am still an academic.

Now, more than ever, I am willing to claim my identity and my space. I am an academic, even if the chorus is telling me otherwise. I can still research thoroughly, think deeply, and teach with enthusiasm. I still have subject matter expertise. I have a terminal degree. What I don't have is access and easy recognition. People don't just see me as the face of an academic. I must constantly explain my identity, and that comes with a cost of time and energy. And sometimes, it produces self-doubt. Is it worth it to explain it this many times? Am I wrong because I don't see what they see? I argue, though, that while constantly asserting yourself can be exhausting, feeling like a piece of yourself has been removed is even harder. I do have to work hard to stay connected to that space, but it is worth the effort because it makes me feel whole. I have something to offer my colleagues in academia as a result of my experience in and beyond the academy. I want to be involved as an academic, even if I'm not in the center of academia. I assume that many of those who have left academia willingly or out of necessity also want to be recognized and included as academics.

SUGGESTIONS FOR INCLUSION

As I've argued throughout, PhDs who follow nontraditional career paths are still academics. If invited, they have much to contribute back to the academy and to their colleagues who are still operating within institutions of higher education. For that reason, I offer suggestions for improved integration of those academics who follow nontraditional career paths within the academic space. I categorize these tasks based on the responsible party.

All Academic Institutions and Academics

Redefine *academic* . . . again. Anyone who wants to be and attempts to be actively involved in the work of scholarship should be able to claim the identity of *academic*. For those operating in spaces seemingly far-removed from the center academia, a term like "noninstitutional academic" would be more inclusive.

Universities

Create access to information through open-access publications and databases. This is one area in which universities are already beginning to excel, but it needs to be continually emphasized. As the system currently stands, scholars operating outside the academy cannot do research without a significant financial investment. Folks in traditional academic roles typically have access to journals and academic publications that are expensive and often not circulated by public libraries.

Designate spaces for traditional and nontraditional academics to interact. Traditional academics, alternate academics, and noninstitutional academics lack sponsored spaces where they can freely discuss and problem-solve together. Creating these spaces and advocating for their use by all types of academics will enable collaboration among peers with differing perspectives.

PhD Mentors

Foster networking. Introduce current students and noninstitutional academics, as well as noninstitutional academics and colleagues with similar interests. As we know, not all current graduate students will be able to find work as tenure-track professors; they need options, and talking to someone with that kind of experience can provide valuable guidance. Additionally, just because someone leaves the university, it doesn't mean they're no longer interested in research. There are unique perspectives that can be explored by teaming up traditional and nontraditional academics.

Alt-Acs and Noninstitutional Academics

Make a conscious effort to stay connected in the limited ways possible. The quickest way to find yourself excluded from academia is to remove yourself from your network of academics. Noninstitutional academics must find ways to stay in touch, whether that's occasional emails and phone calls, interacting on social media (personal learning networks), or finding ways to get to conferences and academic events.

Express needs and wants. I believe much of the separation between traditional and noninstitutional academics happens because we think our needs and wants are different. After all, the aims of the marketplace are so different than the aims of academia (or at least that's the common narrative). If you want to continue publishing, let your contacts in academia know that. If you need help writing a proposal for a conference, let your contacts in academia know that. Again, most people want to help, and if they can't help, they may be willing to point you to someone who can.

Self-identify explicitly. While those closest to the center of the traditional academic identity may never have to explicitly claim that they are academics, noninstitutional academics do. Leaving traditional academia behind may be mistakenly interpreted as a desire to separate oneself from the academic community entirely. Noninstitutional academics have to be vocal about the fact that they are, in fact, still academics and wish to be recognized as such. They must help to reshape the face of the academic if they want their faces to be reflected.

WHEN WE'RE ALL ACADEMICS

While universities have made large investments in educating their graduate students, they are entirely complacent about the lack of return on investment that occurs when those students leave the formal space of academia behind entirely. Perhaps it would be fine to accept the status quo if people were willingly leaving the search for academic jobs because they simply no longer wanted to be academics; however, we know this isn't the case. There is a body of knowledge and untapped potential left with those who have had their "academic" identities denied. Identifying noninstitutional academics as academics, however, moves toward reintegration, and in that reintegration is the opportunity for unique instances of collaboration. If you look again at figure 1, you'll see it looks a lot like the rings on a tree. A tree cannot grow unless it builds new rings, much like the academy cannot continue to expand its sphere of influence if it doesn't leverage the outer rings of noninstitutional scholars.

NOTES

1. Richard C. Larson, Navid Ghaffazadegan, and Yi Xue, "Too Many PhD Graduates or Too Few Academic Job Openings: The Basic Reproductive Number R_0 in Academia," *Systems Research and Behavioral Science* 31, no. 6 (September 9, 2013): 745–750.

2. Meredith Beck Sayre et al., "Toward a Trackless Future: Moving beyond 'Alt-Ac' and 'Post-Ac,'" *The Process of Discovery: The CLIR Postdoctoral Fellowship Program and the Future of the Academy* (Alexandria, VA: Council on Library and Information Resources, 2015).

3. Jason Kim, "Defining Alt-Ac before We Systematize Alternative Academic Career Guidance," *Inside Higher Ed* (blog), November 25, 2018, https://www.insidehighered.com/blogs/technology-and-learning/defining-alt-ac-we-systematize-alternative-academic-career-guidance.

4. Wilfred Toboggan, December 2018 comment on Jason Kim, "Defining Alt-Ac before We Systematize Alternative Academic Career Guidance," *Inside Higher Ed* (blog), November 25, 2018, https://www.insidehighered.com/blogs/technology-and-learning/defining-alt-ac-we-systematize-alternative-academic-career-guidance.

5. Harry Denny, *Facing the Center: Toward an Identity of Politics of One-to-One Mentoring*. Logan: Utah State University Press, 2010.

6. Denny, *Facing the Center*.

BIBLIOGRAPHY

Denny, Harry. *Facing the Center: Toward an Identity of Politics of One-to-One Mentoring*. Logan: Utah State University Press, 2010.

Kim, Jason. "Defining Alt-Ac before We Systematize Alternative Academic Career Guidance." *Inside Higher Ed* (blog), November 25, 2018, https://www.insidehighered.com/blogs/technology-and-learning/defining-alt-ac-we-systematize-alternative-academic-career-guidance.

Larson, Richard C., Navid Ghaffazadegan, and Yi Xue. "Too Many PhD Graduates or Too Few Academic Job Openings: The Basic Reproductive Number R_0 in Academia." *Systems Research and Behavioral Science* 31, no. 6 (September 9, 2013): 745–750.

Sayre, Meredith Beck, Marta Brunner, Brian Croxall, and Emily McGinn. "Toward a Trackless Future: Moving beyond 'Alt-Ac' and 'Post-Ac.'" *The Process of Discovery: The CLIR Postdoctoral Fellowship Program and the Future of the Academy*. Alexandria, VA: Council on Library and Information Resources, 2015.

Toboggan, Wilfred. December 2018 comment on Jason Kim, "Defining Alt-Ac before We Systematize Alternative Academic Career Guidance." *Inside Higher Ed* (blog). November 25, 2018. https://www.insidehighered.com/blogs/technology-and-learning/defining-alt-ac-we-systematize-alternative-academic-career-guidance.

5

You're OK, I'm Always OK

Educational Development and Emotional Labor

MARTHA DIEDE

This chapter is a mirror image to the unfinished thoughts that I was trying to turn into another book chapter. That chapter was supposed to be about connecting people—academic and administrative units, students and faculty, legislators, and alumni in higher education. Every time I sat down to write it, I was suddenly, deeply aware of fatigue. Every. Single. Time.

Why?

Emotionally, I was spent. A few years ago, I, a tenured full professor, department chair, and institutional faculty development lead, made a presentation to a faculty development committee. My task: present survey results about faculty workloads. Having been diagnosed with cancer two months prior, I'd had surgery and two rounds of chemotherapy, to which I reacted with all of the reactions in the fine-print fast speech in the commercials. With chemo-dry eyes, I strained to see the projection, blurry though I stood next to the screen. The provost mocked the figures as completely inaccurate because faculty reported working more hours than literally available in a 24/7 week. This degree of multitasking made visible, he willfully ignored. My charge was to articulate understandably faculty work strain to an administration that wanted to increase faculty workload, despite awareness that workloads were already heavy with 4/4 teaching, community and institutional service, and research expectations. Regardless of how I felt at the time (angry, frustrated, fearful faculty member) and regardless of how other members of the committee were feeling (frustrated, fearful), our job was to control our personal emotional states in favor of presenting the story that our data told. In those moments and shortly after, I considered my options: I could stay in the professoriate, a place that came with myriad conflicting demands and in which I didn't feel an easy fit, or I could use what cancer was giving me—a chance to change directions. I could find a position that demanded a PhD and fit me better. I decided on a shift into the alt-ac track.

The most important lesson that I took with me to my new career track was that of always-already being OK. Especially as a professor-educational developer, I observed that those people who survived and thrived as staff in the academy shared an important characteristic: they were always OK. They were ready with smiles to tell their supervisors that they would find a way to move an initiative ahead or to bring the next idea to fruition. One of them suggested that the way to encourage administrators to respond positively was to communicate "love" for the institution and the administrator's idea, no matter how ridiculous. Interestingly, in more than one example, staff with this attitude were held up to faculty as models for their cheerful "can-do" response to ideas and plans that were at odds with solid evidence and/or accepted norms, sometimes laws. These decisions that staff were expected to "love" included such plans as cutting an already decimated library staff and hiring an underqualified white female for a position when a fully qualified woman of color was in the candidate pool. (The then-director refused to hire the underqualified white woman and hired the fully qualified woman of color for the position. Administrators shortly thereafter forced a change in leadership.) Transitioning from faculty to alt-ac meant that I, too, would have to come to each encounter with faculty members, administrators, and staff ready to evoke the proper feeling, regardless of my personal opinions, feelings, or sense of well-being. Just as in that meeting where I couldn't see the data that I was presenting but did so anyway, I had to be always-already OK.

So what does being always-already OK mean for an educational developer? That's complicated.

Always-already OK means insisting on scholarship foundational to the practice while accepting comments and inquiries such as "so what does an educational developer do?," particularly when I come from a "traditional" discipline (Shakespeare studies), where a scholarly foundation counts its age in centuries. Educational development is fully an academic discipline on its own. Like other academic disciplines, it has foundational texts, ways of thinking, a significant literature base, peer-reviewed journals, national and international conferences, and standard practices. For those who have deeper interest, a *Guide to Faculty Development* is also available in a third iteration. Unlike other academic disciplines, most of the practitioners do not have PhDs or EdDs in higher education, though having a PhD is a frequent requirement to entering the field. While experience as a faculty member is almost equally a disciplinary requirement, educational developers do not teach classes in faculty development, nor do they teach faculty. These scholars more frequently teach students in their disciplinary "homes." Nonetheless, educational developers are not quite faculty. Developers provide consultations, workshops, observations, institutes, academies, and work groups for faculty. Developers support faculty, never training or teaching them. These staff-faculty bridge the gaps in faculty preparation, providing services to move faculty forward into best and/or innovative teaching practices responsible to that faculty member's discipline, supporting faculty in resolving challenges in classroom presentation and/or management, applying scholarly protocols to studying their teaching practices, often offering leadership development for those who become department heads or deans, and encouraging research and publication by offering writing groups, sometimes working with faculty to support and prepare grants as well.

Moreover, the schedule and described engagement with the work of faculty development can present challenges. Educational development work continues year-round in great part because the faculty individual must determine when to engage with the educational developer, so developers work on other people's timetables and respond to requests for individual consultations and work with various groups. Development activities may also occur around the clock, from breakfast coffee groups to honorary receptions and dinners. Further complicating the role of the educational developer is the way in which faculty and administrators describe engagement in developmental activities: words like *remedial* and *corrective* far outnumber terms like *innovative*. The very term *development* can have implications that faculty don't particularly like, as the long-term investment in building expertise does not feel like it should need development in an ancillary area. Moreover, teaching may not be explicitly rewarded in tenure, promotion, and retention policies, a fact that may create unintended barriers to investment in teaching. Even if a department head or three-year-review committee directs a faculty member to visit the campus center for teaching and learning, the department culture may not support professional work on teaching, prioritizing research productivity, number of students taught, or service activities instead. Indeed, some departments actively discourage their faculty from working on their teaching, particularly before contract renewal or tenure. This attitude may increase stress for faculty members in those departments who find themselves working with an educational developer, even if the faculty member chooses to do so without direction, referral, or implied threat. Of course, in these moments, faculty developers must always-already be OK no matter how colleagues describe their work in their hearing or how a faculty member is "referred" to them.

Educational developers support faculty in ways additional to individual and group consultation: as the field continues to show institutional benefit, institutional-level groups find that they, too, want to include the educational developers' perspectives and evidence-based practices. For this reason, educational developers find themselves on committees working with campus space planning units, especially when classroom renovations are scheduled. Developers may also engage with information technology (IT), working toward supporting faculty as they incorporate technology with pedagogy and encouraging IT professionals to think through the implications of their decisions for faculty and students. Developers also work on diversity initiatives and with diversity offices, and increasingly, they work on organizational development initiatives, creating pathways and pipelines to develop academic leaders.

So how does this description play into my deep fatigue every time I sat down to write that chapter on connecting people and bridging gaps as an educational developer?

As I planned how to write the chapter you are reading now, I thought about the many times that my colleagues and friends in different roles in the academic venture ask me if I'm tired. Most of the time, I dig deep and say, "No, I'm not tired," and I say that no with a smile, reminding myself to smile with my eyes, creating the Duchenne smile that science indicates most humans perceive as the most genuine. Always-already OK means that I'm not tired. Ever. Intellectually I assent that at the end of a twelve-hour day consulting with faculty individually, giving presentations, and providing suggestions on class construction and syllabi, I should be tired. If I've spent my day working through administrative processes, managing institutional politics, and moving from meeting to meeting, I should be tired. Coming to terms with the fact that I'm engaged in deep emotional labor required to change my feelings so that I can honestly respond positively to the varied stimuli that come my way helps me to comprehend my fatigue and my inability to recognize it consistently. I've become so accustomed to emotional labor, however, that I am more worried about whether my interlocutors perceive that I am tired as opposed to my actually being tired. Explicitly to myself I worry about how my audiences may perceive my responses, and occasionally, I'll return to a response or statement to clarify so that the conversational partner hears my response in a particularly helpful or kind way as opposed to a sarcastic, negative way. Given the depth and breadth of the people with whom I work, as an educational developer, I must be prepared to "create a publicly observable facial and bodily display" toward people whom I may not know well.[1] This description, literally, is the definition of emotional labor. One of the challenges, of course, is that this emotional labor is hidden from view, sometimes even from my own view.

How might an educational developer's emotional labor occur daily, especially if that labor is invisible? Mindful that departmental, institutional, national, and international contexts are important and that no two institutions of higher education are exactly alike, let's consider some of the people and activities that might fill an educational developer's day and demand always-already OK as a constantly maintained state of being.

First, educational developers inhabit intersecting liminal spaces within institutional power structures. Prepared as faculty, sometimes teaching as faculty, they work as staff and occasionally as administrators. As educational developers engage with administrators, that developer must be always-already OK, ready to advocate for faculty and to advance institutional change as necessary. Administrators hold the purse strings and can be powerful supporters. Because the work of developers and centers may often go unseen—relationship building is not always visible—and because resources are limited, educational developers must also modulate their presence with administrators, knowing how to make their cases for what they need but never pushing too hard or too fast. Although this seems to describe the posture of most academic middle managers, those with higher-profile faculty positions can get away with more strident requests for faculty, staff, and space. I've watched deans ask—straight-faced—for $6 million to fund faculty lines in order to support an important university initiative. Educational developers cannot get away with that. Concurrently, educational developers cannot be too chummy with senior administrators, lest their faculty clientele fear that the developers have joined with administrators to force through changes or to create the possibility for additional faculty work. Faculty partnerships help developers to extend their reach by participating as panelists, lending expertise to research projects, or mentoring colleagues. And while the current climate of higher education requires that everyone be creative with their funding and ways to use it, many educational developers find themselves in positions of figuring out how to reach faculty and to provide necessary programming on budgets that support only center staff. Restricted budgets do not include possibilities such as bringing in well-known presenters or hosting guest developers with additional specialties to spark faculty interest. Some developers find themselves in centers of one or even as that single faculty member assigned half-time to the center as its sole personnel. Regardless of institution type, a single educational developer, or even a half-time one, may support 100, 200, 500, or 1,000-plus faculty. For these reasons, educational developers find themselves managing to be always-already OK with and between administrators and faculty. This posture is an essential professional skill.

Complicating these broadly written positions are the myriad ways in which educational developers inhabit positions within institutions. As universities merge, developers may find themselves working between multiple campuses. Some educational developers drive from place to place. Others find themselves developing faculty remotely by using online conferencing tools, especially as faculty can teach online and live separately from the universities that employ them. The COVID-19 pandemic accelerated the trend toward remote development and significantly increased the demand for educational developers to engage in intellectual and emotional labor. Indeed, educational developers and their IT colleagues had to demonstrate the kind of grit and resilience that Dave Webster and Nicola Rivers have problematized since 2017,[2] well before COVID-19. Even in a pandemic, we must be always-already OK. Despite the challenges that accompany such changes, developers are employed to ensure that the faculty with whom they consult are prepared to engage beneficially with students in classrooms that may or may not suit the faculty's teaching style or preferred methods. The educational developer's role is to observe such changes approaching and to prepare strategies to support faculty across the institution(s) to meet these changes. For example, the General Assembly (GA) in North Carolina decided to reduce tuition—not fees—to $500 per semester for in-state students as a way to combat the rising costs of education and to meet the demands for a more highly educated workforce. The GA chose three campuses at which to implement this plan, and I was the center director at one of those campuses. While I knew that this move could potentially address multiple challenges to higher education at one time, I also realized that once prospective students understood the savings that they could appreciate, they would apply, potentially becoming students. This potential (now very real) influx of students would change working conditions for faculty, altering the number and mix of students in classrooms, likely increasing demands for blended and online classes, and creating opportunities for departments to offer classes at a satellite campus and for faculty to live in different states, teaching only online.

Engaging faculty in professional development opportunities in the face of change at this scale meant that, as an educational developer, I had to see the benefits of such changes and emphasize them in consultations and workshops. To approach this perspective genuinely, I had to acknowledge the challenges that the changes represented for campus units and think creatively of ways to accent the positive. I had to be always-already OK with the plan and the implications that I foresaw.

As part of that determinedly positive attitude, creating partnerships with multiple units across campus becomes even more important, particularly because centers for teaching and learning offer expertise in important campus matters that affect student and faculty experience, such as classroom furniture choice and design, technology choice and implementation, and diversity, inclusion, equity, and access. Partnering across multiple units, however, requires a delicate mix of availability and boundaries. Indeed, it requires the developer genuinely to engage positively with the ideas that partners present without falling into the trap of over-promising and under-delivering. Even if the educational developer must decline an opportunity, that "no" must come with a sense that the educational developer very much values the collaboration. The "no" is not permanent.

Building partnerships also means showing up at various committee meetings and events, placing emotional demands to present affect positively on the educational developer. For example, many educational developers have some responsibility to IT and may also have responsibility for organizational development. The developers may, then, respond to budget requests from multiple units, presenting budgets to IT, academic affairs, and administrative affairs. The processes for each of these units may differ significantly, requiring that at each committee meeting and presentation, the developer adopt a different, yet generally positive posture. Being between high-level units may also mean attending meetings for these units on the same day. Thus educational developers may find themselves engaged in academic code-switching, yet another facet of invisible, emotional labor.

As part of that challenge, many developers have responsibility for high-level faculty opportunities, including teaching awards and leadership development, which also means maintaining the always-already OK state. Developers who "own" teaching awards may create and disperse awards, maintain processes for awards, or create packets to promote their institution's faculty at system or national levels. A faculty member who is a phenomenal researcher and teacher may not be the easiest person with whom to work, especially when the educational developer is not a faculty member, not a student, and not entirely staff. Nevertheless, the educational developer is sometimes tasked with cajoling faculty members to spend their precious time on applications for awards and shepherding the awards through the process. Should a nominated faculty member win, the educational developer may have to be content with sitting in a separate room watching an important ceremony resulting from their time and effort on close-circuit television to make room at the ceremony itself for high-level administrators. Having responsibility for leadership development also demands that the educational developer think through the needs of the administration, the kinds of work that will benefit faculty regardless of their decisions to move into chair, dean, or other administrative roles or to move from institution to institution as part of an individual career path. In these positions, educational developers may find themselves engaging with broader issues in higher education such as changing student demographics and wearable technologies. Equipping faculty to lead from their faculty positions and to think of themselves as leaders equally requires a positive attitude that does not ring hollow. Faculty, as highly trained critical thinkers, press: they ask questions. As a result, educational developers in this arena must be prepared to respond to teaching questions and to leadership questions, sometimes in the same meeting. For the kinds of responses that both situations demand, operating from the inside-outside position is a benefit, in great part because of the neutrality that comes with being in such a space. Still, this intersectional, neutral place requires always-already being OK. No one has the time to get to the point of being alright when faced with tough questions. Educational developers must come ready.

Coming ready also means understanding administrative needs at faculty levels. Some faculty members—excellent classroom instructors and researchers—challenge their department heads and program managers. Despite receiving concrete direction from a department head regarding ways to address a specific institutional issue in class in order to be consistent with institutional values and direction, the faculty member decides that they can trust their own skills and their class to engage in a difficult conversation. Emotions run high; students complain; the faculty member is frustrated and hurt; the department head is equally frustrated. So the team decides to consult an educational developer. The students want to see consequences for the faculty member; the faculty member wants a return to the classroom "normal"; the department head wants to protect the students, the faculty member, and the reputation of the department. Bridging the gaps between these different people and desired outcomes requires not only the expertise of the educational developer regarding best teaching and learning practices and deep understanding of the academic enterprise, but also a genuine willingness to engage with all parties, to validate the concerns of all parties, and collectively to develop a resolution that works for all parties. Simultaneously, the educational developer needs to establish expertise consistent with this alt-ac position—focused on teaching and learning, focused on organizational development, and with disciplinary background appropriately deep to hold ground as a faculty member.

To do this kind of work, the educational developer must not allow personal opinions to interfere. Regardless of outrageous statements that any of the involved parties might make, the educational developer can react with only the blandest response, consciously performing a calm, warm demeanor that will provide each party with a neutral ally who can guide activities in building bridges. Determining what demeanor will suit the occasion and the audience and performing that behavior consciously requires emotional labor. This labor cannot be visible, however, because the very visibility of the labor destroys the effect of it. The combination of work to gain expertise in teaching and learning and labor to be always-already OK, regardless of opinion or emotion on the matter, means that the educational developer's emotional labor makes the state of being OK consistently available. The developer must be always-already OK.

Once partner units and faculty members realize that the developer is always-already OK, then educational developers find that this state becomes a valuable asset in their work. Because much of the work depends on individual and group relationships, maintaining those relationships is key to the continued success of development initiatives.

As part of those efforts, developers may find that they don't get to have bad days. So when campus building maintenance refuses to replace windows so cracked that exhaust from passing cars can be smelled (sometimes seen) indoors, when the center's proposed location changes to a brick basement room in a hard-to-find building, the developers cannot allow themselves to be angry. Instead, they must reassess the situation and determine how best to proceed in order to meet their ultimate goal of maintaining themselves as a persistently supportive, essential presence.

Along with days that involve these kinds of opportunities for emotional labor, educational developers may also find themselves interrupted by faculty members. Because faculty members *are* their work, developers always have time for faculty needs. They must be prepared at any time to provide answers to challenges that faculty present, especially as campus incivility increases, particularly between students and faculty and between students themselves. Despite the push for efficiency, which would seem to necessitate workshops and other types of development opportunities, developers often work individually with faculty members, answering questions that are personal to that individual and working with individuals directly to implement best practices and to highlight the ways in which that individual is already implementing strong teaching practices that match that person's style. Thus educational developers may find themselves, as one developer that I observed did, cussed out by a faculty member for observing professional protocols—advising and coaching but not intervening directly. Despite the incivility of the faculty member, the developer remained in the situation, engaging with the faculty member to support a return to a steadier state. The developer adopted the posture of understanding that faculty members had other challenges and was releasing those other challenges onto the developer. That same developer received a visit from a dean. Again following professional protocols, the developer provided coaching, but did not intervene directly. That dean became exceptionally frustrated and yelled at the developer. Again, the educational developer met the frustration with calm, never rising to the frustration. Eventually, the dean apologized while the faculty member did not. Nonetheless, the developer's emotional labor to maintain professional calm in the face of surprising visits filled with uncivil behavior testifies to the need for the developer to be always-already OK.

The persistence of emotional labor extends even to my recovery from cancer. Surviving cancer is never not a part of my identity. Regularly that survival becomes part of my work as an educational developer. Because I have experienced profound challenges, I can draw on the lessons from that challenge when building relationships with faculty. Those faculty who experience profound life-upheaval may find working with a developer who grasps the complications that such upheavals present easier. Deciding how much to reveal, when in the consultation or workshop and if so, what, is another way in which I engage in the emotional labor of acting as if I am OK when, perhaps that day, I am not. Yet I am paid to build relationships with faculty, departments, deans, and schools so that I can support them in adopting better teaching and learning practices. I'm always-already OK.

Deepening the complicating factors around emotional labor is its cost to the educational developer. Choosing when and how to reveal that I was a full professor and gave that up willingly is a fraught decision, just as choosing to reveal that I have survived cancer is. In an environment of accreditation and assessment that requires documentation of return on and value for investment, the educational developer's work is slightly problematic. Documenting the numbers of workshops given, the numbers of attendees at workshops, and the numbers of consultations will not fully capture the return on and value for investment in educational development. Beneficial changes to teaching practices and to organizational development mature over time. Like students, faculty members may not be fully prepared after a workshop, book group, or consultation to articulate what they have learned, much less to implement it. At some institutions, budget requests for additional personnel require documenting how long each task takes in fifteen-minute increments in order to demonstrate that, indeed, educational developers cannot take on additional institutional responsibilities without a staffing increase. In such environments, invisible, emotional labor, costly to the employee but not directly costly to the institution, complicates matters. The task itself may take only an hour while, depending on the degree of deep- or surface-level acting, the developer may need additional recovery time. Such work doesn't fit neatly on a time sheet in tracking software. The return on and value for that investment of time, however, can be great. The developers' time and emotional labor may be a factor in helping faculty of diverse identities find belonging at an institution. That time and emotional labor may be the difference between losing faculty because of poor evaluations and keeping faculty because they show consistent effort in becoming better teachers, researchers, and university community citizens. The indirect nature of the educational developer's emotional labor—that which allows developers to say, "You're OK. I'm always OK"—may not always show results in the near term. That does not make it any less worthy or any less effortful.

Along with each of the aforementioned moments and challenges is the social construction of the transition from faculty member to the alt-ac track that my cancer occasioned. The acculturation to academic work that I received as a graduate student and the reality of the kind of work that I now do—and which, to be honest, fits me much better—is the cultural conflict between the two. In graduate school, alt-ac was for those who didn't make the transition from graduate student to faculty member. In fact, some alt-ac positions existed, but they were considered beneath the faculty to discuss as possible career paths. Moving from tenured full professor to all that alt-ac requires means always being ready to present development and the accompanying, unacknowledged affective labor as "true" academic work for faculty. Educational development also means working a/effectively against implicit bias to those in academia deemed unworthy because they did not want to pursue a faculty career or because they went into graduate school knowing that they wanted an alt-ac position. Thus, my job is always-already outside, to maintain academic structures, supporting those who want to remain "inside"; to accept the label "alternative" while contributing to the literature/discipline of faculty development; and to sustain myself and colleagues as we argue that our work—affective by nature—is truly "academic." Of course, while having the conversation(s) that dismiss my work as insufficiently academic, I must maintain a calm demeanor, and perform warmth and openness so as not to distance that administrator or faculty member. In a move characteristic of deep emotional labor,[3] I remind myself of all that this view has behind it: fear perhaps of change, senses of not measuring up to expectations from a variety of sources, feelings of being overwhelmed by increasing demands, discouragement occasioned by events beyond their control, or simply a bad day.

Unlike the provost who scoffed at the number of hours faculty worked because that number of hours was not clearly available in a 24/7 week, those who hire educational developers must recognize that the emotional labor demanded by the bridging position that they occupy may be invisible, perhaps even invisible to them. Educational developers may need to think through their work, particularly the emotional labor, and plan for rejuvenation involved in their work that will go unseen, although that unseen emotional labor and recovery from it is a significant part of their job, one for which they're paid, and one that they may be explicitly required to perform. As a faculty-educational developer who has now directed two different centers for teaching and learning, I have come to value the relationships that being always-already OK brings and the bridges that such work builds and supports. I've even written about its value,[4] and I honestly believe that building bridges is important. But this mirror-twin of a chapter won't go away. The display of positive calm comes at a cost that cannot be ignored. Even if I don't want to admit it, the incivilities of the academic workplace, the need consistently to document the worth of relationship-building activities in numeric terms, and the construction of my work as not entirely up to academic standards takes a toll. At some point, I/we must find a pathway to acknowledge and reward the emotional labor required for us to be truly OK.

As my fellow educational developers and I work to make our faculty OK, we can engage in some measures to help ourselves to be genuinely OK, or—at least—to restore some equilibrium when we are honestly not OK or emotionally depleted. Having had to be in circumstances where I had to be always-already OK from 8 a.m. to 5 p.m. for days on end, I learned some techniques that help me to refresh my resources to have sufficient emotional energy to engage in the kind of emotional labor that being a faculty developer demands. In no particular order, I'll list some techniques that work for me.

- Educate ourselves and our supervisors about emotional labor while using language that positions that labor as part of professional work. Unfortunately, as conversations about gender and gendered work have increased, the term *emotional labor* has crept out of the professional workspace and into additional spaces. As a result, some discussions of emotional labor have become more about working with employees navigating their home lives rather than understanding the emotional toll of certain work environments.[5] Alas, that conversation may be nearly impossible to have because of the kind of emotional labor that faculty developers do. So call attention to the emotional labor of others in public ways. Emails work for this because they can be forwarded and kept for the annual review meeting.
- Take control of the calendar. I block off the beginnings and ends of my days. When asked about those blocks, I reply that they are the times in my day when I answer emails and plan for the next day. I block the day after my vacation so that I have time to weed through my email and to address any big challenge that has arisen while I've been away. I also try not to work outside my work hours. These choices keep me from being always in an always-already

OK mode. I did not arrive at these practices overnight. I had to transition myself into being OK with walking away from the office at the end of the day. And, I try to take all of my vacation time.

- Look for friends at work and cultivate them. Having a meeting with a friend who might help me to think through a challenge and to accomplish a goal when I don't have to do as much emotional labor lessens that labor and provides some down time. Having someone whom I can email or call when I need another ear is also a helpful break. Cultivating friends is just as important as cultivating clients for educational development.
- Avoid the energy vampires. Some people suck the life right out of the room. I cannot always avoid these people as they may be colleagues or clients. What I can do is minimize my contact with these folks as much as I can. If I know that I have a meeting with an energy vampire, I plan to have a few post-meeting minutes to make some notes about what went well and what didn't. Getting my thoughts out and visible helps me not to take anything personally and reserve some energy for the rest of my day. If possible, I schedule these meetings between meetings in which I can recharge or schedule extra time after those meetings to get myself a cup of coffee and recharge.
- Negotiate for flexible working arrangements. I can work from spaces that are comfortable for me and allow me to accomplish center goals without necessarily being in the office all of the time.
- Control the cell phone. Just because the phone rings doesn't mean that I have to answer it. If I know that my resources are depleted and that I could make a mistake, I can let the person leave a message. Then, when I am in a better head/emotional space, I can respond. The same is true for emails. I spend less time cleaning up a mess I made if I take a minute first. Unless absolutely necessary, I don't give out my personal cell phone number.
- Schedule a retreat. In order to recharge the batteries, I try to find some times to be away in places where I do not have to expend emotional energy. I use these times to think and to plan for myself as well as for my center. I have also used walking between meetings to recharge quickly when I don't have any other moments in my day. Even three deep breaths in a bathroom stall refreshes my mind and allows a quick reset.
- Have a personal professional development project. In order to keep myself fresh and moving ahead, I need to have a project in which I think about what I do. For me, that also means finding

a way to write about it. Perhaps for others, it means presenting at conferences; attending conferences, workshops, or webinars; having a professional coach; completing a certification; or reading a book. Whatever that project is, encouraging your own professional development is an important way to refill your emotional gas tank and to prepare for the next moment when you have to present as OK.

Perhaps one of these techniques will work for you. Perhaps this list sparks your thinking, and you imagine another technique that helps you to perform the emotional labor to be always-already OK. No matter what technique(s) we use, we must find ways for ourselves to recharge emotionally. Simply having conversations about the intersections between the kinds of experiences and identities that we bring to our work and the kinds of work that we perform can help us to remain mindful of how we work. Perhaps, just perhaps, we can find ways for ourselves to be genuinely OK.

NOTES

1. Arlie Hochschild, *The Managed Heart: Commercialization of Human Feeling*, 20th anniversary ed. (Berkeley: University of California Press, 2012), 19.

2. David Webster and Nicola Rivers, "Critiquing Discourses of Resilience in Education," May 14, 2017, https://davewebster.org/2017/05/14/a-contrary-view-critiquing-discourses-of-resilience-in-education/.

3. Alicia A. Grandey and Gordon M. Sayre, "Emotional Labor: Regulating Emotions for a Wage," *Current Directions in Psychological Science* 28, no. 2 (2019): 131–137.

4. Gayle Maddox and Martha Diede, *Bridges Not Blockades: Transcending University Politics* (Gorham, ME: Myers Education Press, 2020).

5. Julie Beck. "The Concept Creep of 'Emotional Labor,'" *Atlantic*, November 26, 2018, https://www.theatlantic.com/family/archive/2018/11/arlie-hochschild-housework-isnt-emotional-labor/576637/.

BIBLIOGRAPHY

Beck, Julie. "The Concept Creep of 'Emotional Labor.'" *Atlantic*. November 26, 2018. https://www.theatlantic.com/family/archive/2018/11/arlie-hochschild-housework-isnt-emotional-labor/576637/.

Grandey, Alicia A., and Gordon M. Sayre. "Emotional Labor: Regulating Emotions for a Wage." *Current Directions in Psychological Science* 28, no. 2 (2019): 131–137.

Hochschild, Arlie R. *The Managed Heart: Commercialization of Human Feeling*, 20th anniversary ed. Berkeley: University of California Press, 2012.

Maddox, Gayle, and Martha Diede. *Bridges Not Blockades: Transcending University Politics*. Gorham, ME: Myers Education Press, 2020.

6

Plays Well with Others

Practicing Emotional Labor in the Writing Center

KAREN ROSENBERG

When I first took my position as academic staff directing a university writing center, I was only dimly aware of the hierarchies between (and among) faculty and staff. Yet when I look back on my interview marathon, I remember a faculty member asking me several times if I was aware that I was interviewing for a staff position. I remember a staff member telling me that I couldn't expect to act like a faculty member, and did I understand that? (I in fact had no idea what she was talking about, but the question was more like a command, and I pretended to agree with her.) There were signs—so many signs!—that working as academic staff with a PhD came with its own complex set of power dynamics. It has been twelve years since then and I've wrestled with what this alt-ac business means to me. Over the past several years I've come to realize that academic staff roles afford some advantages that faculty roles typically do not. I have become something of an alt-ac enthusiast. And this, in part, is tied to my ever-evolving relationship with emotional labor. In this chapter I will share my experience as an alt-ac, briefly discuss how emotional labor plays into my alt-ac landscape, and argue for a recognition of emotional labor as an important component of academic work, one that should be made more visible and recognized.

When I look back on it, it seems clear that I set out to become an alt-ac. I certainly didn't have that language and likely would have rejected it if I had it (I'm still not crazy about it), but when I entered my doctoral program in women's studies I never intended to suit up for the tenure track. I entered graduate school to get tools to sharpen my activist work, to better understand how to work for a society that supports and fosters healthy relationships. I was immersed in the feminist antiviolence movement and wanted the time and space to make sense of the stories women shared with me in that work.

I have pivoted many times since then. Pivoted away from full-time antiviolence research after the birth of my first child. Abandoned my dissertation research for two weeks to prepare an application for a writing center director position that I was told I was unqualified for. Got said writing center director position. My dissertation advisor told me that I would become "stale" if I stayed in that position for more than a year. I stayed anyway, but I felt keenly aware that my expiration date had come and gone. Even though I didn't want a tenured faculty position, I had been marinating in the hierarchy of the academy for so long (yes, even in women's studies!) that I felt inferior because I wasn't at the top.

After six years, I quit.

The emotional labor I took on as an alt-ac played a part in my decision to quit. The service provision aspects of directing a writing center involve relentless relationship-building and managing emotions (mine, faculty members', students', other staff members'). I had grown weary of stuffing my own emotions when faculty complained that students "couldn't even write a sentence," made racist comments about international students, or railed against the writing center because their students didn't master standard edited English after one or two sessions with a peer writing tutor. It's not that I didn't call the faculty members out—I did. I just did it while swallowing my feelings and working to forge and preserve relationships in the process. This often involved creating more space for faculty members to vent while finding ways to praise their intelligence and downplaying my own. It's tiring work. It's also simultaneously invisible, taken for granted, and asymmetrical.

After I quit my full-time staff position, I worked part-time, taught part-time, and upped my volunteer game at my kids' school. As the parent with more flexible time, and the one bringing in less income, I felt pressure to excel in the dark arts of the domestic sphere, which, to put it mildly, is not where my skill set lies. While I love the hands-on parts of parenting, the duties involved in running a household bring me little joy or sense of engagement. I found my affective labor load was still quite high, though now it was mostly unpaid.

I also experienced the marginalization of working as a contingent faculty member during that stint. Having slid from my doctoral program into my role at the writing center, I had only taught as a graduate student or under the umbrella of my staff position. I experienced the awful mismatch between the amount of self and effort I put into my classes and my compensation.

A year after I quit, I got a call asking if I wanted to return to my previous position. Other people were leaving or shifting roles, and they needed to fill the writing center director hole. That conversation led to a journaling, list-making, walks-with-friends-to-discuss frenzy. *Why did I leave? Did I feel like I could make an impact in the role? If I could do it all over again, what would I do differently?*

I realized that many of the aspects that I missed in the role were enhanced or enabled by my alt-ac status: my relationship with students in the writing center, which was not mediated by the currency of grades; the space I could carve out to sit with and support students, faculty, and other staff without the rhythms and pressures of a full-time teaching load; my stable position within a student support unit, from which I could advocate for institutional change. I envisioned returning to the position with a refreshed clarity and sense of purpose. The emotional labor entailed in managing faculty relationships did not excite me. But I hoped I could enter into those interactions differently, with more power and grace.

I negotiated for the position to be reopened (the only way I could return in a permanent status instead of the interim position initially proffered). I applied for the job that very much still felt like "mine" and interviewed with colleagues who put on stony faces and performed not knowing me for the interview. I got my job a second time.

My year away felt like a sloppy sabbatical. I am now into my fifth year during my second stint in my writing director position, and loving it. What changed? Many things, including a healthy dose of humor, continued focus on the issues I care about, and finding ways to speak up and speak out when I need to do so. I also made myself vulnerable in new ways, and this has created openings. For example, I forged deep relationships with tenured colleagues, and we strategically deployed our institutional locations to foment a feminist antiviolence movement on campus[1] and bring an intersectional feminist analysis to usage of our campus's math tutoring services.[2]

I am now an alt-ac advocate. Part of this, I am sure, is a self-protective "glass half full" mindset. It sure beats thinking of myself as ten years past my expiration date. And though I adore my position, it is not without the typical pitfalls of the alt-ac in academia: less prestige, less cash, less visible power on campus . . . and no paid sabbaticals. But in my experience the alt-ac role is less scripted and more amenable to improvisation than many straight-up faculty roles. I have been courtside for enough of my friends' tenure processes to reaffirm my desire to sidestep that game. I also want to frame the alt-ac as a legit choice, not just the safety net if you fail to catch the swinging trapeze of tenure.

To advance my argument that alt-ac roles in academia can be unabashedly rewarding, I will discuss the elephant of emotional labor. Many of the alt-ac roles are feminized and framed as "service provision" roles, and emotional labor is unavoidable. In this chapter I will discuss emotional labor and the conditions that make it particularly toxic. I will then discuss the concept of *emotional intelligence* and ask if this term affords a way of recognizing and rewarding the aspects of emotion work that should be more visible and valorized throughout academia.

WHAT ARE WE TALKING ABOUT WHEN WE TALK ABOUT EMOTIONAL LABOR?

When sociologist Arlie Hochschild first coined the term *emotional labor* in the early 1980s, she used it as a way to conceptualize the emotional self-regulation work flight attendants needed to do in order to provide "service with a smile." I was reminded of this when I heard a story on the podcast *The Moth* by a flight attendant. She describes what for her was a highlight of the initial training.

> When the founder and CEO of the airline gave a speech to our training class, I knew I was in the right place. He said, "Every one of you is here for a reason, and that reason is your ability to smile and be kind. We can teach you how to evacuate an airplane. We can teach you how to handle a medical emergency. . . . But we cannot teach you to smile and be kind. Your mother did that. Please thank her for me.[3]

What struck me about this statement, aside from the fact that she could have leapt out of Hochschild's original study, was the queasily feminized, naturalized way the CEO described the emotional labor requirements of the job. The folksy "Your mother did that. Please thank her for me" got at a deeper truth: for many of us hardcore emotional laborers, our training started before we could talk; it was baked into our early socialization. And if we were raised female, it's more likely that we learned to be attuned to others' emotions and to regulate our own.

The term *emotional labor* has traveled far and wide since Hochschild first used it. It has been used to describe everything from making dentist appointments to arranging for family photo shoots. Hochschild has lamented this concept creep, arguing that it detracts from the analytic power of the term.[4] Indeed, emotional labor has become a "floating signifier," a term that circulates without a fixed meaning. I am not concerned here with pinning the fluttering "emotional labor" butterfly to the page in order to advance a singular definition. Instead I am interested in how many of us have encountered the term and seen something of ourselves and our circumstances in it. For many of us, it has given us language to talk about bodies of taken-for-granted work, work we may not have even acknowledged to ourselves. When thinking about emotional labor for myself, my truest definition is, "I know it when I see it. . . . I feel it when I do it."

There is something stubbornly preverbal about emotional labor for me. But "I feel it when I do it" is a particularly unsatisfying set up for a chapter, so I conceptualize emotional labor both in Hochschild's original casting as emotional self-regulation *and* helping others manage the emotional content that they introduce into our field of interaction.

THE HEART OF THE WRITING CENTER: EMOTIONAL LABOR IN PRACTICE

A hallmark of much emotional labor is that it is taken for granted and "invisibilized," even to those of us doing it. But it doesn't have to be that way. For the most part, I love the emotional labor I do in the course of my work. I love supporting students as they wrestle with both the emotional and cognitive aspects of their writing assignments. I love providing faculty with a space where they can explore and express their emotions around teaching. With faculty this comes up as we review assignments, grading policies, and their reactions to student writing. And I love being able to use my prior work as a feminist antiviolence activist to create space for students to talk about their relationships with me. I am not a therapist, and I refer early and often to counseling services. However, I also allow students latitude to talk about their relationships and tease out what feels healthy to them and what doesn't. (People disclose to me because I share my prior work background and I believe in breaking silences around abusive relationship dynamics.) I am deeply committed to my role in supporting students and faculty colleagues.

However, I have also emotionally labored in situations that have bewildered and distressed me. For example, Joan (not her real name) is a midcareer faculty member who would pop by my office, close my door, and sit down. She'd often start in with a writing pedagogy-related question but quickly detour. "I'm so tired and stressed out," she began one day, and then shared many (many!) details about her marriage, her child's diarrhea, her irregular periods, her frustration with her colleagues, her elation and frustration with her research, the ways she felt unappreciated in her department, and so on. "Oh my goodness," she finally said. "It's been an hour! I have to go grade papers! Thanks so much for listening." I felt like I had been emotionally mugged. After that day, I practiced my breathing as she monologued in my office. I then began to set expectations before she sat down: *I have a meeting in a few minutes. I have a paper I need to finish. I'm so behind on my email.* I worked not to alienate her, due both to our asymmetric power dynamic and my own firmly socialized need to be liked. But it wasn't fun.

I also file an incident with a senior faculty member in the "unfun" category. She berated me when I asked her if I could use her writing exercises in tutor trainings. "They are not exercises," she informed me. "They are *encounters* and they are *my* intellectual and creative property."

"My apologies. I just thought—"

"Clearly you didn't think. Do you know how I feel? Let me tell you. Over the past twenty years, I have. . . . "

I sat and listened as she shared her pain and anger around the lack of recognition for her work. Unwittingly, my request to use her writing prompts (I cannot bring myself to call them encounters) triggered a whole host of emotions. If I had had more structural power in the situation (i.e., if I were not an alt-ac) I might have told her what she could do with her body of work. Instead I apologized and murmured sympathetically when she recited past injustices. Over the next half hour she switched between treating me like a would-be thief and a confidante. She met my forays into participating in the conversation with hostility, so I just sat and took it. When she finished, she thanked me coolly and left my office.

I have come to consider these instances of toxic emotional labor. For me, toxic emotional labor has four characteristics: power asymmetry between participants; a lack of reciprocity; a lack of recognition (it is often invisible); and a lack of value assigned to the work, when it is made visible. These characteristics help explain why alt-ac roles are structurally vulnerable to toxic emotional labor. I will briefly describe each one of these characteristics of toxic emotional labor.

Alt-acs have less structural power than their faculty counterparts (with some exceptions—contingent faculty arguably have less structural power than full-time alt-acs in academia). Alt-acs are limited in the roles they can play in faculty governance (e.g., I sit on some faculty bodies, but I do not have voting rights). Alt-acs are generally not considered for positions in upper administration on the academic (not student affairs) side of the house. Alt-ac voices often do not carry the same weight as faculty voices. And alt-acs cannot get tenure and the job security that goes along with it. When thinking about toxic emotional labor, power asymmetries are the most difficult to change. But when acknowledged directly, differentials in power need not lead to toxic emotional labor conditions.

A lack of reciprocity can foster toxic emotional labor conditions between alt-acs and faculty members. There does not need to be full reciprocity, but neither should there be a complete imbalance. The faculty member who came into my office to monologue about her work and personal life without allowing for dialogue illustrates how a lack of reciprocity can contribute to toxic emotional labor. My role in those meetings was reduced to head nodding and "uh huhs," dispensed in ways to help me manage both my own emotions and hers. Not only does this feel emotionally distancing to me, but the one-sided rants precluded the development of a healthy working relationship, something that could benefit both of us. I now elbow my way into these conversations with more intentionality and vulnerability. I am also better about extricating myself from one-sided rants.

Toxic emotional labor is often not recognized. It is both "invisibilized" and, when rendered visible, not valued. In addition to the toxic emotional labor that happens behind closed doors or goes unacknowledged in other arenas, emotional labor has little currency in most academic settings. I cannot, for example, tout the emotional labor I performed on my annual review or in applications for grants or fellowships.

By creating this taxonomy of toxic emotional labor practices, I imply that there is such a thing as healthy emotional labor. I'm not sure this is the right move. I am trying to find a way to shed light on the crappy ways alt-acs are pressed into emotional labor while at the same time I want to value the role of emotion work in academia. I definitely do think that emotional labor—managing our own emotions and helping others manage theirs—is crucial work whenever we are in community with each other, including in the workplace. Rather than remain unacknowledged or dismissed as an unfortunate by-product of alt-ac roles, this work should be recognized, valued, and rewarded. It should also provide an entryway into discussions around how we can best care for each other in community. Care feminism has made related claims and provided some useful theoretical framing and blueprints to consider.[5]

But here's where I get stuck: if we're trying to differentiate between toxic and healthy emotional labor, and the term has become so identified with the former, should we leave "emotional labor" as shorthand for the problems with emotion work and find a new term to connote "healthy" emotion work in academia? And what happens if we lasso the concept of "emotional intelligence" to help us do this work?

The argument that being able to manage emotions is crucial to individual and institutional success is baked into the term *emotional intelligence,* often referred to as EQ or EI. First appearing in a 1964 research paper, the concept pushed back against the idea that an individual's IQ was the best predictor of their success. In 1995 journalist Daniel Goleman popularized the term with his best-selling *Emotional Intelligence: Why It Can Matter More Than IQ.*[6] This has spawned a cottage industry of emotional intelligence quizzes, roadmaps, courses, and case studies. Like the term *emotional labor* it has become a floating signifier, used in so many contexts that it no longer has a singular meaning. Can we use this to our advantage? Can we mobilize the term to raise the value of emotion work done by alt-acs and others in the academy?

If we strategically deployed the language of emotional intelligence, it could raise the profile and status of the aspects of emotional labor that we want to foster and keep. We could, for example, advocate for emotional intelligence to be a competency listed in position qualifications and linked to performance reviews. Even if we are not successful in these efforts or if the language of "emotional intelligence" doesn't carry helpful connotations in particular institutional locations, it could serve as a way to start a conversation and find allies. It could also give us language to speak up (or at least mark for ourselves) when we're pressed into toxic emotional labor dynamics.

Our university held a two-part, six-hour training on emotional intelligence for staff. Although I wish that the training would have had both faculty and staff working together, the training underscored the overlap between the emotional labor (with its largely negative connotations) and emotional intelligence, which was presented as an underutilized superpower that we could learn to develop (growth mindset, anyone)?

The rhetoric of emotional intelligence can help steer us away from two of the toxic elements of emotional labor that I discussed earlier: a lack of recognition of the work and a lack of value assigned to the work when it is made visible. I have begun to name instances of emotional labor and emotional intelligence that I experience around me. I praise writing center staff members for their emotional intelligence when I see them interact skillfully with students who are stressed out, confused, or despairing. I name the emotionally intelligent work I observe, such as active listening, identification of feelings, and suggestions for regulating emotions. I also commend staff members' emotional intelligence in reviews. I have found that simply tying emotion work to the signifier "intelligence" is a useful intervention in academic spaces. I hope that if enough of us adopt language that valorizes this work we can co-create more compassionate academic workplaces.

However, emotional intelligence discourse falls short when it comes to the other two elements of toxic emotional labor I mentioned: asymmetric power relations and a lack of reciprocity. Though braiding emotional intelligence discourse into conversations with colleagues can raise the visibility of emotion work, it is not going to remediate the profound power imbalances within academia. Neither does it offer tools to increase reciprocity.

Perhaps, then, it is the work of volumes like this to provide a platform for academic staff to reflect on our emotional labor to help us navigate this tricky terrain. Perhaps sharing our stories will help us see new ways we can move through academia, ways that feel healthier and emotionally cleaner. At the very least, by sharing our stories we make emotional labor more visible and can help us support one another within and across our academic spaces.

NOTES

1. Lauren F. Lichty, Karen Rosenberg, and Kyra Laughlin, "Before There Is a Table: Small Wins to Build a Movement against Sexual and Relationship Violence in a University Context," *Journal of Family Violence* 33, no. 8 (2018): 629–645.

2. Robin Angotti and Karen Rosenberg, "Strategic Collaboration for Richer Assessment: Educational Data Mining to Improve Learning Centers," *Learning Assistance Review (TLAR)* 23, no. 2 (2018): 115–132.

3. Faye Lane, "Fireworks from Above," *The Moth*, https://themoth.org/stories/fireworks-from-above.

4. Julie Beck, "The Concept Creep of 'Emotional Labor,'" *Atlantic*, November 26, 2018.

5. Joan C. Tronto, "Creating Caring Institutions: Politics, Plurality, and Purpose," *Ethics and Social Welfare* 4, no. 2, 158–171.

6. Daniel Goleman, *Emotional Intelligence* (New York: Bantam, 2006).

BIBLIOGRAPHY

Angotti, Robin, and Karen Rosenberg. "Strategic Collaboration for Richer Assessment: Educational Data Mining to Improve Learning Centers." *Learning Assistance Review (TLAR)* 23, no. 2 (2018): 115–132.

Beck, Julie. "The Concept Creep of 'Emotional Labor.'" *Atlantic*. November 26, 2018.

Goleman, Daniel. *Emotional Intelligence*. New York: Bantam, 2006.

Lane, Faye. "Fireworks from Above." *The Moth*. https://themoth.org/stories/fireworks-from-above.

Lichty, Lauren F., Karen Rosenberg, and Kyra Laughlin. "Before There Is a Table: Small Wins to Build a Movement against Sexual and Relationship Violence in a University Context." *Journal of Family Violence* 33, no. 8 (2018): 629–645.

Tronto, Joan C. "Creating Caring Institutions: Politics, Plurality, and Purpose." *Ethics and Social Welfare* 4, no. 2 (2010): 158–171.

7

The Difficulties of Removing the Pink Collar

Affective Labor and Educational Development

LINDSAY BERNHAGEN AND
EMILY O. GRAVETT

In 2017 we published the article "Educational Development as Pink Collar Labor: Implications and Recommendations" in the journal *To Improve the Academy.* It explored the predominance of women, as well as the gendered labor those women perform, in the alt-ac profession of "educational development," also called faculty development or academic development.[1] Known for its liminality,[2] educational development is a field of professionals (sometimes faculty, sometimes staff) who advance the professional development of the university workforce through pedagogical, leadership, and organizational expertise. That same year, our article won the POD Network's 2017 Christine A. Stanley Award for Diversity and Inclusion Research in Educational Development. It has since been cited in other publications, mentioned in national presentations, and identified by senior scholars in the field as a "must-read."

This piece was largely theoretical; that is, we analyzed the place of women in "pink-collar" professions. The women in these professions perform affective or emotional labor, as they care, serve, and support others. As is widely known, women in these fields are often underappreciated and underpaid, despite providing essential, emotional work for and on behalf of others.[3] This is the case even for women in academia, who are often relegated to undervalued professions (like education) and positions (like adjuncts). As we turned our focus to the field we inhabit, educational development, we noticed that it, too, is dominated by women and performs, as articulated in the center mission statements, job ads, and the literature that we analyzed, labor on behalf of others. The thrust of our argument was that these demographics and this discourse may be one of the reasons, heretofore unconsidered in the literature of the field, for the well-documented difficulties of educational developers getting "invited to the table," contributing to organizational development, and advocating for ourselves.

In our article, we wondered, "Are educational developers often consigned to the peripheries of change at our institutions in part because the ranks are mostly populated with women? Is this marginalization exacerbated because educational development work is frequently characterized by relational and emotional labor, labor that all too often goes underappreciated, in part because it is associated with women?"[4]

We ended the article by offering a number of concrete recommendations for readers, including being explicit about the importance of emotional labor, simultaneously being cautious about representing our work as solely service-oriented, and being more explicit about the myriad other roles we assume, which go beyond pink-collar labor. These recommendations, however, were more about the ways we represent, articulate, and encourage others to perceive our work as a field, rather than specific reflections from or advice for individuals deeply entangled in the *doing* of emotional labor, service provision, and care for others. We simply did not have the space in that more theoretical piece to delve into the more personal resonance of the topic.

Yet we are two women who work in educational development. Our social identities, as well as our lived experiences, were, in part, what called us to write the article in the first place. The topic wasn't just interesting to us in a theoretical way; it was deeply personal. How does this pink-collar labor show up in our own lives? Simply because we had become aware of the implications and repercussions of how we represent our labor as well as how our labor is perceived by others does not mean that it has been easy for us to exercise agency and intentionality over when and how we do the important work that earns us our pink collars. After all, the performance of pink-collar labor is not necessarily the result of a lack of awareness, but rather a consequence of a complex confluence of factors: "Women, whether as an innate characteristic or as a consequence of socialization, pay attention to and tend to others' needs in a way that makes them vulnerable to overextending their giving and subjugating their own needs and desires."[5] Because of that complexity, we all have a responsibility to generate more balance in terms of emotional labor—who does it, under what circumstances, and how it gets recognized and valued.

In an effort to explore our own complicity in keeping our pink collars securely fastened around our own necks, it is important to move beyond the theoretical and to dig into real, rich, and personal experiences. While it would be impossible to comprehensively represent the variety of experiences in our field with pink-collar labor, and while we recognize the limits of our particular standpoints (e.g., we are both white, cisgender, able-bodied women in our thirties), we nevertheless share below our struggles in complicated, emotionally laden situations in order to demonstrate how difficult it is to follow our own advice for getting out of the "pink ghetto."[6]

LINDSAY'S STORY

I currently work at an institution facing profound budgetary shortfalls, which are resulting in program consolidation, discontinuance, and reorganization, along with the elimination of faculty and staff positions. Working in this environment, where I direct the Center for Inclusive Teaching and Learning (CITL), is difficult, regardless of one's position. Tensions are high, people are nervous, and everyone wants to point to another area of the university that is more expendable than their own. As is typical in higher education, there is deep suspicion of anything that suggests "administrative bloat,"[7] and since I am in a staff—rather than a faculty—position, I count as "administration" to many of my colleagues. What magnifies my own challenges in this environment is that I run a relatively new unit. In fact, I started my position shortly before the seriousness of our university's financial challenges (which preexisted the COVID-19 pandemic) were really known. As soon as those details became public, colleagues—those with whom I had worked hard to form relationships in a short time—started naming my unit (and thus my position) as one that could be eliminated in order to spare faculty layoffs. (I am privy to this information because Wisconsin, the state where I work, has very robust public records laws, and thus committee and governance conversations are recorded in great detail and made widely available.)

Given this fraught context, I have felt that I had no choice but to work even harder to justify my continued employment. I did this not only to temper calls that I should be let go but also so that those who remained at our institution (assuming I did too) would not spend years resenting me for being spared. It became quickly apparent to me that one of the best-received arguments for my position was to tout myself and my center as "in service" to the faculty for *whatever* they might need. While the CITL offers plenty in terms of strategic leadership, bringing those contributions to wider attention only taps into resentment about the perceived growth in administration at the expense of faculty. After a particularly terrible moment in which a faculty member publicly and angrily accused me of many untrue things, including facilitating administrative takeover of the general education curriculum, I felt a need to publicly downplay—though, of course, not abdicate—those critical and demanding aspects of my job.

At the same time, I started saying yes with palpable (and, in some cases, patently artificial) enthusiasm to anything that would demonstrate my servility to the faculty: Run another learning community? Sure! Take over the management of a training that is distinctly not within my center's mission? Well, someone has to do it, and I want to be a good team player! Make weekly trips to a new branch campus we inherited by administrative fiat? Okay! I can't wait to meet these new constituents! Take over a course—one that tackles the controversial topic of sexuality, no less—midterm because the instructor got sick? I'd love to! Thank you for trusting me! Chair two search committees while hiring for a position in my own unit? It would be my pleasure to give back to our campus in this way! Become interim chair of a shared governance committee on diversity and inclusivity? I am flattered by the opportunity! The challenge is not just in keeping all of these plates spinning in the air but to do it with humility and a smile on my face so as not to seem ungrateful for my continued employment.

The emotional labor of this balancing act, which I felt compelled to perform with an unwavering can-do, positive attitude, became deeply apparent at the first meeting of the group of faculty, deans, and upper administrators that was charged with determining which departments and positions to eliminate. I was not on this committee, but I was invited by the provost to facilitate a ground rules exercise for the group, so that they would have a framework for the difficult conversations that would lie ahead. Not only was this already a difficult situation because of the elevated emotions and sheer status of those in the room, but my heart dropped when I saw that the invite list included multiple faculty members who had explicitly suggested that my position be eliminated; a campus leader who, shortly after I was hired, advised that I would have to prove my worthiness for the position because they'd chosen me over a very strong candidate with "more experience" (this is not accurate; he was just an older white man) despite their reservations; my boss; and my boss's boss.

If the definition of emotional labor is, as Arlie Hochschild says, "the work, for which you are paid, which centrally involves trying to feel the right feeling for the job [which] involves evoking and suppressing feelings . . . crucially being hired and monitored for your capacity to manage and produce a feeling,"[8] then I can think of no more pointed example of when I had to rely heavily on my own ability to provide that labor—to manage my own emotions so that I could manage the emotions of the others in the room just to get the ground rules exercise done to the satisfaction of my superiors. Fortunately, I was able to maintain a positive, empathetic, and supportive demeanor throughout and accomplish the task at hand—but it was absolutely draining! There are countless smaller examples. I have pretended not to know who said what about my position and my center. I have downplayed my personal professional accomplishments (e.g., publishing—because others might question how and why I have time to engage in such "nonessential" tasks) and job responsibilities that are not obviously deferential to others' needs (e.g., serving on strategic planning groups). I have said yes to the point of tears many weeks, done my best to remind myself that I am lucky to have a job at all in this climate, scolded myself for not taking the advice that Emily and I offered in our original article, and then woken up the next day and put a forced smile on my face so that I could kindly and warmly demonstrate my utility all over again.

One of the challenges I have in curbing my own complicity with this pattern is that expending all of this emotional labor to keep those around me happy has worked really well for me, and I enjoy doing much of the work I've discussed above. It's the sheer volume that is the problem. I have a reputation as a positive force, someone who is good at building relationships, and—as I continue to learn when my skills are called upon again and again—someone who is skilled at facilitating difficult conversations. Quite honestly, my aptitude for emotional labor has, in some ways, made me more valuable to my institution.

EMILY'S STORY

Fortunately, my institutional situation is much more secure than Lindsay's. I am an assistant director in the Center for Faculty Innovation (CFI), as well as a faculty member in the Department of Philosophy and Religion, at James Madison University (JMU), a public institution in the state of Virginia. The CFI is a holistic professional development center for college faculty, which means we provide support not only for teaching but also for research/scholarship as well as career planning. The majority of full-time professionals in our office are women, including our executive director (and both previous executive directors). The CFI's position is not perilous, to my knowledge, as JMU just achieved the highest level of financial autonomy from the state and all employees received raises this year. And, while I am not a tenured or tenure-track faculty member (when I arrived, I chose a renewable term appointment, as opposed to a tenure-track position, due to the scholarship that my department would allow to count toward tenure), I haven't been given any reason to believe that my own position is in any jeopardy. My experience of pink-collar labor in the context of educational development is thus not as colored by institutional vicissitudes as Lindsay's.

Yet I still find myself performing a great deal of work that could be considered "emotional labor," including ego-stroking (particularly of male colleagues), complimenting and (re)affirming, gently reminding others of tasks/deadlines that are not my own, allowing people to "pick my brain," pretending I am not bothered by slights or insults (inadvertent or intentional), faking happiness, putting a smile on my face, feigning interest, listening and nodding my head, providing positive feedback or appreciation, rewriting emails to ensure they sound enthusiastic enough, even just showing up when I'm having a tough time. Of course, to quote an article recently published by the BBC, there is also "the extra emotional labour you shoulder if you're a person of colour, a LGBTQ+ person, or a person with a disability. That's the emotional labour you're expected to perform at work on a daily basis, pretty much every time you're faced with uncomfortable or offensive situations—which is, unsurprisingly, quite often. Plus, there is the added expectation that you will repeatedly, yet politely, correct and 'teach' the offending colleague."[9] While I am privileged that I do not bear the burden of this additional work, each and every day, simply by virtue of my gender, I still perform emotional labor that is perennially—though not exclusively—expected of and associated with women.

In a former job, for example, I felt unable to express my true emotions or to offer my genuine reactions and opinions, especially to an older male boss who I quickly came to learn did not respond well to anything that could be interpreted as negative, critical, disagreeable, or even gently dissenting. Yet, even in my current position, in a much healthier environment, I frequently feel unable to express my real reactions to and with the faculty I work with because I worry those reactions will lead them to become turned off from the center altogether. If they get a bad impression from/of me, will they still want to participate in teaching-related professional development programming? If they don't like me, will they not like or trust the unit I work in or my colleagues? I do not know how legitimate these worries are.

To be clear, I don't find all of these behaviors or moves problematic, burdensome, or undesirable all of the time (with the exception of those that require me to be inauthentic). Emotional labor isn't a bad thing, per se, an inherent evil to be avoided at all costs—despite its bad reputation. (And it's certainly not something only women perform, as other authors in this volume will attest.) I enjoy smiling; I like listening to interesting stories or to the people I care about; I think it's important to express gratitude; I want others to experience me as kind and friendly and generous and uplifting. In general, I hope that people feel more joyful after they've interacted with me. Yet too many of these behaviors, for too long of a duration, can certainly sap me.

One part of emotional labor that frequently goes unacknowledged, which I typically find draining and demoralizing, is (not) saying no—in general and to any particularly emotionally laborious tasks. In fact, it seems like saying no is the opposite of emotional labor. It is denying when the expectation is embracing or validating. It is cutting a conversation short when the expectation is indulgent listening. It is refusing to smile when the expectation is a happy face. It is disagreeing when the expectation is agreeing. It is acting frustrated when the expectation is to not rock the boat. It is a bucking of expectations. Emotional labor is an affirmative stance; it is assent or acceptance; it is a saying yes, even when you might want to say no, or saying probably not so gently that the recipient leaves the interaction still feeling warm toward you. The orientation is toward the other and the other's wants or needs, rather than a prioritizing of oneself. Lindsay knows this all too well.

Because of the reputation, credibility, and the longevity of the CFI—conditions very different than those informing Lindsay's experience—my colleagues and I are heavily involved in cross-campus initiatives. In the past academic year alone, for instance, members of our full-time staff served on over two-dozen committees, including highly visible leadership roles on sensitive, important, and emotionally laden topics (e.g., the task force on racial equity). In many cases, these were not invitations to be considered and accepted out of interest or alignment but rather responsibilities that members of the CFI are "voluntold" to do. Like Lindsay, we in the CFI were saying yes out of necessity, in many of these cases, but for very different reasons.

Given the high demand for the CFI's services and a history of routinely saying yes (perhaps a carryover from when we were a new center that needed to establish credibility and utility, as Lindsay is experiencing), but also our limited resources (financial and personnel) and our commitment to work-life balance, we have recently been having conversations in our center about our ability and latitude in saying no. We find it difficult to turn people away who make requests of us, even if they are unreasonable or made at the last minute or downright disrespectful. Of course, it is especially difficult when these requests come from the provost or even the president. Yet it is not simply that, as a center, we experience difficulty saying no. It is also that many individuals on our team—women, in particular—have difficulty saying no. This is certainly true for me. There are a variety of factors that may contribute to this hesitation, including that we might actually appreciate the work and *want* to do it: previous work experience in customer service, position in the center and institutional hierarchy, perception of a lack of autonomy or agency, desire for acceptance/sense of belonging, fear of letting others down, fear of missing out, the (maybe misguided) assumption that it's better for one's career to say yes, exhaustion or guilt (i.e., asked so many times that it's just easier to succumb and say yes), an inflated/misguided sense of one's own potential impact, the sense that someone "has" to do it, or even personality. Indeed, every time I take the Gallup Strengths Finder test, one of my top five signature themes is always "harmony."

Yet I can't help but wonder how much gender is bound up in these impulses or proclivities too—that is, how personality-based they actually are. After all, we know that women, in particular, are socialized to fear (and sometimes are punished for) being perceived as "bitchy," "bossy," "abrasive," "ambitious," or just plain "not nice."[10] We certainly don't want anyone to think of us as "too emotional" or "hysterical."[11] Chimamanda Ngozi Adichie in *Dear Ijeawele, or A Feminist Manifesto in Fifteen Suggestions* writes, to her friend upon the birth of a baby girl, that we should teach our daughters to *reject* likeability.[12] I am simultaneously convinced by this recommendation and not yet able to act upon it. I identify as an approval seeker or a people pleaser. Likewise, Lindsay has been told that she "leads with love." So, it is not simply that saying no is difficult. It is that I feel the need to say no without seeming unable, unwilling, unhelpful, even unappreciative. It is that there is a subtle pressure to say no the "right" way, the palatable way, the way that won't offend anyone. That is the most laborious part.

CONSEQUENCES

Some of the consequences we face when taking on too much emotional labor as educational developers are explicit and immediate. We can get spread too thin; if we say yes to too many commitments, then each is inevitably only getting a small piece of us. We cannot possibly be doing our best work for all of these—and it is plausible that we could gain a reputation for not doing great work as a result. Another consequence of not saying no is that we worry about enabling others. That is, if we do the work that others are supposed to be doing, they will never learn how to do it themselves or they will not experience the consequences of work done poorly . . . or not at all. Finally, we worry about compassion fatigue; indeed, an entire session at a recent POD Network conference was solely devoted: "Mattering to Ourselves: Confronting Burnout and Compassion Fatigue for Educational Developers."[13]

There are also longer-term, more insidious consequences, we fear, of routinely engaging in emotional labor as a primary part of our jobs. These include exhaustion and burnout; the work spilling over into our personal lives; professional derailment (if we are so busy doing all this other stuff, then there is no time to do what's important); others might get credit for our work; we may get pigeonholed; the work itself may be seen as unprofessional—and thus we may be seen as unprofessional too; resentment; diminishment or even destruction of professional relationships; a reinforcement of existing power structures; and the possibility that people will take advantage of us.

In many cases, we may even be *rewarded* for performing emotional labor—even if not in tangible or even particularly helpful ways, as in promotions or raises. People may compliment us or offer appreciation otherwise, they may provide us with additional opportunities or responsibilities, they may recommend us to others, they may invite us to social events, and so on. On the one hand, this is a testament to how critical the work of emotional labor is. On the other hand, these "rewards" may actually further compound the initial problem. Indeed, once we perform emotional labor, we notice that people get accustomed to it and then it becomes very difficult to pull back or bow out gracefully. This is one of the ways the problem gets reconstituted. In fact, on one of Emily's recent internal performance evaluations, after a year in which she had made it known one of her goals was to say no more often, one piece of feedback she received from a colleague was the implicitly dissatisfied question: "What is she saying yes to?" Would anyone have noticed or made that comment if there had been clear boundaries from the get-go?

CONCLUSION

Our intent in this chapter is not to suggest that doing emotional labor is inherently bad. To the contrary, we believe that emotional labor is critical to the successful functioning of all complex human interactions and organizations. In fact, we find much of this work enjoyable, fun, and fulfilling. What concerns us, however, is how we moderate the amount of emotional labor that gets done and by whom, and how we can recognize and value the importance of that work. The gender imbalance in who is doing the bulk of the emotional labor is a systemic problem, and not one that can be fixed by individual action alone. Collective awareness of the issue is a good first step, but we need to do more in order to reward this critical work, to allow women to set boundaries without penalty (and with encouragement!), and—on a more individual level—to become more self-aware and less habituated to saying yes.

If we fail to moderate our contributions of emotional labor, then we risk running out of time and energy to commit to other parts of our job. We have both lost hours (and sometimes even entire workdays) to empathetically listening to and counseling (often male) colleagues about a wide array of personal and professional issues as we've tried to find ways to gracefully shoo them out of our offices. As women, especially, we have to be aware of our own care-taking tendencies and perhaps challenge ourselves to err on the side of doing what feels like "too little" or saying no "too much"; we have to interrogate our compulsion to be so agreeable or "nice." We also have to hone our abilities to distinguish when we actually *do* need to perform emotional labor versus when we really do have the choice to opt out without inviting serious professional repercussions. Developing a strong network of mentors—regardless of gender—can be a useful strategy here. For example, Lindsay was recently asked to teach yet another course without compensation. Though she was tempted to say yes, she first consulted three friendly colleagues to get their take. With their support, she was able to turn down the opportunity without becoming awash in guilt for saying no and found herself, to her relief, facing no negative consequences as a result. The department in question was very understanding.

Finally, and perhaps most importantly, there are personal and emotional benefits to setting boundaries around one's expenditure of emotional labor—and labor in general. The more we feel like we have choice over how we're spending our time, the better we will feel. Saying yes strategically (which means saying no sometimes, too) gives us increased agency in our professional lives and communicates to others that our time and efforts are valuable. By reframing no in this way, rather than as something to feel guilt or anxiety over, we have the opportunity to turn it into an act of empowerment. None of this comes easily, but with practice and support from our colleagues, it is possible to create a more equitable work environment where pink collars can be worn as a matter of personal style rather than as a compulsion.

NOTES

1. See, for instance, Kathryn E. Linder, Kevin Kelly, and Thomas J. Tobin, *Going Alt-Ac: A Guide to Alternative Academic Careers* (Sterling, VA: Stylus, 2020).

2. Deandra Little and David Green, "Betwixt and Between: Academic Developers in the Margins," *International Journal for Academic Development* 17, no. 3 (2012): 203–215.

3. "Pink-Collar Workers Fight to Leave 'Ghetto,'" *Seattle Times*, January 8, 2006, https://www.seattletimes.com/business/pink-collar-workers-fight-to-leave-ghetto/.

4. Lindsay Bernhagen and Emily O. Gravett, "Educational Development as Pink Collar Labor: Implications and Recommendations," *To Improve the Academy* 36, no. 1 (2017): 9–19.

5. Amanda Owen, *The Power of Receiving: A Revolutionary Approach to Giving Yourself the Life You Want and Deserve* (New York: Random House, 2010), 16.

6. "Pink-Collar Workers Fight to Leave 'Ghetto.'"

7. Jenny Rogers, "How Many Administrators Are Too Many?" Chronicle of Higher Education, January 7, 2013, https://www.chronicle.com/interactives/administrative_bloat.

8. Quoted in Julie Beck, "The Concept Creep of 'Emotional Labor,'" *Atlantic*, November 26, 2018, https://www.theatlantic.com/family/archive/2018/11/arlie-hochschild-housework-isnt-emotional-labor/576637/.

9. Sophie Wilkinson, "Why Was Everyone Talking about Emotional Labour

in 2018?" BBC, December 24, 2018, https://www.bbc.co.uk/bbcthree/article/5ea9f140-f722–4214-bb57–8b84f9418a7e.

10. See, for instance, Sheryl Sandberg, *Lean In: Women, Work, and the Will to Lead* (New York: Alfred A. Knopf, 2013); and Kim Scott, *Radical Candor: Be a Kickass Boss without Losing Your Humanity* (New York: St. Martin's Press, 2017).

11. Therese Huston, *How Women Decide: What's True, What's Not, and What Strategies Spark the Best Choices* (Boston: Houghton Mifflin Harcourt, 2016), 6.

12. Chimamanda Ngozi Adichie, *Dear Ijeawele, or a Feminist Manifesto in Fifteen Suggestions* (New York: Alfred A. Knopf, 2017).

13. Allison Boye, "Mattering to Ourselves: Confronting Burnout and Compassion Fatigue for Educational Developers," POD Network Conference. Montreal, QB, October 2017. https://podnetwork.org/content/uploads/POD-Program-2017-Draft-10-21-2017.pdf

BIBLIOGRAPHY

Adichie, Chimamanda Ngozi. *Dear Ijeawele, or a Feminist Manifesto in Fifteen Suggestions*. New York: Alfred A. Knopf, 2017.

Beck, Julie. "The Concept Creep of 'Emotional Labor.'" *Atlantic*. November 26, 2018. https://www.theatlantic.com/family/archive/2018/11/arlie-hochschild-housework-isnt-emotional-labor/576637/.

Bernhagen, Lindsay, and Emily Gravett. "Educational Development as Pink Collar Labor: Implications and Recommendations." *To Improve the Academy* 36, no. 1 (2017): 9–19.

Boye, Allison. "Mattering to Ourselves: Confronting Burnout and Compassion Fatigue for Educational Developers." POD Network Conference. Montreal, QB, 2018. https://podnetwork.org/content/uploads/POD-Program-2017-Draft-10–21–2017.pdf.

Huston, Therese. *How Women Decide: What's True, What's Not, and What Strategies Spark the Best Choices*. Boston: Houghton Mifflin Harcourt, 2016.

Linder, Kathryn E., Kevin Kelly, and Thomas J. Tobin. *Going Alt-Ac: A Guide to Alternative Academic Careers*. Sterling, VA: Stylus, 2020.

Little, Deandra, and David A. Green. "Betwixt and Between: Academic Developers in the Margins." *International Journal for Academic Development* 17, no. 3 (2012): 203–215.

Owen, Amanda. *The Power of Receiving: A Revolutionary Approach to Giving Yourself the Life You Want and Deserve*. New York: Random House, 2010.

"Pink-Collar Workers Fight to Leave 'Ghetto.'" *Seattle Times*. January 8, 2006. https://www.seattletimes.com/business/pink-collar-workers-fight-to-leave-ghetto/.

Rogers, Jenny. "How Many Administrators Are Too Many?" Chronicle of Higher Education. January 7, 2013. https://www.chronicle.com/interactives/administrative_bloat.

Sandberg, Sheryl. *Lean In: Women, Work, and the Will to Lead.* New York: Alfred A. Knopf, 2013.

Scott, Kim. *Radical Candor: Be a Kickass Boss without Losing Your Humanity.* New York: St. Martin's Press, 2017.

Wilkinson, Sophie. "Why Was Everyone Talking about Emotional Labour in 2018?" BBC. December 24, 2018. https://www.bbc.co.uk/bbcthree/article/5ea9f140-f722–4214-bb57–8b84f9418a7e.

8

Affective Labor and the Balancing Act for Women in Academic Technology

CELESTE TU'Ờ NG VY SHARPE AND CARLY J. BORN

❖ ❖ ❖ ❖ ❖ ❖ ❖ ❖ ❖ ❖ ❖ ❖ ❖ ❖ ❖

Academic technologists inhabit unique positions at their institutions. We are experts in pedagogy, but not *quite* in the same way as teaching, tenure-track faculty. We are often generalist experts with wide-ranging technical skills, and specialists in a few discrete disciplinarily informed areas. We are academic staff, or "alt-ac" professionals, and described in a variety of ways by those faculty with whom we work: academic technologists are guides, resources, shepherds, innovators, support, magicians.

Here, we think it best to describe our own positionality to inform the following discussion. Celeste is a woman of color who holds a PhD in history and stepped into an academic technology role after several years working on digital humanities projects and teaching K–16 educators how to incorporate technology into their classrooms. Carly is a white woman who has worked in instructional technology for fifteen years. She has an MA in teaching Japanese as a foreign language, specializing in computer-assisted language learning, and a graduate certificate in instructional design. As our brief biographies show, there is no one path to academic technology jobs. Balanced expertise between pedagogy and technology defines the field, but being successful as an academic technologist also means delicately navigating institutional and societal views of technology in education.

The composition and role of information technology (IT) in higher education, and faculty views on the place of technology in their teaching practice, creates a challenging landscape for academic technologists to navigate. Recognition of our professional expertise is contingent upon careful negotiations of institutional hierarchies, affective labor, and gender performances. As a result, there are particular costs and pressures on women in these roles. Women are simultaneously asked to perform affective labor with faculty to soothe tech-induced anxieties and present expertise in a nonthreatening manner, while feeling pressured to acquire more deep technical knowledge (or "hard skills") to prove our place within an IT department.

There have been some small gains in efforts to increase the number of women in IT jobs in higher education. A study published by the Educause Center for Analysis and Research (ECAR) found that the number of women in IT jobs continues to grow, albeit slowly, among managers and staff, but not at the highest levels of leadership in the field (chief technology officer, chief information officer, etc.). In other areas of diversity, however, higher-education IT jobs continue to underperform: the IT workforce remains predominantly white (83 percent). The percentage of higher-education IT employees who identify as LGBQ is around 9 percent, and around 8 percent of respondents reported having been diagnosed with a disability or impairment.[1]

While the sector of jobs as a whole is only slowly diversifying, the nature of work in higher-education IT is shifting. The ECAR report found that there is growing recognition of the value of communication and relationship management skills in IT executives, managers, and staff. Given the demands of constantly evolving technologies, it makes sense that an ability to communicate effectively with campus constituents would be valued. This is the context in which we are most used to thinking about performing affective labor. Additionally, a majority of staff surveyed "rated managing inside relationships as key to their professional success."[2] These inside relationships—relationships within an IT department—are another key place where we perform (or are expected to perform) affective labor to some degree due to the relationship between academic technology and the IT department.

The organizational structure of IT departments in higher education varies depending on institution size, type, and leadership. Generally, academic technology is situated in one of three possible places: within IT, within a merged library and IT unit where librarians and technologists make up the core staff, or within a teaching and learning center. For the purposes of this chapter, we discuss how academic technology fits within a small private four-year liberal arts college organizational structure. At our college, academic technology sits within Information Technology Services (ITS) and reports to the chief technology officer, who in turn reports to the dean of the college.

ITS serves both the administrative and academic pursuits of the college and is made up of five main sub-departments: academic technology, enterprise systems, systems integration group, technology support group, and web services. All ITS sub-departments, except academic technology, work closely with the administrative offices and the business processes of the institution. Technology adoption has understandably varied between the administrative and academic areas of the college. The digitization of business processes in administrative offices is pushed both by shifts in marketing strategies (college branding, social media outreach, etc.) and by the desire to reduce staffing costs by automating some formerly arduous processes. In these offices, tech innovation is a business win, and employees must learn to adapt and continue to develop digital skills. No intrinsic motivation is necessary.[3]

Academic technology (AT) is the only group that focuses exclusively on the academic work of the college: teaching and learning and research. To be sure, all of the other groups support some aspects of academic activity, such as classroom technologies, server provisioning, web development and governance, and so on. But AT is the primary resource for faculty and students' scholarly forays into technology use. As a result, our work is wide-ranging. We support the college's learning management system and facilitate simple to elaborate pedagogical uses of the platform. We provide expertise in developing course assignments and projects, data management and research design, and experimenting with emerging technologies. The adoption of technology in the academic realm, however, is motivated in a substantially different way than the administrative.

According to Joel Smith and Lauren Herckis, two researchers at Carnegie Mellon University's Simon Initiative on technology-enhanced learning, faculty typically form a very strong mental model of what constitutes quality instruction in their discipline, based on their own personal educational experiences.[4] It's easy to imagine that most professors remember the one or two really great instructors from their own educational experiences. Naturally, many will attempt to emulate their mentors, replicating their own experiences for their students.

This model of education has been quite effective historically. The rate of change in pedagogical trends was rather slow until the development of psychology as an analysis of how the human brain works in the latter part of the nineteenth century.[5] Prior to that time, only select, largely homogenous populations enrolled in institutions of higher education.[6] And the technology of education (the book) remained largely unchanged for centuries. As the field of psychology developed, commentary from authors such as Vygotsky, Skinner, and Pavlov started to interest educators, who took their ideas further and created new fields of learning sciences. The advent of learning theories, alongside the increasingly rapid development of widely available digital technology products, has changed the game of education. Researchers are now drawing upon a great number of disciplines in the investigation of technology enhanced learning (TEL).[7] Gráinne Conole points out that the advent of "Web 2.0" technologies—those that evolved the web-based medium into an interactive and collaborative space—requires educators to radically rethink their approaches to teaching and to student learning.[8]

Rethinking one's approach to teaching is a lot to ask of educators. Smith and Herckis found that faculty are often quick to reject ideas about effective learning if they do not line up with their own beliefs, even in the face of evidence to the contrary. Critically, faculty are beholden to the tenure and professional review processes, which are still largely based on traditional educational paradigms. In our experience, few institutions encourage or even recognize contributions to learning that involve digital projects. Smith and Herckis cite the faculty professional performance surveys from 1999, 2000, and 2002, which found that only 32 percent of faculty agreed that their institution "appropriately rewards contributions made to digital pedagogy."[9] While professional organizations such as the Modern Language Association and the American Historical Association have created guidelines for tenure and promotion for digital humanities work, it is still rare for scholars to be promoted for digital pedagogy and projects.[10] In the end, faculty in higher education are often not encouraged or motivated to make significant changes to their teaching methods in general, let alone rewarded when they do.

Academic technology is one of the newer fields that have emerged in the past few decades. Additionally, it carries the added complication of making use of tools that did not necessarily grow out of academic fields. As computers started to become mainstream in the 1960s, pop culture began to reference what was then considered fantastical applications of technology in the near future (e.g., *The Jetsons, Star Trek,* etc.). Decades later, some of these predictions have actually manifested, but in a far less impressive fashion. Next to a virtual reality game system, the ability to lock and unlock your home from your smartphone is less awe-inspiring. Digital worksheets are still collections of problems designed to give students more practice delivered via a screen instead of paper. New technologies are often difficult to learn, change rapidly, and do not often fit into a faculty member's ideas about what makes quality teaching and practices. Combined with the lack of incentives to use technology to innovate or enhance pedagogies, faculty are often ambivalent about incorporating technology into their teaching or research.

Our positions are campus-facing, meaning that we are the points of contact for faculty for almost any kind of IT question; we refer when necessary and coordinate support with other professional staff on campus, such as the research and instruction librarians and writing center staff. People in our roles often become pedagogically informed technology champions, not just enthusiasts. Faculty who are unwilling to adopt or are intimidated by technology will not come to the workshops or roundtables, no matter how interesting they may turn out to be. And pre-tenure faculty are often warned away from tech innovation in their teaching because of how much work it can be and how it will not help their tenure case. In some situations, we are not seen as qualified academics and peers, despite advanced degrees and years of teaching experience, because we report to the IT department and do not hold faculty status.

In our context, faculty have a large degree of autonomy over what and how they teach, and technology adoption is *almost* optional. At our institution, we have had a learning management system (LMS) for over ten years that has grown more robust each year. At the same time, ours is a residential college with small class sizes and an emphasis on a high-touch experience for the students; there is little need to rely on technology to communicate with students or collect assignments. Adoption of the LMS for even the basic task of distributing course readings began very slowly here. Only in the past year or two have we started to see interest in some of the more advanced tools in the LMS, such as those that facilitate peer review workshops. In higher education, this is one of the most basic points of entry for faculty to incorporate technology into their classes, one that is often discussed as a way to move to deeper conversations about digital pedagogy.[11]

Often we hear technology-related inquiries from faculty at the point of need, which is often right up to the night (or hour) before the class session. This presents us with a double-edged consideration: (1) do we turn the faculty away, citing the time crunch and potentially risk losing ground and harming the relationship with that person, or (2) do we move heaven and earth to respond to the request, thus perpetuating the bad habit of integrating technology into the curriculum at the last minute and putting the onus on staff to smooth the results? This is a dilemma we face nearly every day, and it's never an easy answer.

Team discussions, and discussions with peers at similar institutions, often center on how to handle a particular person's request given the time, personnel, and technology constraints. We need to be fully aware of all of the possibilities but not take the lead unless explicitly asked. The personality dynamics and history of interactions are also key factors. We are told to not be "too forward" in encouraging faculty to come to us. "Forwardness," or assertiveness or dominancy, can be perceived differently for women than men, resulting in backlash for explicit assertiveness, though less so for implicit assertive actions.[12] Confidently presented evidence-based advice and arguments that some technologies and pedagogies can improve student learning only go so far, and they can easily backfire depending on how the faculty perceives what we say.

Requests or questions that involve technology take on a different flavor than other kinds of requests from alt-ac professionals due to the prevailing industry culture that tells us technology exists to make things simple in an intuitive and instantaneous way. This view shapes understanding of and responses to technology in the academic sphere. An acceptable response time is perceived to be minutes, and the emotional escalation of the problem is exponential and connected to how much time passes.

For example, I (Celeste) answered a call by a professor who couldn't remember how to import resources from a previous year's course in the learning management system. I talked her through the basic steps, but some checkbox unseen by both of us thwarted the initial attempt. The lack of immediate success frustrated the professor, who then unleashed a more emotionally charged lament about how technology just makes things worse. Five minutes and one more attempt through the process later, the resources were imported and the professor expressed relief that everything looked good and worked as desired, and the call ended on a cheery note. During that five minutes, however, I used several different strategies to soothe the emotions of the professor: I listened and repeated back the frustration to validate it; I reassured her that this wasn't a personal failing and that the technology was not targeting her specifically; and I restated that she was not alone, that I was there partnering with her to resolve the issue. I adopted a light tone throughout and shifted from an authority posture to one of a fellow traveler who would take the journey with them.

This is one example of the many kinds of affective and emotional labor we perform on a day-to-day basis. When tech-related issues occur—or are perceived to occur—the incidents elicit an emotional response: it is now a problem to be fixed, or a mess to be cleaned up. "Mess," as Paige Morgan writes, "has negative connotations that intersect with gendered labor: messes are things that women clean up; emotional labor, if we think of it as merely dealing with emotions, is just another type of mess that people assume women can/should handle."[13] To be sure, our male colleagues occasionally encounter these responses and requests, but they are more consistently able to deflect the emotional labor threads and focus on the technical. Setting boundaries is respected in our male colleagues but is unevenly received for us.

When it comes to exploring and incorporating new technologies into a course or research project, the motivations for adoption are nebulous. At our college, individual faculty have wide latitude to decide which technologies they use and how they implement them into their pedagogy. And as we work with faculty, our emotional labor can be a significant factor in the decision-making process. Morgan describes, "While I can make strong recommendations, the scholars I work with are the ultimate decision makers; and this is why my work is emotional labor, as opposed to pure technical advice."

The power dynamics and hierarchies at our institution, like many others, places staff in a precarious state where we can almost never be the decision makers, even in a nominally collaborative interaction or project. Whereas faculty are viewed by the institution as the central "stars," professional staff (both in IT and in other academic support roles) are viewed as second-class and always of lesser importance. In response (or defense), we couch our professional input and expertise in our emotional labor. In many ways, the effectiveness of our emotional labor is the lynchpin for our interactions with faculty, which Morgan neatly summarizes: "People will make better decisions if they are feeling steady, resilient, and energized, rather than depleted, by their work."[14]

In my (Celeste) interaction with the professor, the emotional labor helped her feel steady and willing to continue using the technology; in contrast, if I hadn't addressed the emotional register of the interaction then it is possible that the faculty would have abandoned the technology altogether. Professors often describe losing interest in digital assignments or projects when a staff person they have worked with leaves or is no longer able to be a collaborator. What is telling is that professors describe feelings of personal abandonment, uncertainty, and loss—of feeling alone and unsteady rather than lacking the knowledge or capability.

As academic technologists, we are often the conduits and translators between faculty and ITS. When working with our ITS peers, the attitudes and assumptions of male colleagues is a hurdle. Forty people are employed by ITS, and the gender breakdown is 70 percent male (28) and 30 percent female (12). Academic technology, however, is the only group that approaches gender parity: 57 percent male and 43 percent female.[15]

Getting a response from ITS peers to a request or issue can be a careful dance. We often find ourselves resorting to a range of affective strategies to get our requests taken seriously and given appropriate prioritization. These strategies include phrasing requests with soft language that appeals to our listener's ego and stressing the stakes that are most recognizable to the individual to feel rewarded or as though they are contributing in a heroic role. The delivery of the communication also matters: often, in-person requests are necessary to humanize the request for our male peers. Showing up in someone's office to communicate the same request can be more effective because we can leverage tone, body language, and calibrate the message in the moment and activate some kind of emotional investment or response.

A different calculus occurs when discussing technical issues that fall between us and our male coworkers. The default or implicit assumption is that because we are women in campus-facing roles, we are less technically skilled and able to make technical fixes. Often these are benignly communicated, such as "I can just take care of that." And sometimes those assumptions are benign. Friction occurs when those assumptions are not able to adapt to evidence to the contrary.

For example, I (Carly) was recently given superuser privileges to the LMS staging server to debug plug-in functionality and read/write privileges for the LMS production server. I have managed the LMS for over ten years, but this was unprecedented access to the servers. The access was given by the main server admin for the LMS. This was not just a matter of mere delegating—it was recognition that I was more than capable. Previous people in that role reacted very differently and repeatedly deflected requests for access. I found it difficult to convince previous staff people that I was fully capable of handling this access and would not do anything that might jeopardize the stability of the server. I have no formal IT or programming training, and I identify as more of an academic than an IT support person. So, on paper I did not have "authority" to be worthy of direct access. Self-deprecation is a key part of the college culture; one must be thoughtful in how knowledge and expertise is presented. This value on self-deprecation is challenging to negotiate for staff who are viewed as subordinate within the hierarchy of the college. As discussed earlier, the negotiation with faculty is delicate. With staff peers, it can also reinforce assumptions and negative stereotypes and work against recognizing the evidence of skill and capability.

Assumptions across groups persist that a woman in technology must have a technologically adept man in close proximity. I (Carly) have heard many times over the years about how clients on campus assume my spouse is also in the field of technology. This assumption continues to persist even after I correct them. The only reason I do not hear it much anymore is that we are now well-known in this small town after many years of living here. I (Celeste) have also been asked probing questions about people—really, men—in my life who may be responsible for my interest in and aptitude with technology.

Some of these questions may stem from the lack of diversity in technology jobs: it is a long-standing problem that technology-dominant fields have trouble attracting and retaining women. The state in which we work and live, Minnesota, is no exception. The Minneapolis–St. Paul–Bloomington metro area is ranked forty-fourth out of the top one hundred largest metropolitan areas in the United States for women's share of technology jobs. Women occupy 48.4 percent of total jobs but only 26.2 percent of computer and math occupations.[16] What is less understood is what technology jobs are like for women in higher education—what challenges, demands, and opportunities for women exist.

Critical examinations of alt-ac labor within the context of information technology and technology culture writ large are nascent. This chapter is an initial foray into the particular context of academic technologist affective and emotional labor, as well as the gendered dynamics of simultaneously negotiating academic and tech culture. We have identified several key factors in these dynamics, including assumptions about technology (as "magic," as utility, as unnecessary) and the latent technology culture (speedy, reckless, masculine) that individuals bring to their interactions with us that shape our labor to a significant degree. While we read and benefit from the growing literature by librarians and faculty developers that bring those critical perspectives to bear, we also seek to encourage further study and consideration of how tech culture and gender play out in the context of higher education context.

NOTES

1. Joseph D. Galanek, Dana C. Gierdowski, and D. Christopher Brooks, "The Higher Education IT Workforce Landscape, 2019." Research report. Louisville, CO: ECAR, February 2019.

2. Galanek, Gierdowski, and Brooks, "The Higher Education IT Workforce Landscape."

3. "Four Ways CFOs Can Avoid a Digital Talent Crunch," Deloitte Network, *Wall Street Journal*, June 14, 2017, https://deloitte.wsj.com/cfo/2017/06/14/as-finance-goes-digital-does-a-talent-crunch-loom/.

4. Joel Smith and Lauren Herckis, "Understanding and Overcoming Institutional Roadblocks to the Adoption and Use of Technology-Enhanced Learning Resources in Higher Education," Carnegie Mellon, 2018, https://www.cmu.edu/simon/projects/flagship-projects/barriers-to-tel.html.

5. "Educational Psychology," Encyclopedia.com, https://www.encyclopedia.com/social-sciences-and-law/education/education-terms-and-concepts/educational-psychology. Accessed July 12, 2019.

6. "National Assessment of Adult Literacy (NAAL)," https://nces.ed.gov/NAAL/lit_history.asp. Accessed July 12, 2019.

7. Gráinne Conole, "Theory and Methodology: The Interdisciplinary Nature of the Field," in Gráinne Conole, ed., *Designing for Learning in an Open World*, 15–31 (New York: Springer, 2013).

8. Gráinne Conole, "Open, Social and Participatory Media," in Gráinne Conole, ed., *Designing for Learning in an Open World*, 47–63 (New York: Springer, 2013).

9. Smith and Herckis, "Understanding and Overcoming Institutional Roadblocks."

10. Modern Language Association, "Guidelines for Information Technology Access and Support for the Modern Languages," February 22–23, 2013, https://www.mla.org/About-Us/Governance/Committees/Committee-Listings/Professional-Issues/Committee-on-Information-Technology/Guidelines-for-Information-Technology-Access-and-Support-for-the-Modern-Languages; Modern Language Association, "Guidelines for Evaluating Work in Digital Humanities and Digital Media," February 2012, https://www.mla.org/About-Us/Governance/Committees/Committee-Listings/Professional-Issues/Committee-on-Information-Technology/Guidelines-for-Evaluating-Work-in-Digital-Humanities-and-Digital-Media; and American Historical Association, "Guidelines for the Professional Evaluation of Digital Scholarship by Historians," September 2015, https://www.historians.org/teaching-and-learning/digital-history-resources/evaluation-of-digital-scholarship-in-history/guidelines-for-the-professional-evaluation-of-digital-scholarship-by-historians.

11. Jeffrey Pomerantz and D. Christopher Brooks, "ECAR Study of Faculty and Information Technology, 2017," https://www.educause.edu/ecar/research-publications/ecar-study-of-faculty-and-information-technology/2017/lms. Accessed July 17, 2019.

12. Melissa J. Williams and Larissa Z. Tiedens, "The Subtle Suspension of Backlash: A Meta-Analysis of Penalties for Women's Implicit and Explicit Dominance Behavior," *Psychological Bulletin* 142, no. 2 (2016): 165–197.

13. Paige Morgan, "Not Your DH Teddy-Bear; or, Emotional Labor Is Not Going Away," July 29, 2016, https://acrl.ala.org/dh/2016/07/29/not-your-dh-teddy-bear/.

14. Morgan, "Not Your DH Teddy-Bear."

15. See https://apps.carleton.edu/campus/its/about/staff/.

16. Mark Muro, Sifan Liu, and Jacob Whiton, "Gender Bias Plays out in the Digital Workforce, but Not in Every Industry," *Brookings* (blog), January 18, 2018. https://www.brookings.edu/blog/the-avenue/2018/01/18/gender-bias-plays-out-in-the-digital-workforce-but-not-in-every-industry/.

BIBLIOGRAPHY

American Historical Association. "Guidelines for the Professional Evaluation of Digital Scholarship by Historians." September 2015. https://www.historians.org/teaching-and-learning/digital-history-resources/evaluation-of-digital-scholarship-in-history/guidelines-for-the-professional-evaluation-of-digital-scholarship-by-historians.

Conole, Gráinne. "Open, Social and Participatory Media." In Gráinne Conole, ed., *Designing for Learning in an Open World*, 47–63. New York: Springer, 2013.

———. "Theory and Methodology: The Interdisciplinary Nature of the Field." In Gráinne Conole, ed., *Designing for Learning in an Open World*, 15–31. New York: Springer, 2013.

"Educational Psychology." Encyclopedia.com. https://www.encyclopedia.com/social-sciences-and-law/education/education-terms-and-concepts/educational-psychology. Accessed July 12, 2019.

"Four Ways CFOs Can Avoid a Digital Talent Crunch." Deloitte Network, *Wall Street Journal*. June 14, 2017. https://deloitte.wsj.com/cfo/2017/06/14/as-finance-goes-digital-does-a-talent-crunch-loom/.

Galanek, Joseph D., Dana C. Gierdowski, and D. Christopher Brooks. "The Higher Education IT Workforce Landscape, 2019." Research report. Louisville, CO: ECAR, February 2019.

Modern Language Association. "Guidelines for Evaluating Work in Digital Humanities and Digital Media." February 2012. https://www.mla.org/About

-Us/Governance/Committees/Committee-Listings/Professional-Issues/Committee-on-Information-Technology/Guidelines-for-Evaluating-Work-in-Digital-Humanities-and-Digital-Media.

———. "Guidelines for Information Technology Access and Support for the Modern Languages." February 22–23, 2013. https://www.mla.org/About-Us/Governance/Committees/Committee-Listings/Professional-Issues/Committee-on-Information-Technology/Guidelines-for-Information-Technology-Access-and-Support-for-the-Modern-Languages.

Morgan, Paige. "Not Your DH Teddy-Bear; or, Emotional Labor Is Not Going Away." July 29, 2016. https://acrl.ala.org/dh/2016/07/29/not-your-dh-teddy-bear/.

"National Assessment of Adult Literacy (NAAL)." https://nces.ed.gov/NAAL/lit_history.asp. Accessed July 12, 2019.

Pomerantz, Jeffrey, and D. Christopher Brooks. "ECAR Study of Faculty and Information Technology, 2017." https://www.educause.edu/ecar/research-publications/ecar-study-of-faculty-and-information-technology/2017/lms. Accessed July 17, 2019.

Smith, Joel, and Lauren Herckis. "Understanding and Overcoming Institutional Roadblocks to the Adoption and Use of Technology-Enhanced Learning Resources in Higher Education." Carnegie Mellon. 2018. https://www.cmu.edu/simon/projects/flagship-projects/barriers-to-tel.html.

Whiton, Mark Muro, Sifan Liu, and Jacob Whiton. "Gender Bias Plays out in the Digital Workforce, but Not in Every Industry." *Brookings* (blog), January 18, 2018. https://www.brookings.edu/blog/the-avenue/2018/01/18/gender-bias-plays-out-in-the-digital-workforce-but-not-in-every-industry/.

Williams, Melissa J., and Larissa Z. Tiedens. "The Subtle Suspension of Backlash: A Meta-Analysis of Penalties for Women's Implicit and Explicit Dominance Behavior." *Psychological Bulletin* 142, no. 2 (2016): 165–197.

9

Emotional Labor in Open Access Librarianship

JENNIFER HODL SOLOMON AND
REBEKAH KATI

As librarians working in the scholarly communications subfields of open access (OA) and institutional repositories, we regularly engage in emotion management. Libraries are not neutral, nor are the interactions librarians have with faculty, whether in-person, online, or asynchronously. Drawing on Arlie Hochschild's definition, emotional labor is "labor that requires one to induce or suppress feeling in order to sustain the outward countenance that produces the proper state of mind in others."[1] In this chapter, we explore and critically examine the emotional labor of scholarly communications librarianship in the course of our daily work and in the wider scholarly communications community. In particular, we focus on the complexities of emotional labor within the OA cross-section of scholarly communications work.

The term *open access* refers both to the movement(s) to challenge existing models in scholarly publishing and to "literature [that] is digital, online, free of charge, and free of most copyright and licensing restrictions."[2] OA is a component of scholarly communications and is "the system through which research and other scholarly writings are created, evaluated for quality, disseminated to the scholarly community, and preserved for future use. The system includes both formal means of communication, such as publication in peer-reviewed journals, and informal channels, such as electronic mailing lists."[3] One of the challenges that we have faced, and see reflected in conversations and literature by our peers, is the difficulty in how to do OA (1) at all, and (2) correctly. Within library and information science literature, scholarly communication is often characterized as an ecosystem in which researchers, publishers, and libraries are the actors and research, publication, access, and discovery are the activities. As it exists today, the system is broken; we argue that change needs to be implemented at the macro level for it to become more effective (e.g., changes to the faculty tenure and promotion system to include expectations for OA publishing). For those of us working on the frontlines, how do we do this in the microcosm of one campus, one academic department, or even one researcher?

On our own campus, receptivity and interest in OA has been gradually increasing. In 2016 the Faculty Council at the University of North Carolina–Chapel Hill (UNC–Chapel Hill) approved an OA policy, which states that faculty[4] must deposit articles that they have written into an OA repository. As part of the implementation plan, UNC–Chapel Hill Libraries hired two new positions in 2017: OA librarian and institutional repository librarian. These positions[5] primarily focus on faculty outreach and operational support service, specifically raising awareness of the policy, encouraging faculty to consider the Carolina Digital Repository (CDR) to host their policy-compliant scholarly work, and improving the functionality of the CDR.

Rebekah is currently the institutional repository librarian at UNC–Chapel Hill. She identifies as a white, cisgender, straight woman. Jennifer was the OA librarian at UNC–Chapel Hill from 2017 to 2019. She identifies as a white, cisgender, queer woman. We were both attracted to the field of scholarly communications and OA because we believe that scholarship should be openly available to everyone. We acknowledge that there are many perspectives that we are missing and that as white, middle-class women, we are speaking from positions of privilege. Unlike our colleagues who are people of color, first-generation college students, working class, disabled, or otherwise marginalized, our privilege allows us to interact with other white, middle-class people, without worrying that someone will challenge our "right" to occupy the space. We can walk across a campus that has visible historic links to enslaved people in the United States, and has been lately perpetrated violence to current students who voice their opposition to the continued presence of these links, without the constant reminder of our own oppression. In the field of librarianship, which is still dominated by white women, and academic librarianship in particular, it is easy for us to appear, and feel, that we belong.

In the following sections we will illuminate our experiences engaging in emotional labor as scholarly communications librarians and explore how Hochschild's theory of emotional labor and Kimberle Crenshaw's radical framing of intersectionality[6] affect our work. Hochschild's observations about the ways flight attendants performed emotional labor and its effects on their well-being speak to our experiences, especially the concepts of deep and surface acting. Hochschild describes *deep acting* as the process of internalizing feelings to the point where we actually feel them. This is in contrast to *surface acting,* where we pretend the feeling. Both forms of acting are used to navigate feeling rules, which govern how one is expected to act in certain situations. When our emotions violate a feeling rule, we employ deep or surface acting to reconcile the difference. Deep acting may require playing a role to help bring forth the expected feeling. Additionally, status plays a part in Hochschild's work, as she described the ways in which customers' wishes were prioritized over those of the flight attendants. Hochschild also describes the act of detachment, where emotion workers depersonalize their work to protect themselves from burnout. We will describe specific ways in which we engage in these acts in the following sections.

Although we mentioned that as white, middle-class, cisgender women, we are in positions of privilege relative to many other people within library work and throughout the United States, we also recognize the ways that intersectionality affects our work experiences, and particularly in the production of emotional labor. Crenshaw was the first scholar to explicate how Black women's "intersectional experience is greater than the sum of racism and sexism, [and] any analysis that does not take intersectionality into account cannot sufficiently address the particular manner in which Black women are subordinated."[7] We aim to make visible the ways that our multiple identities bring about different emotions and expectations of emotions. In some examples this is how our roles as women impact our interactions with masculine bodies and cisgender men. At other times, we recognize that our whiteness may be a barrier to forming relationships and trust with people of color. Further, in our recommendations, we draw from Crenshaw's clear directive to "[begin] addressing the needs and problems of those who are most disadvantaged and with restructuring and remaking the world where necessary, then others who are singularly disadvantaged would also benefit."[8]

Finally, we include recommendations for managing emotions and navigating the complexities of emotional labor for people doing OA and identify strategies that we can use to improve our practices, in pursuit of the elusive effortless deposit.

MASTER'S REQUIRED, EMPATHY PREFERRED

It seems that this should not need to be stated, but we are passionate about our work and want to help make OA a sustainable publishing model. We also want to make working in OA valuable, rewarding, and restorative. Much has already been written on librarianship as a calling, which aligns with many of the tropes we have heard throughout our own experiences in library school and into our careers from friends, mentors, and colleagues. But as Fobazi Ettarh writes, "'vocational awe' refers to the set of ideas, values, and assumptions librarians have about themselves and the profession that result in beliefs that libraries as institutions are inherently good and sacred, and therefore beyond critique."[9] In examining the work we do in OA librarianship, we translate these assumptions and beliefs into our work, which is both implicit and explicit in our emotional labor.

At the core of our jobs, we are responsible for OA awareness, adoption, and advocacy. We educate faculty about the OA policy (awareness), help faculty deposit in the CDR (adoption), and encourage them to increase their use of OA resources throughout their teaching, research, and publishing goals (advocacy). We are expected to have the skills and motivation to accomplish behavioral and cultural changes across a large research campus, with diverse disciplines, faculty, students, and staff. These are not effortless tasks or often straightforward ones. In order to achieve awareness, we must develop relationships with our faculty partners and maintain them through increased contact to facilitate adoption and possibly enable advocacy. We accomplish this through the use of emotion work, while mindful that our employers dictate the boundaries of our work and our resources.

Often, the stress becomes too much and we detach from our work as a coping strategy. We strongly feel that the act of detachment should include periodic assessments and reevaluation of the definition of "success." Our current success measures for the OA policy at UNC–Chapel Hill were drafted before we were hired, when the university was close to purchasing a faculty activity tracker, which would have collected and deposited faculty work to the CDR en masse. As of this writing, that purchase has not yet occurred. Therefore, we have not met the success criteria as originally defined. It was not a failure on our part as there was no feasible way that we could have done so. Now we need to reassess and determine tasks that are feasible to accomplish under the current conditions. This means that we need to detach from the older, established conditions and definitions of success. This process feels like failure, and we feel like we are letting the library, the OA initiative, and the whole OA movement down.

A key part of reassessment is obtaining buy-in from managers and administrators. Often it is easier for administrators to put OA work on entry-level library staff and allocate it some slim budget lines, than to do the work of incorporating it into a larger strategic plan and engaging the faculty on an institutional level. Change in this field will only come from above. As of this writing, institutional change in OA shows signs of movement at UNC, and we hope that the trend continues.

APPEALING TO FACULTY

In libraries in the United States, arguments for the open availability of scholarship rest on three pillars: the good of humanity, researcher labor, and funding on the federal or state level. Here, we focus on the "good of humanity" pillar, as it is a key part of our engagement with emotional labor in the field. This pillar argues that making scholarship openly available is the right thing to do for society. OA advances and democratizes knowledge because the products of knowledge gathering are available to everyone, instead of limiting access to only those who can afford the fees or are affiliated with an institution that can.

One might expect faculty to readily engage with this pillar. After all, isn't the mission of a university, especially a public one, to democratize knowledge? If the price of democratizing knowledge is to fill out a form to deposit a paper, shouldn't that be easy to do? Yet, repositories in general suffer from limited faculty engagement. Ruth Tillman found that 25 percent of repositories surveyed reported no monthly self-deposits by faculty, even if the repository was well-established.[10] In our conversations with faculty, we identified reasons why they don't deposit. Some are not aware of the issues in OA. Some do not have the time. Some find filling out forms tedious. Some do not care. Faculty indifference causes us to engage in deep and surface acting to project the feeling of ease and simplicity onto the deposit process, making it convenient and more enticing for them to participate.

Another facet of OA faculty engagement is challenging the myth that OA journals are low quality. In our outreach to faculty, we have heard multiple faculty describe their impressions of OA journals as predatory, lacking academic rigor, or lacking relevance to a tenure-track position. These impressions are incorrect. While some publishers have used OA to promote low-quality journals, most high-quality journals support some form of OA. These sentiments are demoralizing to us. How do we overcome such deeply entrenched myths to reach faculty who don't seem to want to listen?

A complication in engaging faculty with OA is that compliance can be confusing. The OA landscape is filled with jargon, restrictions, and complicated nuances, which complicate our goal to make faculty compliance effortless. Notably, Green and Gold OA are two prevalent and visible ways to deliver OA content, and are the methods that we most often recommend to faculty.[11] Green OA is "when an author archives a version of their work in an OA repository, irrespective of where it is finally published."[12] Typically, the version deposited in the repository is the version that the author submitted to the journal prior to peer review. Gold OA is "when an author publishes in an OA Journal."[13] This is the final published version of the article, and authors may be charged a fee or article processing charge (APC) for the article to be made available to the public. Publisher policies dictate which version an author is allowed to deposit in a repository, although UNC's OA policy gives UNC faculty a large degree of freedom for their post-2016 work. Keeping track of these restrictions and whether one is compliant is confusing. Many faculty do not have the correct version to upload or the funding to pay an APC.

Another reason for faculty disengagement in OA is tenure and promotion.[14] The criteria for tenure and promotion actively disincentivize publishing in OA journals, as they can be incorrectly seen as less prestigious than traditionally published journals. The democratization of knowledge becomes less important when participants cannot move forward in their careers. Furthermore, the "good of humanity" pillar resonates with some disciplines more than others. When speaking to faculty members about OA and depositing their work, we found that humanities and social sciences faculty use articles, posters, and conference papers to develop arguments and workshop their ideas. They are reluctant to post these materials openly before their ideas are fully developed.

Despite many of the challenges of working in OA, we also have very rewarding experiences engaging faculty. Some faculty members do believe in the "good of humanity" pillar and recognize that depositing their work openly can lead to increased reach. When we have an initial conversation with a faculty member and they begin to see the value of making their work accessible, we feel a sense of joy or success. For example, we were contacted by a researcher who wanted assistance with publishing their own project. This was a unique opportunity to work closely with them throughout the entire publishing process; from copyediting to indexing. Another faculty member decided to deposit their works into the repository because they felt that it was the right thing to do, and they wanted to set an example for their peers and students. We have also experienced excitement and hope through teaching graduate student workshops and collaborating with graduate student workers to prepare them for OA and scholarly communications careers. When we help faculty successfully engage in OA work, we no longer need to employ deep or surface acting. We genuinely feel the euphoria of success.

REACHING OUT

Outreach to faculty can take the form of presentations at department meetings, workshops, one-on-one instructional or training sessions, emails, activities, and more. During outreach activities, we engage in surface acting. We project the feeling that OA and the repository are exciting, interesting, and wonderful! This is not to say that we don't find these topics interesting, but we recognize that faculty, for the most part, do not share our interest. Their display of boredom is at odds with the role-specific feeling rules that we should feel and exhibit excitement for OA. Perhaps if we pretend that everyone finds these topics interesting at all times, the faculty will be more receptive to our message and want to hear what we have to say. Our surface acting as emotional labor will bring actual feelings in line with the feeling rule, enabling us to promote the pro-OA paradigm that our employer would like us to sell.

Not all outreach is successful, which adds complexity to our emotion work. During a department faculty meeting, we were met with a surprising level of concern and fear. Pre-tenure and tenured faculty were shocked to hear about the OA policy for the first time and were worried about the implications. While collectively they seemed interested in making their work accessible to more people, they were reluctant to deposit in the CDR for reasons of personal safety and professional clout. We were forced to backtrack and used surface acting to soothe their anxieties.

Our outreach activities also force us to embody other roles, which helps us feel emotions we display during deep acting. We become salespeople when we try to convince faculty that the repository is a good place to store their content. We are project managers as we plan upgrades and new features to the repository. We play the role of assistants when we do work for faculty that they could do for themselves. We feel supported when our managers play the role of advocates as we try to convince library and university leadership to give us more staff and resources as budgets shrink and other priorities take precedence.

INVISIBLE LABOR

At UNC, librarians have faculty status and can serve on faculty council.[15] Unlike many of our faculty colleagues, we are not tenured and instead have multi-year, renewable contracts. In order for our contracts to be renewed, we must engage in the nebulous category of professional service, which includes publishing articles, serving on committees, and/or community engagement.

In part due to our "not-really-faculty" status, relations with tenured faculty can be fraught. Faculty don't always see us as peers or as experts, just as people who facilitate access to the research they need. Our status as "not-really-faculty" adds a layer of difficulty to interactions with faculty when we ask them to send us their curriculum vitae, fill out a form to deposit, or allow us to talk at their faculty meetings or other activities that would enable us to complete our daily work. We can only ask nicely and hope that they comply. Often, this approach is unsuccessful and our requests are put aside. Being seen as not-real impacts our ability to do our jobs and the form of deep acting that we display. It also affects the strategies we use to get buy-in from faculty and department administrators.

In an effort to make depositing in the repository seem more appealing, we feel faculty discomfort and engage in surface acting by apologizing to alleviate their concerns. We make several types of apologies in our interactions with faculty and staff: that they have to fill out yet another form to deposit, that the institutional repository system doesn't match the expectations that they might have, and that the repository doesn't have a feature that they want. This is an example of Hochschild's observations about status, as the faculty's wishes and importance are enhanced over ours in this interaction.[16] Sometimes their concerns are addressable, but they may want something that we are not prepared to give them. However, we want that person—who is right in front of us, in the moment—to have a positive experience. It is difficult to step back and think about whether the request is reasonable and if the problem is something that others might be experiencing too, or if the problem represents a personal preference of that particular user. These interactions manifest a type of emotional labor: we are the faces of the OA program and the repository, and we must take on all these expectations and frustrations into ourselves, as a form of deep acting. We feel these interactions: the user's frustration, our confusion while deducing the cause of the issue, or everyone's discouragement as we give a vague answer. We can't promise anything, because we may not be able to deliver and that would be unthinkable. We must remain professional while absorbing feelings that could be considered unprofessional.

The emotional labor of OA comes with a price for us, including burnout, frustration, and demotivation. Sometimes we feel like we are doing the faculty's work for them in the interest of achieving our goals of making their work discoverable. In one instance, we deposited a faculty member's manuscript that would have cost $8.99 to access on the publisher's site or $144 for an annual subscription. We estimate that our emotional labor cost is somewhere in between.

Emotional labor is inherent in the job that we do, which we accept. However, we would like for it to be recognized as an intrinsic part of the job on the part of library and university administration, and valued accordingly when we are being assessed for promotion and raises. Managing emotions is just as much of a skill as liaison work, software development, or acquisitions. Yet, in our experience, as with other forms of gendered labor, it seems to be ignored or taken for granted. If we did not do this work, few would use the repository system or engage in OA activities. We know this because it was the status quo before our jobs were created.

GENDER AT WORK IS WORK

Our gender presentations affect the ways in which we interact with others at work and contribute to our engagement in emotional labor. The desire to appear smart, well-informed, calm, passionate, authoritative, and kind is a strenuous juggling act. The field moves very fast, and it is challenging to keep up with all the news, twists, turns, and hot takes while also performing our day-to-day work at a high level. This happens in face-to-face interactions with faculty and also within online spaces with other scholarly communications librarians. Our desire to be immaculately professional coincides with keeping up with the pace, colliding in feelings of inadequacy and impostor syndrome that prevent us from participating in larger discussions.

Professional interactions in scholarly communications have a gendered aspect. Many prolific commenters in scholarly communications spaces are male. Clayton Hayes and Heidi Elaine Kelly analyzed conversations on the SCHOLCOMM listserv, a key venue for scholarly communications discussion, and found that although only 35 percent of the participants on the listserv were male, their comments accounted for over 50 percent of the activity, including 60 percent of the replies.[17] Anecdotally, the promotion of male voices has proliferated into other scholarly communications spaces as well, including blogs and Twitter. Although library work is a feminized operation,[18] this leads to the assumption of male voices as authorities, an observation shared by Hochschild as she discovered that passengers assumed that younger male flight attendants were the managers of their older, female colleagues.[19] In scholarly communications employment, this means literal promotion of male bodies into managerial or other higher-paying positions. As women in this space, who want to be seen as professionals but suffer from imposter syndrome, it is difficult to speak up—especially if we are challenging the perceived authority of the male commentariat. Therefore, we find ourselves staying silent and don't participate when perhaps our voices would be needed. This affects our career prospects and the price that we can command for our emotional labor.

RECOMMENDATIONS

Drawing upon our experiences, observations of closely related situations within the scholarly communications community, and Hochschild's analysis, we have developed a set of recommendations for coming to terms with emotional labor in OA work. We acknowledge that these recommendations are not new, but we hope that by placing them within this context they will reach others. Furthermore, these strategies are continuous, evolving, and overlapping.

Institutional Change

Scholarly communications librarians would benefit from changes within the institutions where they are employed by centering OA as a key component of the university's mission. This could include investments in infrastructure, human resources, collections management policies, and leadership. OA librarians could be better supported and spend less energy on managing emotional labor if the organizational culture embraced OA. This would mean a shift from viewing OA as an add-on or afterthought to a necessary facet of teaching and research.

Managerial Support

Managers and supervisors could provide much-needed support to scholarly communications librarians by formalizing the emotional labor required for these positions, though inclusion in performance goals and appraisals. Rather than a one-size-fits-all approach, a manager should work with the employee to create goals appropriate for that person, which will vary widely depending on their identity and experience, especially in regard to intersectionality of multiple identities. Managers should acknowledge that emotional labor is draining, and they should proactively offer options for support. Compensation should be commensurate with other "skilled" work and demonstrate that this is important and valuable.

Collaboration with Faculty

Faculty can also help change the role of emotional labor when interacting with scholarly communications librarians. By recognizing the types of deep and surface acting that librarians engage in during conversations and outreach work, faculty could empathize and may see reflections of their own emotional labor in performing rigorous academic work. Faculty who recognize that this labor is not easy or seamless may better appreciate the ways that librarians aim to provide services and work collaboratively.

Building Community

As a community of scholarly communications librarians and practitioners, we need to spend more time recognizing privilege and actively being more inclusive. We need to take a hard look at who is talking in public forums and whose careers are advancing. We need to stop hiring rock stars and inviting ninjas to speak at conferences. We need to stop trolling each other on listservs and discussion forums and be supportive of our diverse peer group. We need to stop treating scholarly communications as a special membership, in which only we get the jokes and references, and only members of the in-group get opportunities for advancement.

Personal Change

As scholarly communications librarians, we think it is important to normalize emotion work in our roles. Our work can be made visible by discussing it with supervisors and colleagues, including strategic ways for professional goals, and openly recognizing the emotional work of others. In addition, detachment can be an effective tool for managing emotional labor, as Hochschild observes.[20] Both of us have used this strategy in our work, although we are often unsuccessful, and we experience feelings of phoniness as Hochschild cautions. Finally, we can work to accept imperfections, allow ourselves to experience wrong feelings or unsuccessful ones, and give ourselves permission to not be effortless.

CONCLUSION

In writing this chapter, as with many projects, we started with one vision and ended up with a very different thing. In examining our own work and lives from the past two years, we experienced many of the emotional highs and lows all over again. At certain points, we spoke of sections as too whiny or full of rage to be included in scholarly work. At times, we self-censored or felt embarrassed. We cut many sections that were important and needed to be heard but did not fit within our narrow scope for this essay. We know that our work will continue to evolve and, over time, the way we view these interactions and events will change as well. However, emotional labor is a constant within OA work and the scholarly communications ecosystem. We affirm that this is necessary, challenging, and often rewarding part of the job, and as such should be recognized and validated.

NOTES

We would like to thank Stefanie Knauer for her amazing suggestions to improve this chapter. Anne Gilliland and Julie Rudder have been wonderful supervisors and incredibly supportive of us.

1. Arlie Russell Hochschild, *The Managed Heart: Commercialization of Human Feeling* (Berkeley: University of California Press, 2012), 20, http://ebookcentral.proquest.com/lib/unc/detail.action?docID=870020.

2. Peter Suber, "Open Access Overview," https://legacy.earlham.edu/~peters/fos/overview.htm. Accessed June 30, 2019.

3. Association of College and Research Libraries, "Principles and Strategies for the Reform of Scholarly Communication," http://www.ala.org/acrl/publications/whitepapers/principlesstrategies. Accessed June 30, 2019.

4. The OA policy applies only to tenure-track faculty, though everyone at the university engaged in scholarly work is encouraged to use the CDR.

5. At other institutions, these roles are often combined into a single position that engages very different skill sets.

6. Kimberle Crenshaw, "Demarginalizing the Intersection of Race and Sex: A Black Feminist Critique of Antidiscrimination Doctrine, Feminist Theory and Antiracist Politics," *University of Chicago Legal Forum* 1989, no. 1 (1989): 139–167, http://chicagounbound.uchicago.edu/uclf/vol1989/iss1/8.

7. Crenshaw, "Demarginalizing the Intersection of Race and Sex," 140.

8. Crenshaw, 167.

9. Fobazi Ettarh, "Vocational Awe and Librarianship: The Lies We Tell Ourselves," The Library With the Lead Pipe, 2018, http://www.inthelibrarywiththeleadpipe.org/2018/vocational-awe/.

10. Ruth K. Tillman, "Where Are We Now? Survey on Rates of Faculty Self-Deposit in Institutional Repositories," *Journal of Librarianship and Scholarly Communication* 5, no. 1 (2017): eP2203.

11. University of North Carolina at Chapel Hill, "Open Access Policy," https://unc.policystat.com/policy/5104632/latest/. Accessed June 30, 2019.

12. Association of College and Research Libraries, "Scholarly Communication Toolkit: OA Policies & Publishing," https://acrl.libguides.com/scholcomm/toolkit/openaccess. Accessed June 17, 2019.

13. Ibid.

14. We deeply empathize with contingent faculty, postdoctoral researchers, and graduate students who may want to engage in OA publishing for personal and professional reasons but also need to build a path toward secure employment.

15. We define "librarians" as "positions within the University Libraries which UNC–Chapel Hill has classified as EHRA non-faculty." Differences between librarians and library staff can be a minefield. We know "staff" who have MLS

and other graduate degrees. We know "librarians" who have degrees other than MLS/MIS. Many of the staff positions today do work that librarians did 15–20 years ago, in some organizations even more recently than that.

16. Hochschild, *The Managed Heart*, 97.

17. Clayton Hayes and Heidi Elaine Kelly, "Who's Talking about Scholarly Communication? An Examination of Gender and Behavior on the SCHOLCOMM Listserv," *Journal of Librarianship and Scholarly Communication* 5, no. 1 (2017): eP2171.

18. Seventy-nine percent of librarians and 76.5 percent of library technicians surveyed identify as women. AFL-CIO, "Library Professionals: Facts & Figures," https://dpeaflcio.org/programs-publications/issue-fact-sheets/library-workers-facts-figures/. Accessed June 30, 2019.

19. Hochschild, *The Managed Heart*, 119.

20. Hochschild, 28.

BIBLIOGRAPHY

AFL-CIO. "Library Professionals: Facts & Figures." Department for Professional Employees. Accessed June 30, 2019. https://dpeaflcio.org/programs-publications/issue-fact-sheets/library-workers-facts-figures/.

Crenshaw, Kimberle. "Demarginalizing the Intersection of Race and Sex: A Black Feminist Critique of Antidiscrimination Doctrine, Feminist Theory and Antiracist Politics." *University of Chicago Legal Forum* 1989, no. 1 (1989): 139–167. http://chicagounbound.uchicago.edu/uclf/vol1989/iss1/8.

Ettarh, Fobazi. "Vocational Awe and Librarianship: The Lies We Tell Ourselves." *In the Library with the Lead Pipe*. January 10, 2018. http://www.inthelibrarywiththeleadpipe.org/2018/vocational-awe.

Hayes, Clayton, and Heidi Elaine Kelly. "Who's Talking about Scholarly Communication? An Examination of Gender and Behavior on the SCHOLCOMM Listserv." *Journal of Librarianship and Scholarly Communication* 5, no. 1 (2017). https://iastatedigitalpress.com/jlsc/article/id/12782/.

Hochschild, Arlie Russell. *The Managed Heart: Commercialization of Human Feeling*. Berkeley: University of California Press, 2012.

"Open Access Overview," Peter Suber, accessed June 30, 2019, https://legacy.earlham.edu/~peters/fos/overview.htm.

"Open Access Policy." University of North Carolina at Chapel Hill. Accessed June 30, 2019, https://policies.unc.edu/TDClient/2833/Portal/KB/ArticleDet?ID=132180.

"Principles and Strategies for the Reform of Scholarly Communication." Association of College and Research Libraries. Accessed June 30, 2019. http://www.ala.org/acrl/publications/whitepapers/principlesstrategies.

"Scholarly Communication Toolkit: OA Policies & Publishing." Association of College and Research Libraries. Accessed June 17, 2019, https://acrl.libguides.com/scholcomm/toolkit/openaccess.

Tillman, Ruth K. "Where Are We Now? Survey on Rates of Faculty Self-Deposit in Institutional Repositories." *Journal of Librarianship and Scholarly Communication* 5, no. 1 (2017). https://www.iastatedigitalpress.com/jlsc/article/id/12796/.

10

Telling Alternate Stories

Academic Advising, Student Fear, and Living Our Parallel Plans

ELIZABETH LUNDBERG

"These are my favorite classes, but I don't know if I want the major. What can you do with a degree in gender studies?"

"Let me know when you find out, because I've got one."

The student just stared at me until I mumbled something about working with the Career Center. I don't know how much of a selling point it is that she could be like me. Certainly this exchange wasn't as bad as when another advisor in my office, working at an admissions event, got caught in the middle of a dispute between a parent and student inquiring about business and art majors respectively. "What can you even do with an art degree?" the dad sneered.

"I have an art degree," the advisor responded.

The dad pointedly looked him up and down before taking a business checklist and handing it to his daughter. These are the hazards of using our stories.

Still, our stories have a place. In academic advising, we spend a lot of time talking with students about their "parallel plans": if they don't get into this business school, or that medical school, or this grad program, then what? We call them *parallel* plans and not *backup* plans to emphasize that they can be just as good—just as fulfilling, just as exciting, just as worth pursuing—as the thing the student originally thought they wanted. Students are not always convinced by the "parallel" thing. It's okay. I'm not always convinced myself. The point is that alt-ac advisors are especially good at having the conversation. We have sat where they sit now. We are living our parallel plans.

UNDER PRESSURE

College students are, more than ever before, feeling the pressures of economic instability, rising education costs, and a crippling student loan crisis. Millennials, workaholics because of the economic disasters they've endured and a culture that promotes being "on" at all times, are just now old enough to have their own kids in college, emulating those same behaviors in response to largely the same—if anything, accelerating—economic and cultural forces.[1] Anne Helen Peterson describes burnout as "the millennial condition. It's our base temperature. It's our background music."[2] One of the primary reasons for this perpetual feeling of burnout, she explains, is that "I've internalized the idea that I should be working all the time. Why have I internalized that idea? Because everything and everyone in my life has reinforced it—explicitly and implicitly—since I was young." And just as millennials were parented "intrusively," their education and activities "optimized" to get them ahead, they too have used "intensive" and "vigilante" parenting strategies that will supposedly prepare their children to weather the storms of adulthood.[3] College students today have spent their whole lives, as many of their parents did before them, viewing everything they do in terms of investment, efficiency, and risk management.

These pressures can be felt in increasing mental health needs on campuses across the United States. As Lois M. Collins documents, since 2013 there has been an alarming uptick in the number and severity of student mental health needs, a situation Collins calls "a burgeoning crisis."[4] Experts point to the nature of college as a transitional time of life as a factor that makes students vulnerable, but Kelly Davis at Mental Health America argues, "It's not just the challenging life stage. College life—the world, for that matter—has changed greatly in just a generation," and she points specifically to "events just since the year 2000."[5] Collins goes on to list the things students reported worrying about when asked about their anxiety in one social work class at the University of Utah:

> Fear of being seen, imperfections and all. Fear of being invisible. Feeling uncertain and helpless with issues as diverse as environmental degradation and political discord. Fear of missing out. Fear of failure. Job competition. Substance abuse. Fear of being judged or excluded. Too many demands for time, for money, for "success" in its assorted definitions. Constant change. The cost of everything, from tuition to housing. Personal safety, including sexual assaults and school shootings. Peer pressure. Parental expectations. Inability to handle adversity. Social media comparisons. With the professor as scribe, the list blanketed the whiteboard spanning a wall in the spacious classroom.
>
> At the end, a student looked at the list and sighed aloud. "The bar is just so high for everything," she said.

In addition to the strain placed on colleges' mental health services, these pressures can be felt in students' (and parents') academic and career decision making. Anyone who has spent time asking students what they hope to get out of college can tell story after story of students whose aspirations for college are nothing more than "getting a job." Students sometimes report that they want to "make a lot of money," but any time I've asked follow-up questions about what "a lot of money" means to them, I've learned that it means they'd be able to buy a house and support a family. The economic fear and precarity underlying these students' decisions are palpable. Students tell me they've always loved history but think they need business degrees because they're more career oriented. They tell me they want to pursue a career in marketing because it's one of the only safe ways to admit they like to write. They want to be dental hygienists because they've been told they make decent money, so they've never even thought about whether they want to spend their days with their hands in people's mouths. These students are looking for a return on their parents' investments in them, as they've been raised to. They are calculating and practical. Their dreams so often feel small, rigid, and joyless, because they are circumscribed by fear.

The kicker is that while these students have traded their actual passions for what they think will protect them economically, they're wrong. Writing for *Forbes* in 2018, Derek Newton parses data from an underemployment study and concludes that the top two offenders when it comes to graduating students who go on to take jobs that do not require bachelor's degrees are business- and health-care-related programs—precisely the kinds of majors students tell me they are choosing not out of genuine interest, but because they will lead to jobs. STEM majors fare better in the post-college job world, but so do students who major in humanities and languages.[6] A Burning Glass study reports that across all majors 43 percent of college graduates are underemployed in their first jobs, but the authors of that report explain, "While STEM majors outperform others, there are good choices for students in all fields. In their first jobs, liberal arts majors such as philosophy, foreign languages, and English have comparable rates of underemployment to the market at large. Biology majors, although in a STEM field, fare worse with a 51% underemployment rate."[7] If we jump to midcareer data rather than only looking at first jobs after college, a year-long study conducted by PayScale Inc. found 80 percent or higher increases in earnings over time in a variety of majors that might surprise our students: art history, communication studies, film studies, history, international relations, journalism, philosophy, and political science. And if we look at those median midcareer salaries by major, English, coming in at $64,700, is comparable to biology ($64,800) and higher than health-care administration ($60,600), nutrition ($55,300), psychology ($60,400) and even education ($52,000)—the thing you supposedly add onto an English degree to make it more practical and career-focused.[8]

Benjamin Schmidt, in a 2018 piece for the *Atlantic* argues that the humanities are in crisis (as they always seem to be) not because a degree in a humanities field is a "bad investment," but because students and parents *think* it is. Schmidt describes a precipitous decline in the number of students studying subjects like history, philosophy, languages, and literature since 2008, and he argues it is because "students seem to have shifted their view of what they *should* be studying—in a largely misguided effort to enhance their chances on the job market." He continues, even filtering out business and health majors and focusing on STEM versus the humanities: "The difference between humanities majors and science majors, in median income and unemployment, seems to be no more than the difference between residents of Virginia and North Carolina. If someone told me not to move to Charlotte because no one there can make a living, I would never take them seriously. But worried relatives express the same concerns about classics majors every day, with no sounder evidence." Furthermore, Schmidt points out that trying to predict when entering college what jobs will be most in demand four years later and picking a major that seemingly lines up with such a job involves some specious logic and dubious forecasting. At a more basic level, the true shift he locates at the center of the humanities "crisis" has to do with changing philosophies about what education is and is for. In 1970, when surveyed about what they hoped to get out of college, seven out of ten students included among other answers "develop a meaningful philosophy of life," and only four in ten said they hoped to earn more money; by the mid-1980s those percentages had reversed.[9] Students today have carried forward that sense of college as primarily an income-booster rather than an *education,* having learned it from parents who hold the same ideas.

WE ADVISE, YOU DECIDE

The decisions students are making often come out of that understanding of the purpose of college, one we may simultaneously understand and lament, ascribe to and resent. Students have internalized age-old narratives of education as a means of uplift as well as more recent ones about needing to optimize and monetize their every experience just to get by. They stand poised at personal, political, and economic moments of precarity. Former US secretary of education Betsy DeVos explicitly defined them as "human capital" in the same speech in which she also warned, "nothing is free. Someone, somewhere ultimately pays the bills."[10] Students understand education more than ever as an investment that needs to pay off. Considering the lifelong debt sentence they may be taking on just to be here, they are correct when they say, "the bar is just so high." This bundle of economic fears and beliefs is an increasingly large part of what academic advisors have to address when we help students work through their academic decisions—and an especially challenging part, because students who see college as a system to be gamed for economic advantage are not primed to trust advice from people working within that system.

Academic advising is *conceptual* and *informational*. Advisors must master an impressive breadth of knowledge, including theories of student development, advising strategies, characteristics and needs of various student populations, and institution-specific missions, initiatives, cultures, and communities. Advisors are also responsible for knowing and conveying to students institution-specific curricula, policies, regulations, procedures, resources, deadlines, and technologies. Advising is also, crucially, *relational*. In order to convey any of that knowledge to students effectively and actually help guide them through it, advisors must build rapport and trust with their students, which means working with them in developmental and affective ways.[11] It is not merely that advisors convey information to students; we also help them see how that information applies to their situations and, when applicable, process their feelings about that information—as well as their feelings about everything else they go through in college. As Michael Anft explains, writing for the *Chronicle of Higher Education* in 2018,

> Advising and orientation efforts are undergoing a sea change. Gone are the days when the advising office's mission involved little more than helping students register for the next semester's classes or decide on a major. The emerging brand of adviser is still expected to take on those tasks, but also to handle a wider range of student needs—financial concerns, mental-health issues, extracurricular opportunities—and keep students on track.

These growing expectations for academic advising come from several places at once: Anft highlights universities' efforts to support at-risk students and reduce attrition, but also "the increasing demands of students and parents, particularly the return they want to see on their investment in education."[12] Given the generational mindset, economic forces, and mental health crises I cited earlier, it seems that students need more and more *support* because they have less and less *security*. They may not have been primed to trust their academic advisors, but they have been primed to need us. As Peterson puts it, writing about her own students, "They'd been guided closely all their lives, and they wanted me to guide them as well. They were, in a word, *scared*."[13]

Academic advising is still "a field working toward true professionalization," but Erin Justyna, writing for *Academic Advising Today*, argues that "the last 37 years have seen advising move from an afterthought to a recognized, crucial contributor to student success."[14] As academic advising moves toward professionalization, many of the people hired to do advising come to it with degrees in higher education administration or counseling, and/or they have backgrounds in other student service areas like new student orientation, career counseling, or student housing. Anft documents some of the ways schools are moving away from older models of advising in which faculty met advising needs, toward viewing academic advising as a distinct profession and need within college and university communities. Some schools have met advisors' ever-expanding job descriptions with expanded technological tools and training, including training advisors to serve as "academic life coaches," who work "intrusively" to help students manage every aspect of their academic lives.[15] It may seem, given these trends, that an educational background in counseling or higher ed administration and a work history in student services are exactly the right preparation for working as an academic advisor. There are many of us working in the field, however, for whom academic advising is *alt-ac*: we have advanced degrees in unrelated fields and originally set out to be faculty. Our entrée into advising came through college-level teaching, and academic advisor may be the first university staff position we've held. At the University of Iowa, where I work, almost all of us at the Academic Advising Center fit this description, whether we think of ourselves as alt-ac or not.

And as it turns out, we who come to academic advising with an alt-ac perspective—particularly those of us who endured a post-2008 academic job market—are uniquely equipped to navigate students not only through the academic decisions they need to make but also through the affective aspects of these decisions. We've made our own decisions out of precarious places, struggling with constraining narratives about our educations and careers, and finding compromises between passion and pragmatism. We are, so many of us working in alt-ac capacities, inhabiting a space between our ideals and the demands of late capitalism, doing what we need to do to pay the bills while preserving what is left of our arts-and-humanities souls. The bargains we have struck, the positions we have carved out, the enclaves of like-minded academic expats we have found—we are lucky. We are resentful. We are grateful. We are disillusioned. We are living something-like-but-not-exactly a Life of the Mind. Have we sold out? Are we part of the problem? Is our work as meaningful as we once hoped it would be? (The university as an institution exists in a similar place, honestly—a place where lofty ideals meet the need to make money, a place where we want to change the world without giving up our relatively privileged place within it.)

Coming to advising with an alt-ac perspective means the battery of questionable advice to which our students are subjected as they try to predict what will keep them afloat in this economy can be downright triggering. The things we hear from students sound like ghosts of our own pasts. You heard you need a business degree to get a job? I heard my work had to be interdisciplinary but not *too* interdisciplinary, cutting-edge but not risky or faddish, engaged with public discourse but not dated in its politics. You heard a Spanish minor is the silver bullet? I heard the silver bullet was lots of teaching experience—no, peer-reviewed publications—no, the "digital humanities." You heard no grad school will accept you if you complete the BA in psychology rather than the BS? I heard no one would ever hire me to teach again if I took this advising job. Your mom's friend's daughter majored in communication studies, and is now unemployed and serving as a cautionary tale? I sometimes wonder who from my grad school cohort is unknowingly serving in that same role.

TELLING BETTER STORIES

These stories are all just that: stories. They are powerful, though, because stories, as any good English major will tell you, are important. The stories we tell about ourselves—I am a pre-med student, I am a bad test-taker, I am good at math, I am a failed academic—sediment into identity over time, as we repeatedly tell them. The stories we hear from other people—you can't support yourself with a degree in that field, if you accept an alt-ac position you'll never again have a shot on the academic market—can carry the weight of authority and truth because narrative is persuasive. If a statement applies to even one person out there somewhere, it is at least a partial truth, right? If I identify with the protagonist of this story, surely her fate will befall me as well, right? Narratives also feel deterministic because of their temporality: they are thought of as having a beginning, middle, and end, so positioning yourself within a narrative imbues every present action with heavy significance, a fatalistic sense of cause and effect. It also reifies beliefs in linear progress and optimization of experience. Because students and their parents have correctly assessed present-day pressures surrounding education, it can be challenging to show them that the stories they believe about how best to respond to those pressures are flawed. Or that shifting to a parallel plan does not have to feel like failure. Or even that despite the state of the world it is possible to study something simply because you enjoy it and still be okay. Stories are incredibly difficult for advisors to counter—except with other stories. Remember the statistics and figures from earlier in this chapter about underemployment and majors? Me neither. Remember the thing about living in Virginia versus living in North Carolina? Yeah, you do. Because stories are memorable and effective. (Another reason to major in English.)

When we work with students making decisions out of places of economic fear, there are several ways our alt-ac backgrounds can arm us with helpful stories. The first is simply that we can use our experiences to gain credibility, so that when we show students the errors in their thinking they are more likely to hear what we have to say. When we say you do not need a business degree to get a job, students are skeptical, even when we bring data to support our claims. Instead we can try talking about the ways the advice we got about our careers did and did not match up with our lived experience, as well as all the people we know working in fields completely unpredictable based on major alone. We can also draw from our own lives to encourage students to seek out the pocket universes where it is sometimes possible to do work you find meaningful and get paid for it. We can encourage them to choose, find, or make bigger dreams than merely "getting a job" while also empathizing with the pressures and fears shaping their goals. We can suggest what looking back at college and the job market from the other side might feel like, because we are there, on the other side. However our alt-ac stories feel—bitter, triumphant, relieved, nostalgic, disillusioned, grateful—they are our stories to tell, from here on the other side of a fear probably comparable to what our students feel.

Furthermore, we can help students seek out counter-narratives to the constraining ones they have internalized. We can model for them how to write their own narratives about themselves, their present and future major and career paths, and their positions within this economic system they've inherited. We can nudge them toward more critical perspectives where they can analyze and talk back to those narratives. What is alt-ac, after all, if not a counter-narrative? Cultivating a "growth mindset," currently a popular concept within academic advising, involves encouraging students to reframe their ideas about themselves and their abilities, to believe that they are capable of change.[16] If a student says, "I am not a good writer," we might reply, "You are not a good writer *yet*," which is another way of saying: tell a different story about yourself. Shift this plot point from the end to somewhere in the middle.

One strategy we can borrow from narrative therapy involves separating the person from the problem.[17] In an advising context, this practice would look something like encouraging students to create some space between their identity and the major, career, or thing they always thought they would do or be. One way to get at this separation is to pose a thought experiment with no stakes: "What if that thing didn't exist anymore? What would you do or could you be instead? What else are you in addition to that thing?" Such an exercise can give students the permission and safety necessary to envision a different world—or a different place for themselves within this one. At the end of the experiment everything goes back to normal. Students haven't actually declared a new major, dropped all their classes, or even spoken aloud their curiosity about dance or anthropology to anyone outside of the advising center. They haven't changed anything about their lives—except, hopefully, their perspective on the connection between who they are and what they (hope to) do.

Another strategy is to help students frame their situations and stories within a larger sociocultural context. We don't always want (or have time) to connect a student's anxieties about their job prospects to the student debt crisis, the overall devaluing of the arts and humanities, or the monolithic death grip of capitalist thinking. But when we do have the opportunity to suggest the problems students face are systemic and the meanings they ascribe to the events of their lives "do not occur in a vacuum," it can be illuminating and even empowering.[18] As the Dulwich Centre, one of the primary homes of narrative therapy, explains, "There is always a context in which the stories of our lives are formed. This context contributes to the interpretations and meanings that we give to events." Some stories are based on "thin" description and conclusions that allow "little space for the complexities and contradictions of life" and often "obscure broader relations of power."[19] We can help students by finding ways to "thicken" the stories they tell about education and the job market by bringing in social contexts. To know that they are not alone in their fears, that they can do everything "right" and still struggle, that it is not their fault they have to grind so hard for economic stability—ironically, hearing these things can relieve some of the pressure our students feel. Peterson writes, toward the end of her article on millennial burnout,

> But as I finish this piece, I feel something I haven't felt in a long time: catharsis. I feel *great*. I feel *something*—which is not something I've really felt upon the completion of a task in some time. There are still things to tackle after this. But for the first time, I'm seeing myself, the parameters of my labor, and the cause of my burnout clearly. And it doesn't feel like the abyss. It doesn't feel hopeless. It's not a problem I can solve, but it's a reality I can acknowledge, a paradigm through which I can understand my actions.[20]

Students can't solve the problems of economic precarity by choosing the right major or landing the right internship. Thickening the ways they describe those problems by situating them within broader contexts can go a long way toward helping them affectively navigate the decisions they have to make, and toward creating distance between students and the stories they've heard—not letting those stories cement into beliefs about their own identities.

Finally, we can teach students to make room for alternate stories. We can ask where they heard the stories they're repeating to us, if they've heard any others, and if they know people who don't fit those narratives—and we can tell the alternative stories ourselves, providing counterexamples from our own lives. I tell students I know so many people who have jobs without business degrees. Have I told you about my brother, who went to culinary school and now works in IT, or my sister, who trained as an EMT and now works in marketing? I know a project manager whose degree is in social work, someone who works in health care after majoring in Spanish, someone who makes more money teaching aerobics than she did as an academic—and on and on. I have a PhD in English and am working in advising, and, contrary to the warnings I received, I still teach and write regularly. It's not that the people telling stories to our students (or to us) don't know what they're talking about. It's that none of us do. That story about living in Virginia versus living in North Carolina is one way to make sense of the data; there are other equally valid ways. I cherry-picked the data I wanted from those studies as much as the people recruiting students to STEM and business majors do. If a student's dad tells her she has to major in business to get a job and I tell her "no you don't," neither of us is right. We're telling different stories. In this economy there is no safe bet, no winning strategy, no gaming the system. Those storytellers—including me!—are well-intentioned but really just guessing based on limited information. Doesn't it help to know that? Isn't it freeing? Study what you actually want to study! It probably makes no difference!

And let's take those same strategies back to the discourses of alt-ac and our own affective relationships with academia, while we're at it. At its best alt-ac provides an important, previously missing perspective on academia and its connections to the rest of the world. At its worst alt-ac is characterized by a bitter combination of nostalgia, heartbreak, and "you can't fire me; I quit." Part of making alt-ac feel better is telling better stories about ourselves. When I was on the academic market, one of my faculty mentors explicitly told me he thought of me as one of his tragic stories about the state of academia today: that someone with so much talent and promise and drive couldn't get a tenure-track job. He collected these stories—he rattled off three or four other names with mine. Later, when I told him I had gotten a job in advising, he told me he thought it was a good temporary step for me, and he still hoped I would make it. That's his story about me. I've been told there are also faculty in my PhD program who hold up my advising job as a success story. I could resent the fact that very few people in my department narrated my story that way when I was actually pursuing this job and could have used their support. Alternatively, I could agree with them and subscribe to that success story. Or I could write my own story—a "thicker" story—and try to show my students how to do the same. I'm still at the same institution where I earned my PhD, but I'm nowhere I could have predicted. I didn't get the thing I wanted, but I still get to do all my favorite parts of that thing, including writing and teaching within my academic field. It's a weird story. I'm happy to tell it to any student who comes into my office.

NOTES

1. Katie Johnston, "Millennials Aren't Lazy, They're Workaholics," *Boston Globe*, December 19, 2016, https://www.bostonglobe.com/business/2016/12/19/millennials-aren-lazy-they-workaholics/3ZD86pLBYg954qUEYa3SUJ/story.html; Anne Helen Peterson, "How Millennials Became the Burnout Generation," Buzzfeed News, January 5, 2019, https://www.buzzfeednews.com/article/annehelenpetersen/millennials-burnout-generation-debt-work.

2. Peterson, "How Millennials Became."

3. Peterson.

4. Lois M. Collins, "The New Campus Crisis: How Anxiety Is Crippling College Kids across the Country," *Deseret News*, October 3, 2018, https://www.deseretnews.com/article/900034860/the-new-campus-crisis-how-anxiety-is-crippling-college-kids-across-the-country.html.

5. Collins, "The New Campus Crisis."

6. Derek Newton, "It's Not Liberal Arts and Literature Majors Who Are Most Underemployed," *Forbes*, May 31, 2018, https://www.forbes.com/sites/dereknewton/2018/05/31/its-not-liberal-arts-and-literature-majors-who-are-most-underemployed/#4a26021611de.

7. Matthew Sigelman et al., "Majors That Matter: Ensuring College Graduates Avoid Underemployment," Burning Glass Technologies, October 2018, https://www.burning-glass.com/wp-content/uploads/underemployment_majors_that_matter_final.pdf.

8. "Degrees That Pay You Back," *Wall Street Journal*, https://online.wsj.com/public/resources/documents/info-Degrees_that_Pay_you_Back-sort.html. Accessed October 15, 2019. These numbers are for graduates with only bachelor's degrees about ten years after commencement.

9. Benjamin Schmidt, "The Humanities Are in Crisis," *e Atlantic*, August 23, 2018, https://www.theatlantic.com/ideas/archive/2018/08/the-humanities-face-a-crisisof-confidence/567565/.

10. Betsy DeVos, "U.S. Secretary of Education Betsy DeVos Warns of Looming Crisis in Higher Education," US Department of Education, November 27, 2018, https://www.ed.gov/news/press-releases/us-secretary-education-betsy-devos-warns-looming-crisis-higher-education.

11. "NACADA Academic Advising Core Competencies Model," NACADA: The Global Community for Academic Advising, https://www.nacada.ksu.edu/About-Us/NACADA-Leadership/Administrative-Division/Professional-Development-Committee/PDC-Advisor-Competencies.aspx. Accessed September 2, 2021.

12. Michael Anft, "Student Needs Have Changed. Advising Must Change, Too," Chronicle of Higher Education, July 1, 2018, https://www.chronicle.com/article/Student-Needs-Have-Changed/243797.

13. Peterson, "How Millennials Became."

14. Erin Justyna, "On Being an Advising Professional," *Academic Advising Today* 39, no. 4 (December 2016), https://www.nacada.ksu.edu/Resources/Academic-Advising-Today/View-Articles/On-Being-an-Advising-Professional.aspx.

15. Anft, "Student Needs Have Changed."

16. Carol Dweck, "Carol Dweck Revisits the 'Growth Mindset,'" Education Week, September 22, 2019, https://www.edweek.org/ew/articles/2015/09/23/carol-dweck-revisits-the-growth-mindset.html.

17. "Narrative Therapy," Good Therapy, June 18, 2018, https://www.goodtherapy.org/learn-about-therapy/types/narrative-therapy.

18. "What Is Narrative Therapy?," Dulwich Centre: A Gateway to Narrative Therapy & Community Work, https://dulwichcentre.com.au/what-is-narrative-therapy/.

19. "What Is Narrative Therapy?"

20. Peterson, "How Millennials Became."

BIBLIOGRAPHY

Anft, Michael. "Student Needs Have Changed. Advising Must Change, Too." Chronicle of Higher Education. July 1, 2018. https://www.chronicle.com/article/Student-Needs-Have-Changed/243797.

Collins, Lois M. "The New Campus Crisis: How Anxiety Is Crippling College Kids across the Country." *Deseret News*. October 3, 2018. https://www.deseretnews.com/article/900034860/the-new-campus-crisis-how-anxiety-is-crippling-college-kids-across-the-country.html.

"Degrees That Pay You Back." *Wall Street Journal*. https://online.wsj.com/public/resources/documents/info-Degrees_that_Pay_you_Back-sort.html. Accessed October 15, 2019.

DeVos, Betsy. "U.S. Secretary of Education Betsy DeVos Warns of Looming Crisis in Higher Education." *U.S. Department of Education*, November 27, 2018, https://www.ed.gov/news/press-releases/us-secretary-education-betsy-devos-warns-looming-crisis-higher-education.

Dweck, Carol. "Carol Dweck Revisits the 'Growth Mindset.'" Education Week. September 22, 2019. https://www.edweek.org/ew/articles/2015/09/23/carol-dweck-revisits-the-growth-mindset.html.

Johnston, Katie. "Millennials Aren't Lazy, They're Workaholics." *Boston Globe*. December 19, 2016. https://www.bostonglobe.com/business/2016/12/19/millennials-aren-lazy-they-workaholics/3ZD86pLBYg954qUEYa3SUJ/story.html.

Justyna, Erin. "On Being an Advising Professional." *Academic Advising Today* 39, no. 4 (December 2016). https://www.nacada.ksu.edu/Resources/Academic-Advising-Today/View-Articles/On-Being-an-Advising-Professional.aspx.

"NACADA Academic Advising Core Competencies Model." NACADA: The Global Community for Academic Advising. https://www.nacada.ksu.edu/About-Us/NACADA-Leadership/Administrative-Division/Professional-Development-Committee/PDC-Advisor-Competencies.aspx. Accessed September 2, 2021.

"Narrative Therapy." Good Therapy. June 18, 2018. https://www.goodtherapy.org/learn-about-therapy/types/narrative-therapy.

Newton, Derek. "It's Not Liberal Arts and Literature Majors Who Are Most Underemployed." *Forbes*. May 31, 2018. https://www.forbes.com/sites/dereknewton/2018/05/31/its-not-liberal-arts-and-literature-majors-who-are-most-underemployed/#4a26021611de.

Peterson, Anne Helen. "How Millennials Became the Burnout Generation." Buzzfeed News. January 5, 2019. https://www.buzzfeednews.com/article/annehelenpetersen/millennials-burnout-generation-debt-work.

Schmidt, Benjamin. "The Humanities Are in Crisis." *Atlantic*. August 23, 2018. https://www.theatlantic.com/ideas/archive/2018/08/the-humanities-face-a-crisisof-confidence/567565/.

Sigelman, Matthew, Bledi Taska, Dan Restuccia, Soumya Braganza, and Scott Bittle. "Majors That Matter: Ensuring College Graduates Avoid Underemployment." Burning Glass Technologies. October 2018. https://www.burning-glass.com/wp-content/uploads/underemployment_majors_that_matter_final.pdf.

"What Is Narrative Therapy?" Dulwich Centre: A Gateway to Narrative Therapy & Community Work. https://dulwichcentre.com.au/what-is-narrative-therapy/.

11

Both Student and Employee

Uncovering the Affective Labor of Supervising Student Staff

DANIEL DALE

The University of Colorado–Boulder offers supervisors of student employees a helpful handout detailing "strategies for helping supervisors succeed with student employees." One of the first pieces of advice this handout offers is this: "Understand that student employees are students first and employees second. Though it is important to have high standards on the job, it is also important to be flexible to accommodate academic obligations." Shortly after this, the handout takes a different view: "Supervisors who are too lenient are not doing students any favors. Student job [*sic*] are 'real jobs.'"[1] This conflicting view of student employees as "students first" but also employees that have a "real job" is prevalent throughout the alt-ac positions that directly oversee student workers. These workers are viewed as students tied to the educational mission of the university. However, they are also employees of the university whose positions often touch on the "business" side of higher education (attracting prospective students, soliciting donations, increase retention, etc.).

Academics who find themselves supervising student employees must navigate this tension between student and employee. Often, academics who pursue a career in higher education do so because they want to interact with students in an educational context. Because of this, many academics who opt for alt-ac careers seek roles that allow them to work closely with students. To some, the pursuit of an academic career in higher education stems from a passion for teaching, and this does not go away when pushed toward an alt-ac career. However, many academics who come to the staff role from teaching quickly realize that their interactions with students change drastically when students become their employees. How do staff members that come from teaching balance the competing needs of those in the role of student/employee? Often times, it is hard to juggle the job requirements of an employee with the desire to mentor and educate students.

On the one hand, staff members who supervise students feel responsible for their educational and personal development, especially staff members who have a history of interacting with students in a classroom context. On the other hand, the realities of performance-based budgeting, annual reviews, and contingent employment require staff members to utilize students' labor. Additionally, in many cases, student workers are themselves engaging in affective labor by being paid to counsel, mediate, mentor, and teach. In essence, student employees and supervisors are getting paid for the same kind of affective labor.

The aim of this chapter will be to clear a space where staff members who supervise students, and the student employees themselves, can reflect on the affective labor student workers engage in. Through this space, my goal will be to advocate for a greater focus on affective labor when training and supervising student employees. Student employees do not inhabit two distinct spaces, employee while on-the-clock and student while away from work. Supervisors cannot untie the knot and separate these two roles. Rather, a student worker's labor is irrevocably tied to their positionality as student.

Although student labor in higher education takes many forms, this chapter will focus mainly on student workers who work as peer educators. For these student workers, interacting with other students is the focus of their labor. This is not to diminish the importance of student workers who do not directly work with other students. Rather, I am interested in investigating the sticky relationship between supervisors and student employees who are often engaging in the same kind of affective labor within the university.

THE RISE OF PEER EDUCATION IN HIGHER ED

Traditionally, student work has been viewed as inconsequential to the larger educational mission of the university. Previously, while students might have worked with other students as resident advisors (RAs), most student employment was in areas such as food service or clerical work. According to Stephanie Ganser and Tricia Kennedy, after World War II, with the influx of undergraduates to universities, the RA role expanded to become commonplace in most universities. However, this kind of peer educator role did not move beyond the residence hall for some time.[2]

Starting in the 1970s, universities began to create learning assistance centers. While academic support in some form (such as tutoring) has been a part of higher education since the 1600s, academic support has been formalized in higher education only in the past few decades. For the majority of this time, most tutors were professional staff members, and not student employees. However, starting with the formalization of learning assistance centers on campuses, this role began to be overtaken by students who were currently enrolled at the university where they also worked. Only recently have various kinds of academic and nonacademic support roles for peer educators sprung up at universities across the country.[3]

The push to hire more student workers as peer educators has intensified in the twenty-first century thanks to the rise of neoliberalism within higher education. Due to state budget cuts in the wake of the Great Recession, and a decrease in higher education funding more generally, universities are often faced with a shrinking budget. At the same time, universities are providing more support for students, who are now viewed as customers.[4] Laying out the landscape of neoliberal higher education, Alex Kostogriz argues, "Outcomes, effectiveness, performance standards, services delivery to 'clients,' customer satisfaction and accountability are just a few habitually used words that capture the rational-calculative mode of policy-making and managerial practices today."[5] These supports often take the form of expanded first-year services, structured resident hall curriculums, and expanded career coaching. Without the funds to hire full-time professional staff for these positions, many universities employ student labor to facilitate these programs.[6] Often, student workers are asked to supplement the labor of overworked professors who are teaching large lecture hall classes with an increasing enrollment.[7] In both cases, students are being asked to fulfill duties that previously would have gone to a full-time staff member.

While, as Janet Colvin mentions, "this sort of peer interaction may have an even greater impact on students than what happens in the classroom,"[8] any alt-ac staff member who oversees one of these peer education programs knows how important cost savings, budget, and retention numbers are to keeping a program funded, no matter how impactful that program might be. In other words, the driving force behind the growth of peer education in higher education is mainly economic. These competing interests are laid out by David Arendale, who writes, "Institutions cannot waste scarce resources on programs that may not contribute both to increased student success as well as enhancing the institution's economic stability through lower student dropout rates and the loss of tuition dollars."[9] Arendale's language in this passage is fairly telling. Within the current structure of higher education, it is not enough for a program to lead to "increased student success" within the university. Rather, programs need to "both" serve the academic needs of students while still attending to the financial goals of the neoliberal university. The push within higher education to "do more with less" leads to students working as "peer health educators, peer counselors, peer advisers, resident assistants, peer tutors, supplemental instruction leaders, orientation leaders, and group facilitators."[10] While these positions all vary in their responsibilities, they share a heavy level of interaction between the students employed by the university and the larger student population. Furthermore, all these positions require a degree of affective labor that often goes ignored or overlooked.

One by-product of the neoliberal university is an attempt to separate the student and worker sides of undergraduate labor. Many undergraduate employment positions are couched in language that attempts to cover up the knotty entanglement of the competing student/worker dual role. For example, many studies on student workers in higher education turn to the euphemistic term *paraprofessional*.[11] Likewise, the students these peer educators work with are themselves referred to as "clients."[12] While some of the intention behind these labels might be well meaning, I believe this shift to a market-based language is ultimately harmful to the educational mission of peer education programs. Often, students who work as peer educators do so because they have some knowledge or skill derived from their experiences as a student within higher education. However, once students are hired and brought into the administrative side of the university, the "best practices" around managing student employees often requires that supervisors view them through the lens of labor.

Many supervisors find themselves in a similar situation to the one described by Michael Peters. To Peters, "Within universities managerialism and principles of new public choice turn colleagues into line managers who lead double lives: theoretically they espouse the critique of neoliberalism but in practice side with the administration and love the power of hierarchy temporarily grants them."[13] While many alt-ac professionals would disagree with the assertion that they "love the power of hierarchy," many would identify with being caught between the problems they see with the neoliberalism of higher education and the need to fulfill the requirements of their administrative position. While alt-ac professionals might be critical of performance-based budgeting, data-driven assessment, and other qualities brought about by the neoliberal shift in higher education, they nevertheless are responsible for producing budgets and reports that align with this new neoliberal mission. Adding to this frustration is the fact that many of those in alt-ac careers (especially early in their careers) are not in a position to challenge these neoliberal power structures without jeopardizing their position within the university. Nevertheless, it is important for alt-ac staff members to be aware of the ways in which these neoliberal economic pressures make their way into the managing, training, and everyday lives of peer educators they oversee.

PEER EDUCATORS AND AFFECTIVE LABOR

Before sketching out the exact ways peer educators engage in affective labor within the university, I want to quickly define what I mean by *affective labor*. While the term stretches back to the Italian autonomism movement of the 1960s and 1970s, the ideas behind affective labor were more recently explored within the context of late capitalism by Michael Hardt and Antonio Negri. Affective labor is the kind of work that produces an immaterial result rather than a material object. Hardt and Negri see this work happening in the realm of "human contact and interaction. . . . Its products are intangible, a feeling of ease, well-being, satisfaction, excitement of passion. Categories such as 'in-person services' or services of proximity are often used to identify this kind of labor, but that is really essential to it are the creation and manipulation of affect."[14] Affective labor is a social act. It is work that creates relationships, communities, and ways of being.

While the affective and emotional labor of teachers is well-documented,[15] this research has not looked at how peer educators engage in affective labor in their positions within the university. Nevertheless, peer educators and instructors often engage in the same kinds of affective labor. While their labor differs in important ways, the current research on affective labor in education can be used to begin an investigation of affective labor in peer education within the university.

For example, as Kostogriz points out, "It is difficult to determine when the affective labour of teachers begins or ends, thereby rendering its value neither measurable nor manageable by standards and performance indicators."[16] Like a teacher or instructor, a student worker's affective labor evades easy quantification when viewed through the lens of neoliberal higher education. While things like course grades, DFW (D, F, and withdrawal) rates, and retention can be summarized using quantitative data, the effect of affective labor is much harder to quantify. Although nebulous measure of things like "student satisfaction" attempt to put this affective labor into an easy-to-digest number, these measurements often miss the nuanced ways students engage in affective labor during their everyday work. The amount of time a peer educator spends mediating conflict, mentoring younger students, and providing community building are extremely important aspects of a student's lived experience in higher education. These crucial moments are usually overseen by peer educators. Nevertheless, the importance of these interactions ultimately eludes the usual measuring sticks of higher education and are thus less valued than the traditional measure of academic success.

In order to give affective labor more visibility within education, Kostogriz calls for a realigning of the way we view the importance of certain kinds of labor. He believes that we should acknowledge the "primacy of affective labour in the teaching profession, prior to its rationalization."[17] In other words, affective labor should be viewed as a foundational aspect of teaching apart from the ability to measure its effect on teaching through a neoliberal lens. Rather than being a component of teaching that needs to be justified via data, affective labor should be viewed as an always-already present component of teaching. The same could be said of peer education. Like teaching, peer education is irrevocably tied to affective labor. Supervisors of these student workers cannot disentangle the peer educator role from affective labor.

We can see affective labor in the work of peer educators in numerous ways. Managing the emotions of students in a learning community often falls to the undergraduate peer leader in charge of these spaces.[18] Peer tutors aren't just responsible for helping students learn course content, but they are also charged with helping students manage feelings of isolation and anxiety.[19] Likewise, Gregory Blimling sees the resident advisor as someone who assures "students are given the support they need to succeed. . . . They are asked to be informal counselors, friends, confidants, role models, programmers, administrators, rule enforcers, and conflict mediators."[20]

The labor of these resident advisors (and other peer educators) is directly tied to the way they manage the affect of the students they serve. As Hardt and Negri point out, "Images, information, knowledge, affects, codes, and social relationships, for example, are coming to outweigh material commodities or the material aspects of commodities in the capitalist valorization process."[21] To Hardt and Negri, the ability to build and maintain social relationships can be just as valuable (in an economic sense) as a material good. Colleges often derive value through the labor of their student workers by placing them in roles where they are asked to mediate conflict or put students emotionally at ease. While the ethical value of this kind of work is obvious, for a university, there is also the economic value of keeping students academically productive, and thus, enrolled and paying tuition.

Peer educators working in orientation engage in similar affective labor. For one thing, as Ganser and Kennedy point out, "Orientation leaders are now expected to communicate and model institutional expectations, set the tone of campus culture, and build community among new students."[22] Rather than simply showing students around campus or explaining where certain offices are located, student workers who oversee orientation are responsible for creating community. Their paid labor is directly responsible for bringing about certain social relations in the students they interact with. This is not some ad-hoc task that the peer educators can accomplish on their own volition, depending on their own experiences and feelings about the university. Rather, the training, hiring, and supervision of these peer educators is structured to force the creation of social relationships in a specific way that aligns with the overall mission of the university. As Hardt and Negri note, "The production of subjectivity plays a significant role in the creation of economic value."[23] Within higher education, there is a desire to encourage students to embrace a subjectivity that involves positive feelings toward the university, thus creating a revenue stream in the form of increased retention and, later on, alumni donations. Peer educators assist in this process by encouraging students to get involved in student organizations, publicizing campus opportunities, and posing as students who have a positive relationship with the university.

The training and selection of peer educators is directly tied to their ability to effectively utilize affective labor. Steven Ender and Fred Newton, for example, tie peer educator efficiency to characteristics that "include communications and relationship qualities such as empathy, respect, specificity, genuineness, and warmth—qualities . . . that could be enhanced through systematic training."[24] There is a conscious push by supervisors of student workers to harness and direct the affective labor of peer educators to larger institutional goals. Put simply, the best peer educators are the ones who effectively utilize their affective labor when interacting with other students. As Hardt and Negri put it, "A worker with a good attitude and social skills is another way of saying a worker adept at affective labor."[25]

For those in alt-ac positions who manage student employees, it is imperative to be aware of the affective aspects of student labor. This specific kind of labor is not neutral. Workers are invariably affected by the kind of labor they engage in. While some student workers might have some experience managing and navigating the pitfalls of affective labor, other students might be in this position for the first time. In some ways, those in alt-ac positions might be especially equipped to mentor and advise student workers in this position. For one thing, many alt-ac workers find themselves in a similar position to student workers. Alt-ac staff members often come to their role from a teaching background or a desire to work with students in an educational context. At the same time, they are enmeshed in the administrative side of the university, which often takes its cue from market-driven economic policy. Alt-ac staff members straddle the divide between the seemingly disparate business and educational missions of many universities. Student workers are in a similar position. They are plucked from the educational realm of the university and thrust into a role where they are subject to the logic of labor and capital. In essence, student workers and the supervisors who mentor them inhabit a similar space. Thus, it is essential for alt-ac supervisors of student staff to help peer educators mitigate and steer through the stress brought about by their affective labor.

THE OCCUPATIONAL HAZARDS OF PEER EDUCATION

The tension between the neoliberal economic policy of many contemporary universities and the educational mission of alt-ac staff members often trickles down to peer educators. While this tension has not been thoroughly investigated within the realm of alt-ac careers or student workers, it has been viewed through the lens of teaching. Izhar Oplatka, for example, sees an explicit conflict between the administrative mission of an institution (budget, ranking, profile, etc.) and the affective labor necessary to be an effective educator. To Oplatka, "emotion management that is aimed at the achievement of external benefits (e.g., organizational success, impressive management) is incompatible with the ethical and moral aspects of teaching."[26]

Within the realm of supervising student employees, this plays out when we ask peer educators to manage their emotions during their interactions with other students. This often takes the form of asking students to moderate or eliminate the interactions they would have with students if they were outside their role as peer educator. For example, in a peer tutoring session, it would be considered inappropriate for a peer educator to steer students away from taking a certain professor or course. However, this kind of advice would be part of a normal student-to-student interaction. In her expansive study on the airline industry and how the training of flight attendants mandates a certain kind of emotional façade, Arlie Hochschild points out how jobs in the service industries often include "a general source of stress, a thread woven through the whole work experience: the task of managing an estrangement between self and feeling and between self and display."[27] Many peer educators navigate this space on a regular basis. Students often feel solidarity with other students: they are subject to the same power structures and have similar experiences. When they are asked to assume a different role in their interactions with other students, we essentially ask peer educators to interact with students as if they were not students. That is to say, the interactions that students might have with one another are filtered through the professional expectations attached to the labor they perform.

While asking our students to modify their interactions with other students in this way may seem like a small thing, we should be careful not to minimize how it impacts student workers. The stress experienced by workers who have to manage their emotion can prove to be especially acute for RAs, who might feel like they can never drop the "mask" of quasi-professional while interacting with students. While many students truly enjoy being an integral part of their peers' education and college experience, even the best student workers can sometimes be adversely impacted by their labor. This is especially true for students who work in residence education or other student life programs. For one thing, RAs are often expected to be "on the clock" and ready to assist students at all hours of the day.[28] The blurring of labor and recreation is indicative of affective labor as a whole. Within the framework of affective labor, there is an "increasingly indefinite division between work time and leisure time. . . . When production is aimed at solving a problem . . . or creating an idea or a relationship, work time tends to expand to the entire time of life."[29]

Having to manage and enact change in the emotions and subjectivity of their peers can be an exhausting experience, especially when peer educators' affective labor seeps beyond the hours they are on the clock. Additionally, the classic Marxist conception of alienation takes on new meaning when applied to affective labor: "When affective production becomes part of waged labor it can be experienced as extremely alienating: I am selling my ability to make human relationships, something extremely intimate, at the command of the client and the boss."[30] This feeling of alienation can be especially acute for peer educators, who are often put into a position where they are interacting with a student as an employee one day, and as a student the next.

Furthermore, this always-on requirement could result in student workers experiencing secondary trauma, similar to social workers and other mental health professionals, that manifests "when an individual hears about the firsthand trauma experiences of another."[31] While all peer educators are potentially subject to secondary trauma, students working in the resident advisor role are particularly vulnerable. As Ganser and Kennedy see it, "Today resident assistants are typically on the front line in crisis situations and are usually the first to respond even before police or medical professionals."[32] This position as the point person during a student crisis exposes peer educators to experiencing secondary trauma, which may in turn harm their academics and everyday life. With the exception of a recent study by Jason Lynch, scholarship around peer educators and secondary trauma is extremely rare.[33] Additionally, while Lynch provides a framework for identifying secondary trauma in resident advisors, he does not provide any avenues for helping RAs work through this trauma. Those of us in alt-ac positions that oversee student staff in these situations need to do more to train our staffs to recognize and address this kind of trauma. More broadly, the training of peer educators needs to involve an acknowledgment and exploration of the affective labor many peer educators engage in.

FINDING COMMON GROUND: TRAINING STUDENT WORKERS IN AFFECTIVE LABOR

In order to bridge the gap felt between alt-ac staff members and the students they manage, it is imperative that we acknowledge and build upon the shared affective labor that both engage in. Through either training or experience, many alt-ac staff members who have a background in teaching have developed the skills necessary to manage and navigate their affective labor. Often times, the students we manage haven't had this same training or experience.

While we may extensively train our student staff, this training often overlooks or only briefly touches on affective labor. However, as Adrian Kelly writes, education is "an intimate encounter that calls upon professional skill and caring. I do not read these as a set of natural traits inherent in certain individuals but a set of professional skills that need to be developed."[34] In order to create peer educators who can interact with students in a variety of educational, social, and community contexts, we have to train these student workers to be aware that their work goes beyond their educational skills or campus knowledge and continues through to the emotions exchanged in their bodily experiences with other students. Part of this training will involve flattening the space between supervisor and student worker by shedding light on the shared affective labor both undertake. One way to do this is by exploring the specific kinds of affective labor student workers and alt-ac workers share, and how this affective labor fits into the overall mission of the university. In these discussions, we should not cover up the economic forces that bring peer education into being. Rather, we should be open with peer educators about how their labor generates value for the university. The goal of such an uncovering would be to show student workers how their labor is impacted by many of the same forces that affect the labor of alt-ac staff members.

Our training of student workers should also include information on how their affective labor opens peer educators up to the possibility of secondary trauma. For example, part of the training curriculum could focus on the concept of "compassion fatigue," which describes the consequences of repeated interactions with others who are currently experiencing trauma or emotional distress.[35] Within student affairs scholarship, an awareness of compassion fatigue and its consequences is only now just being investigated. However, the scope has currently been limited to full-time professional staff members and has not been widened to include the student workers who are often the first responders to traumatic events. Many of the same observations concerning the effects of compassion fatigue on professional staff members in student affairs can be applied to student staff. For example, Thomas Raimondi argues, "As a helping profession, those who work in student affairs build empathetic relationships with the students they serve; being emotionally affected by the students' problems and trauma is a natural consequence."[36] While Raimondi is talking specifically about professional staff members, his argument is just as valid when applied to student workers. This shared experience provides another opportunity to bridge the gap between student workers and alt-ac staff members. When training student workers, alt-ac staff members can point out how they have dealt with compassion fatigue in their work and offer students potential ways of coping and addressing these feelings.

We also have to be careful in our training of peer educators. While the work peer educators do is important, institutions should avoid what Ariel Ducey calls "the imperative for work to be more than a job"[37] seen in many professions that involve affective labor. To Ducey, this push to make employees view their work as "more than a job" is a way to paper over some inequity within that position (low wages, for example) by instilling a sense of duty beyond the normal wages-for-work paradigm of traditional labor. Ideally, this imperative "will channel engagement into hard work, into the attitude that 'work is more than a job' and therefore requires commitment regardless of the conditions of that work."[38]

While Ducey specifically focuses on health-care workers, we can see something similar in the peer educator role. On the student employment page of Fordham University, for example, working as a student is described as "more than a job. It is an experience which involves a commitment."[39] While this language might seem harmless, as Ducey notes, it actually has a somewhat insidious effect. When it comes to peer educators, the implicit suggestion is that their interactions with students in their work is just as important as their position as student within the university. This can often lead peer educators to sacrifice their own studies and self-care in order to go above and beyond when helping the students they work with. This language that encourages peer educators to treat their position as something that is "more than a job" also muddies the boundaries between student and worker, since the implied message is that their job should extend beyond the hours they are scheduled to work. One consequence of these porous boundaries is the potential for students to be exposed to secondary trauma outside the hours they are paid for their labor. Those who oversee student workers in this situation need to help and support students in creating boundaries that allows them to clear a space for self-care and other steps to counteract secondary trauma and compassion fatigue.

CONCLUSION

The rise of peer education within higher education has brought about some unforeseen consequences for the students working in these positions. While the effects of secondary trauma and compassion fatigue have been recognized within alt-ac positions that work closely with students, these same stressors often go overlooked in student workers who work closely with their peers. Those in alt-ac positions that oversee these student workers are in a good position to help peer educators who might be experiencing secondary trauma or compassion fatigue as a result of the affective labor demanded by their job. Alt-ac staff members are often keenly aware of these effects, and rather than hiding or covering these feelings up, we should use these experiences to build common ground with the student workers who are often experiencing similar emotions.

NOTES

1. "Strategies for Helping Supervisors Succeed with Student Employees," University of Colorado–Boulder. https://www.colorado.edu/studentemployment/sites/default/files/attached-files/strategies_for_supervisors.pdf. Accessed October 30, 2019.

2. Stephanie R. Ganser and Tricia L. Kennedy, "Where It All Began: Peer Education and Leadership in Student Services," *New Directions for Higher Education* 2012, no. 157 (2012): 17–29.

3. Kenneth A. Bruffee, *Collaborative Learning Higher Education, Interdependence, and the Authority of Knowledge* (Baltimore: Johns Hopkins University Press, 1999); Ernest T. Pascarella and Patrick T. Terenzini, *How College Affects Students* (San Francisco: Jossey-Bass, 2005).

4. Daniel B. Saunders, "Neoliberal Ideology and Public Higher Education in the United States," *Journal for Critical Education Policy Studies* 8, no. 1 (August 2010): 41–77.

5. Alex Kostogriz, "Accountability and the Affective Labour of Teachers: A Marxist-Vygotskian Perspective," *Australian Educational Researcher* 39, no. 4 (November 2012): 398.

6. Ganser and Kennedy, "Where It All Began," 18.

7. Janet W. Colvin, "Peer Mentoring and Tutoring in Higher Education," in Mang Li and Yong Zhao, eds., *Exploring Learning and Teaching in Higher Education* (New York: Springer, 2015), 207–229.

8. Colvin, "Peer Mentoring and Tutoring in Higher Education," 207.

9. David R. Arendale, "Access at the Crossroads: Learning Assistance in Higher Education," *ASHE Higher Education Report* 35, no. 6 (April 2010): 27.

10. Steven C. Ender and Fred B. Newton, *Students Helping Students: A Guide for Peer Educators on College Campuses* (San Francisco: Jossey-Bass, 2000), ix.

11. Ganser and Kennedy, "Where It All Began," 23.

12. James Breslin et al., "Students as Colleagues: A Paradigm for Understanding Student Leaders in Academic Support," *Learning Assistance Review (TLAR)* 23, no. 2 (Fall 2018): 41–64.

13. Michael A. Peters, "Affective Capitalism, Higher Education and the Constitution of the Social Body Althusser, Deleuze, and Negri on Spinoza and Marxism," *Educational Philosophy and Theory* 51, no. 5 (April 2019): 469.

14. Michael Hardt and Antonio Negri, *Empire* (Cambridge, MA: Harvard University Press, 2000), 292–293.

15. Colin Beard, Sue Clegg, and Karen Smith, "Acknowledging the Affective in Higher Education," *British Educational Research Journal* 33, no. 2 (April 2007): 235–252; Adrian Kelly, "Intimacy and Emotional Labour in Academic Development," *International Journal for Academic Development* 20, no. 1 (January 2, 2015): 93–104; Kostogriz, "Accountability and the Affective Labour of Teachers," 397–412; Izhar Oplatka, "Emotion Management and Display in Teaching: Some Ethical and Moral Considerations in the Era of Marketization and Commercialization," in Paul A. Schutz and Michalinos Zembylas, eds., *Advances in Teacher Emotion Research: The Impact on Teachers' Lives* (Boston: Springer, 2009), 55–71; Peters, "Affective Capitalism, Higher Education, and the Constitution of the Social Body," 465-473.

16. Kostogriz, 399.

17. Kostogriz, 402.

18. Nancy Sherman Shapiro and Jodi H. Levine Laufgraben, *Creating Learning Communities: A Practical Guide to Winning Support, Organizing for Change, and Implementing Programs* (San Francisco: Jossey-Bass, 1999); Martha L. Loudder and Martyn Gunn, "First Year Learning Communities: From Inspiration to Reality in Three Months," in Nancy Simpson and Jean Layne, ed., *Student Learning Communities, Faculty Learning Communities, and Faculty Development* (Stillwater, OK: New Forums Press, 2006).

19. Nancy Falchikov, *Learning Together: Peer Tutoring in Higher Education* (London: Routledge, 2001).

20. Gregory S. Blimling, *Student Learning in College Residence Halls: What Works, What Doesn't, and Why* (San Francisco: Jossey-Bass, 2015), 162.

21. Michael Hardt and Antonio Negri, *Commonwealth* (Cambridge, MA: Belknap Press, 2009), 132.

22. Ganser and Kennedy, "Where It All Began," 19.

23. Michael Hardt and Antonio Negri, *Assembly* (New York: Oxford University Press, 2017), 75.

24. Ender and Newton, *Students Helping Students*, 5.

25. Michael Hardt and Antonio Negri, *Multitude: War and Democracy in the Age of Empire* (New York: Penguin, 2004), 108.

26. Oplatka, "Emotion Management and Displays in Teaching," 56.

27. Arlie Russell Hochschild, *The Managed Heart* (Berkeley: University of California Press, 1983), 131.

28. Ganser and Kennedy, "Where It All Began."

29. Hardt and Negri, *Multitude*, 111.

30. Hardt and Negri, 111.

31. "Secondary Traumatic Stress," National Child Traumatic Stress Network, https://www.nctsn.org/trauma-informed-care/secondary-traumatic-stress. Accessed October 30, 2019.

32. Ganser and Kennedy, "Where It All Began," 23.

33. Jason R Lynch, "The Development and Validation of the Secondary Trauma in Resident Assistants Scale," *Journal of College and University Student Housing* 44, no. 1 (September 2017): 10–29.

34. Kelly, "Intimacy and Emotional Labour," 12.

35. Charles R. Figley, "Compassion Fatigue as Secondary Traumatic Stress Disorder," in Charles R. Figley, ed., *Compassion Fatigue: Coping with Secondary Stress Disorder in Those Who Treat the Traumatized* (New York: Taylor & Francis, 1995), 1.

36. Thomas P. Raimondi, "Compassion Fatigue in Higher Education: Lessons from Other Helping Fields," *Change: The Magazine of Higher Learning* 51, no. 3 (May 2019): 53.

37. Ariel Ducey, "More Than a Job: Meaning, Affect and Training Health Care Workers," in Patricia Ticineto Clough, ed., *The Affective Turn: Theorizing the Social* (Durham, NC: Duke University Press, 2007), 188.

38. Ducey, 198.

39. "Student Employment," Fordham University, https://www.fordham.edu/info/21343/student_employment. Accessed July 5, 2019.

BIBLIOGRAPHY

Arendale, David R. "Access at the Crossroads: Learning Assistance in Higher Education." *ASHE Higher Education Report* 35, no. 6 (April 2010).

Beard, Colin, Sue Clegg, and Karen Smith. "Acknowledging the Affective in

Higher Education." *British Educational Research Journal* 33, no. 2 (April 2007): 235–252.

Blimling, Gregory S. *Student Learning in College Residence Halls: What Works, What Doesn't, and Why*. San Francisco: Jossey-Bass, 2015.

Breslin, James D., Maryann H. Kope, Joannah L. O'Hatnick, and Anna G. Sharpe. "Students as Colleagues: A Paradigm for Understanding Student Leaders in Academic Support." *Learning Assistance Review (TLAR)* 23, no. 2 (Fall 2018): 41–64.

Bruffee, Kenneth A. *Collaborative Learning Higher Education, Interdependence, and the Authority of Knowledge*. Baltimore: Johns Hopkins University Press, 1999.

Colvin, Janet W. "Peer Mentoring and Tutoring in Higher Education." In Mang Li and Yong Zhao, eds., *Exploring Learning and Teaching in Higher Education*, 207–229. New York: Springer, 2015.

Ducey, Ariel. "More Than a Job: Meaning, Affect and Training Health Care Workers." In Patricia Ticineto Clough, ed., *The Affective Turn: Theorizing the Social*, 187–208. Durham, NC: Duke University Press, 2007.

Ender, Steven C., and Fred B. Newton. *Students Helping Students: A Guide for Peer Educators on College Campuses*. San Francisco: Jossey-Bass, 2000.

Falchikov, Nancy. *Learning Together: Peer Tutoring in Higher Education*. London: Routledge, 2001.

Figley, Charles R. "Compassion Fatigue as Secondary Traumatic Stress Disorder." In Charles R. Figley, ed., *Compassion Fatigue: Coping with Secondary Stress Disorder in Those Who Treat the Traumatized*, 1–20. New York: Taylor & Francis, 1995.

Hardt, Michael, and Antonio Negri. *Assembly*. New York: Oxford University Press, 2017.

———. *Commonwealth*. Cambridge, MA: Belknap Press, 2009.

———. *Empire*. Cambridge, MA: Harvard University Press, 2000.

———. *Multitude: War and Democracy in the Age of Empire*. New York: Penguin, 2004.

Hochschild, Arlie Russell. *The Managed Heart*. Berkeley: University of California Press, 1983.

Kelly, Adrian. "Intimacy and Emotional Labour in Academic Development." *International Journal for Academic Development* 20, no. 1 (January 2, 2015): 93–104.

Kostogriz, Alex. "Accountability and the Affective Labour of Teachers: A Marxist-Vygotskian Perspective." *Australian Educational Researcher* 39, no. 4 (November 2012): 397–412.

Loudder, Martha L., and Martyn Gunn. "First Year Learning Communities: From Inspiration to Reality in Three Months." In Nancy Simpson and Jean

Layne, eds., *Student Learning Communities, Faculty Learning Communities, and Faculty Development*, 1–14. Stillwater, OK: New Forums Press, 2006.

Lynch, R. Jason. "The Development and Validation of the Secondary Trauma in Resident Assistants Scale." *Journal of College and University Student Housing* 44, no. 1 (September 2017): 10–29.

Oplatka, Izhar. "Emotion Management and Display in Teaching: Some Ethical and Moral Considerations in the Era of Marketization and Commercialization." In Paul A. Schutz and Michalinos Zembylas, eds., *Advances in Teacher Emotion Research: The Impact on Teachers' Lives*, 55–71. Boston: Springer, 2009.

Pascarella, Ernest T., and Patrick T Terenzini. *How College Affects Students*. San Francisco: Jossey-Bass, 2005.

Peters, Michael A. "Affective Capitalism, Higher Education and the Constitution of the Social Body Althusser, Deleuze, and Negri on Spinoza and Marxism." *Educational Philosophy and Theory* 51, no. 5 (April 16, 2019): 465–473.

Raimondi, Thomas P. "Compassion Fatigue in Higher Education: Lessons from Other Helping Fields." *Change: The Magazine of Higher Learning* 51, no. 3 (May 2019): 52–58.

"Secondary Traumatic Stress." National Child Traumatic Stress Network. https://www.nctsn.org/trauma-informed-care/secondary-traumatic-stress. Accessed October 30, 2019.

Shapiro, Nancy Sherman, and Jodi H. Levine Laufgraben. *Creating Learning Communities: A Practical Guide to Winning Support, Organizing for Change, and Implementing Programs*. San Francisco: Jossey-Bass, 1999.

"Strategies for Helping Supervisors Succeed with Student Employees." University of Colorado–Boulder. https://www.colorado.edu/studentemployment/sites/default/files/attached-files/strategies_for_supervisors.pdf. Accessed October 30, 2019.

"Student Employment." Fordham University. https://www.fordham.edu/info/21343/student_employment. Accessed July 5, 2019.

12

Leaning toward Joy

Affective Labor, ADHD, and Being Alt-Ac

MATTHEW J. TRYBUS WITH
EMILY O. GRAVETT

There are many professionals who inhabit alt-ac spaces, either by choice or by necessity. Some—like librarians, writing center staff, and digital/networked humanists[1]—have begun to critically reflect on the various roles that they inhabit in these spaces, particularly as it comes to performing often invisible, but critically necessary, affective labor. Those who work in learning centers have tended to focus almost exclusively on students in their scholarship, primarily studying tutors and clients (e.g., their learning, their training, etc.) rather than turning a critical lens on themselves or their colleagues.[2] Perhaps such professionals worry that by exploring their own roles or development, they are taking time away from the students they are supposed to be supporting. This chapter, however, focuses squarely on one man's experiences working in a learning center, an alt-ac space, in the context of higher education, disability, and affective labor.

We have several reasons for writing this chapter. In part, we want to add to the voices participating in alt-ac conversations. Learning center professionals have an important perspective to contribute too.

We would also like to work through the ways that identity, privilege, and oppression intersect, when, for instance, a white man finds himself performing affective labor, typically associated with women and the stereotypically feminine, in an alt-ac space. We would also like to model a certain (perhaps still unusual) coauthorship approach, which, like the "dialogic mode of collaboration" that Lisa Ede and Andrea Lunsford described decades ago, involves fluid roles, a loose structure, and an appreciation of multiple perspectives.[3] Finally, we would like to trouble and move beyond the pernicious "deficit" model of disability—to explore not only the very real challenges and limitations related to affective labor that result from a disability like attention-deficit/hyperactivity disorder (ADHD), but also the many opportunities, advantages, even gifts.

THE WRITING PROCESS

The two of us (Matt and Emily) came together to write for the first time on another piece related to disability—in the context of "educational development," the name for the sort of work that professionals at centers for teaching and learning do (as described in chapter 7 of this collection). Emily invited two colleagues, one of whom was Matt, who were experts in disability and disability studies, to write with her.[4] While she knew the field of educational development well, her knowledge of disability and disability studies was inchoate; she knew she couldn't write that piece alone. After taking some time to ponder the invitation, Matt enthusiastically agreed with the understanding that he would benefit from support throughout the writing process.

Through that collaboration, we each learned how the other one worked. Matt is easily able to share ideas verbally, but doing so in writing has often posed a challenge for him. Indeed, he describes his college experience as "a series of unfinished Blue Book essays." Emily quickly realized that if she wanted to harness all that Matt had to offer, she was going to have to change how she conceived of scholarly collaborations and adjust how she worked with him. Emily's previous experiences of coauthorship had led her to think it meant both people wrote—and usually relatively equally, depending, perhaps, on the order of authorship. Instead, what we did is set up camp in Matt's office regularly, with each of us sharing ideas and Emily transcribing them; later, Matt would read drafts and provide feedback and revisions while Emily helped to give them their final form. While we are both aware of the gendered history of women playing this kind of role (e.g., serving as the underpaid and underappreciated secretaries, court reporters, and so on who support men in more prestigious roles), this is just the sort of task Emily enjoys and excels at. What developed was an equitable, scholarly partnership, deeply informed by our individual working styles and preferences and built upon the strengths and needs of each person.

That experience was both time-consuming and incredibly rewarding. It resulted in the publication of an essay about disability that we hope will inform, perhaps even transform, the field of educational development. It was also incredibly emotional. One day, while working in Matt's office, he began to tear up. Emily wasn't quite sure what was happening, so she sat quietly, waiting for the moment to unfold. Matt eventually explained that he had always had trouble viewing himself as a scholar. He felt that others misunderstood how he worked best or, if they did understand, they did not know how to operationalize it. This was the first time Matt felt like he was engaging in a true scholarly collaboration, in the written form, with someone who really understood him. It was an example of "access intimacy," which is

> that elusive, hard to describe feeling when someone else "gets" your access needs. The kind of eerie comfort that your disabled self feels with someone on a purely access level. Sometimes it can happen with complete strangers, disabled or not, or sometimes it can be built over years. It could also be the way your body relaxes and opens up with someone when all your access needs are being met. It is not dependent on someone having a political understanding of disability, ableism or access. Some of the people I have experienced the deepest access intimacy with (especially able-bodied people) have had no education or exposure to a political understanding of disability.[5]

When Emily saw the call for proposals (CFP) for this volume, she had the idea that Matt could contribute something meaningful—something about his ADHD and the amazing (affective) work he does through his role in the learning centers. Yet she knew he would be resistant, even fearful, at the prospect. The identity of scholar is still an uneasy one for him; he often feels like an "impostor," as, admittedly, many academics do.[6] But Emily also knows that Matt trusts her and that he will seriously consider any idea she brings to him. After a bit of humorous hemming and hawing, which Emily has come to expect, Matt started riffing on the CFP, sharing thoughts and experiences related to the volume's theme.

Due to the vulnerability of putting himself out there on the page, he said he didn't want to work on a chapter alone and asked Emily if she would coauthor with him again. Because Emily loves collaborating with others, especially friends, and because she wanted to help Matt get his ideas out there—ideas that might not have otherwise seen the light—she agreed.

AD(H)D

Just as Matt and Emily had a journey toward coauthorship, Matt had his own journey toward discovering his disability. After years spent wondering whether he might have ADHD, Matt was finally diagnosed by a psychiatrist in 2005. The diagnosis came after a series of clinical screenings (e.g., Thomas Brown's rating scale, Conner's Continuous Performance Test) and interviews—with him, his partner, and even his parents. Part of his goal was simply to confirm what he had sensed for a long time. Over the years, Matt could see himself in students who were struggling and who had ADHD. Matt also thought it might be helpful, based on what was going on in his life at that time, to see if medication would help his symptoms.

Since his diagnosis over a decade ago, Matt has sought to better understand his disability, in part by turning toward resources like Gabor Maté's *Scattered: How Attention Deficit Disorder Originates and What You Can Do about It* and Thomas Brown's *Attention Deficit Disorder: The Unfocused Mind in Children and Adults.* In defining what he refers to as attention-deficit disorder (ADD), Brown did not intend to offer a diagnosis different from Attention-Deficit Hyperactivity Disorder (ADHD) in *The Diagnostic and Statistical Manual of Mental Disorders*; rather, he wanted to "propose a new way of looking at these impairments, of which many, but not all, are encompassed in current diagnostic criteria."[7] According to Brown, those with what he calls "ADD syndrome" have chronic difficulties in: (1) organizing, prioritizing, and getting started (i.e., activation), (2) focusing, sustaining, and shifting attention (i.e., focus), (3) regulating alertness, sustaining effort, and determining processing speed (i.e., effort), (4) managing frustration and modulating emotions (i.e., emotion), (5) utilizing working memory and accessing recall (i.e., memory), and (6) monitoring and regulating actions (i.e., action).[8]

In a typical workday in the Learning Centers, Matt experiences numerous difficulties that fit into Brown's model. Although colleagues like

Emily also experience, at times, some of these same difficulties, Matt is often left wondering just how much the ADHD is a contributing factor. For the sake of this chapter, we will discuss just a few of the areas in Brown's model that are most relatable to him—and potentially to readers. It should be clear, however, that the ways in which these challenges show up are specific to Matt and to the varying contexts in which he finds himself. We are concerned that Brown's model may inadvertently give the impression that ADHD challenges will be present in the same way at all times for people with ADHD, regardless of time or space.

The hardest area for Matt is the first on the aforementioned list of difficulties: *activation*. Brown writes that "those with this syndrome often complain that procrastination is a major problem. . . . They keep putting off important tasks until the task has become an emergency."[9] Matt frequently procrastinates on major tasks, putting them off until the last minute. Deadlines are challenging for him. In years past, he has turned in his annual evaluation a couple of weeks late because he misjudged how much time the task was going to take and because he was working on other projects that required less energy and effort and that he found more interesting. Sometimes Matt's workflow feels like a series of doors or a Rube Goldberg machine; he puts pressure on himself to fully complete one task, jump over one hurdle, before he allows himself to move on to the next, sometimes regardless of importance or urgency.

Matt also experiences challenges in terms of the second area on Brown's list: *focus*. Brown describes "excessive distractibility," that those "persons with ADD syndrome have chronic and severe difficulty screening out those distracting stimuli. They cannot ignore the myriad thoughts, background noises, and perceptions in the surrounding environment."[10] Email notifications pop up on Matt's computer and he gets easily pulled away from what he is trying to focus on. One click on a Wikipedia link or YouTube video can take him down a rabbit hole for hours. During conversations, he regularly finds himself going off on tangents; Emily often has to tell him, "FOCUS!" Brown also notes that "while trying to compose a letter, responses to an essay exam, a report, or some other written project, they find themselves stuck on one phrase or one particular sentence, working and reworking it in an effort to make it perfect."[11] This was part of the struggle for Matt with his annual evaluation and basically anything else he writes, including his master's thesis and even this chapter; he procrastinates, in part, because he wants to make everything perfect.

Like anyone else, Matt sometimes experiences boredom or irritability, though he wonders if this is a way his ADHD affects his *emotions*. At times, his sense of overwhelm about various tasks and deadlines leads to him shutting down, feeling doubt, frustration, stress, and inadequacy as a result. Yet, like many of the people whom Brown studied, Matt experiences a great deal of "insufficiently controlled excitability."[12] Rather humorously, one of his student leaders wrote on an evaluation of his that "sometimes Matt's enthusiasm is scary." Though Brown presents all of these categories in "ADD syndrome" as challenges—and certainly many people with ADHD do experience them in this way—Matt's experiences with the emotional realm, in particular, have been more positive, as we will describe. He has so much capacity for, and love of, emotion and affective labor and he feels that he draws much energy and strength from them.

ALT-AC AND IDENTITY

Currently, Matt works as the coordinator of the Peer Assisted Study Sessions (PASS) program, also known as supplemental instruction, in our university's Learning Centers. Programs like these are often co-housed with writing centers, math and science labs, student success centers, learning assistance programs, English-language learner services, and communication centers—basically, anyone who facilitates student development and academic success by helping students develop appropriate strategies and behaviors to increase learning efficiency.[13] In this chapter, we primarily refer to Matt's position as Learning Centers staff, though he is, technically, a faculty member, because it reflects the name of the unit he works for. The students he supports in the PASS program, "PASS leaders," are more generally referred to as "peer educators." Students who contribute to similar efforts or work in similar programs at other institutions may also be referred to as tutors, consultants, or peer leaders in the literature. This variability, even confusion, in the terminology may be related, in part, to the alt-ac nature of the work and the people who pursue it; nobody is quite sure how to classify or what to call the various professionals in these roles.

The Learning Centers inhabits a liminal space on our campus. Reporting both to Academic Affairs and Student Affairs over the years, the Learning Centers found a new home under the vice provost for Student Academic Success and Enrollment Management within the Academic Affairs division of the university. The broader campus community does not always seem to understand its location in the institutional hierarchy.

The Learning Centers serves both students, through its peer educators, and faculty—either indirectly, by supporting their courses with peer educators, or directly, by offering professional development opportunities (as in writing instruction consultations). It is physically located in our university's Student Success Center, which houses other student-oriented yet nonacademic services, such as the University Health Center, Orientation, Dean of Students, and Counseling and Psychological Services. Many of the faculty with whom Matt and his colleagues work may associate the Learning Centers with Student Affairs, which is not always viewed with as much respect or credibility.

Matt himself inhabits a liminal space within the Learning Centers. As noted, his position is classified as "instructional faculty" and he is a ten-month employee, like most other instructional faculty, yet he does not belong to a disciplinary department, he does not hold professorial rank, he is not on the tenure track, his terminal degree is a MEd, and he is not eligible for promotion. (Before this job, he worked for seven years in another alt-ac space on campus, the Office of Disability Services.) As PASS coordinator, he holds less prestige and power, and earns lower pay, than other instructional faculty (most of whom hold doctoral degrees). It is difficult for him to even get a raise (beyond occasional cost-of-living increases) without acquiring more education (unlikely at this point in his life) or somehow attaining a new title.

Although he works in an underappreciated center on campus and although he identifies as having a disability, which comes with its own set of oppressions, stigmas, and discriminations, Matt recognizes that he is privileged in many ways too. As a white person, Matt wields privilege in this world and on our predominantly and historically white campus. White men dominate academia, benefiting from the entrenched systems of patriarchy and white supremacy in the United States.[14] As Michael Kimmel and Bethany Coston note, "Despite their sometimes stigmatized status, [disabled men] do have access to sites of privilege," simply by virtue of being men.[15] As a man in academia, Matt experiences privilege in many ways. For example, his colleagues and students assume he was hired on the basis of his own merits, not because of affirmative action; if he adjusts his work schedule around child care, people admire him for being a good parent; he can dress informally for work and still be taken seriously; he expects his voice will be heard and that people won't question his expertise; if he is passionate about something, he won't be judged as overly emotional or irrational (except maybe by his students on funny end-of-year evaluations!). We feel it is important to recognize, as Kimmel and Coston do, the "dynamics of having privilege in one sphere but being unprivileged in another arena."[16]

Yet being a man in this particular alt-ac space can be confusing for Matt. Matt works mostly with women: of the PASS leaders, about two-thirds are women, the gender breakdown is similar among his colleagues, and he reports to a phenomenal woman leader. The work that the Learning Centers staff does is focused on helping other people—students and even faculty—so it is similar to other helping, "pink-collar" professions (see chapter 7 in this volume), such as nursing, which are mostly inhabited by women. It is precisely the kind of other- and service-oriented labor that women tend to perform in the United States, at home and in the workplace. And, of course, the qualities necessary for succeeding in this sort of work environment include compassion, empathy, kindness, patience, altruism—all of which are stereotypical "feminine." Matt finds himself working in a space surrounded by women, pursuing a career associated with women, and performing labor that is disproportionately borne by women. While our society tells us that "men, especially disabled men, must avoid emotional expression,"[17] Matt's experience is that such expressions—and their associated labor—are impossible to avoid in his role.

ADHD IN ACADEMIA

Matt's various identities, including ADHD, have affected his work in higher education in many ways. Academia itself is ableist and generally feels exclusionary to Matt—and, we know, to many other faculty and staff with disabilities.[18] As Beverly Tatum writes, "Whether one succumbs to the devaluing pressures of the dominant culture or successfully resides them, the fact is that dealing with oppressive systems from the underside, regardless of the strategy, is physically and psychologically taxing."[19] Given some of Brown's findings—that "it is not unusual for individuals with ADD syndrome to drop out or fail out of college"[20]—it is remarkable that Matt graduated from college at all, let alone going on to earn his master's in education.

In his master's thesis, Matt wrote openly about the challenges he experienced in academia, particularly in the realm of scholarship, due to what he referred to then as ADD. It is worth quoting at length here:

> Like many other ADDer's, my mind lacks a template for order, a mental model of how organization comes about. . . . My challenge is that the

mind-set and hardware to get me where I want to go seem to be missing. At times, it can take me an hour to craft a single paragraph and hours to author a page. The number, breadth, and complexity of my ideas are tangled up in my head like knots. Words, sentences, and paragraphs do not come to me in a linear manner so I wrestle with them doing my best to link them together in a way that most clearly articulates my meaning to myself and to my readers. "Is that what I *truly* believe?" "Is that what I *really* meant to say?" Couple these challenges with the difficulty I have modulating and filtering my attention. Every moment I am faced with a countless variety of internal (thoughts, emotions, physical) and external (tasks, obligations, physical) stimuli, each one of these has the potential to lure me away from writing for second, minutes, hours, days, and weeks at a time. A characteristic observation among members of the ADD community is how much more time and energy it takes us to do things compared to our non-ADD peers. This is just one of the reasons why this is so. When engaged in scholarly writing, I perceive ADD as a dam. It is a barrier across the deep, broad, swiftly moving waters of my "metaphysical life space, the internalized world of individual, philosophical consciousness" that retards and obstructs the flow of my communication with the world outside of myself to a trickle. In spite of this great challenge, I still love words, writing, and expressing myself in this way. I find the writing process intrinsically rewarding and enriching.[21]

Despite his advanced degrees, and despite flourishing in his current position, even thinking about proposing and writing a chapter for this volume was intimidating to Matt. It is not simply that writing is still a struggle for Matt, as he experienced with his thesis many years ago. The call for proposals, though written by a scholar who herself identifies as having ADHD, included language that felt alienating to him, such as: "the ever-popular and much-derided 'quit lit' is an example of the affective impact of the choice to opt out of the tenure-track rate race." He found himself asking questions like, "What does the CFP even mean?" and "Why is so much of the writing in higher education inaccessible, even to those of us in it?"

Unlike students, who may be supported by units like our Office of Disability Services, faculty and staff in higher education may not always find dedicated systems in place to help them navigate academia with a disability. At our institution, like many others, the entity that employees with disabilities are supposed to turn to is Human Resources (HR). Notably, Matt has chosen not to seek any "accommodations" through HR so far. Having to "out" himself to the institution feels like it would be a time-consuming, onerous process—more of a barrier than any of the benefits he might be qualified to receive. It is his personal protest against the system, which seeks to help but can actually create more problems for those who need it. (We both have colleagues who fear attitude shifts, retribution, even job loss as a result of disclosing their disabilities, so we understand that legal protections and HR accommodations are essential.) Matt has also been fortunate to work with people, like his current director, who have been willing to create work environments that allow him to function well, which has prevented him from needing any legal accommodations through the framework of HR.

It is also the case that, throughout his life, Matt has figured out enough ways to navigate the world that he can't foresee any accommodation helping him. He has developed numerous skills to compensate for his ADHD. Yet Emily wonders if these skills are really compensatory or if they are actually the *result* of the ADHD. Matt has an ability to connect deeply with others, to empathize, to lead with love. These are a gift. And Matt is not the only one who has viewed this disability in such a light. There are numerous online articles, editorials, and blog posts devoted to the beauty and the benefits of living with ADHD.[22] These writings suggest that those who have ADHD also excel in spontaneity, imagination and creativity, energy, innovation, perseverance and resilience, compassion, empathy, laser- or hyper focus, problem solving, observation, humor, a zeal for life, even love. In his work with students (as well as colleagues, as Emily can attest), Matt brings an unbridled positivity and energy. It is as Thich Nhat Hanh has written: "Roses and garbage inter-are. Without a rose, we cannot have garbage; and without garbage, we cannot have a rose. They need each other very much. The rose and the garbage are equal. The garbage is just as precious as the rose."[23] So, as challenging as ADHD and affective labor can be, for Matt, he also views them both as key to teaching and learning. He chooses to lean toward joy.

AFFECTIVE LABOR

Being coordinator of the PASS program entails a range of responsibilities, most of which require affective labor of some sort. It occurs to us that the liminality of alt-ac spaces, such as the Learning Centers, may actually facilitate the sorts of close, emotional relationships with students, and the accompanying affective labor involved, that more "traditional" academic spaces, like the undergraduate classroom, may not. For instance, many professors are hesitant to get to know their students personally or to recognize them as whole human beings. Yet Matt has had a chance to get to know students deeply, making lasting emotional connections with the PASS leaders whom he supervises, especially. These PASS leaders are primarily responsible for tutoring their fellow students, mainly in STEM courses. The seventy-three PASS leaders who Matt supervises typically support about fifteen courses, fifty unique faculty members, and over 4,500 unique students. The impact they have on campus is hard to convey. In the past academic year alone, Matt spent over two hundred documented hours in trainings, meetings, observations, discussions, and other mentoring activities related to his work with students, sometimes late into the evenings or over the weekends. Although Mary Ellen Guy and Meredith Newman claim that "caring work is exceptional or optional for men, while it is obligatory for women,"[24] Matt's particular position also requires it.

Acting as their cheerleader and keeper of the program's overall goals, Matt encourages and supports students in the ways that they want to grow. As Sarah Rose Cavanagh shows convincingly, "emotions enhance learning" because they can harness attention, maximize working memory potential, enhance memory consolidation, and inspire motivation (both individual and communal).[25] Matt brings emotion and energy to his interactions with students, he motivates, he keeps up the vision as well as the momentum, and he asks a lot of questions of his students (e.g., what do you want to work on? what are your hopes? how are you doing?). In his annual evaluations (which Matt was embarrassed to include here, but which Emily thought were an apt indication of the affective labor he performs), his PASS leaders note that he is inspirational, compassionate, caring, friendly, personable, encouraging, welcoming, and kind. These are, in fact, many of the same "traits most predictive of teaching success" as reported by Cavanagh: active and enthusiastic, mindful and humorous, supportive and warm, confident and optimistic.[26]

Here are some comments that illustrate how Matt shows up emotionally to support his students:

> Matt is the most inspiring individual I have ever worked with, and this is no understatement. He has seen me through so many highs and lows and has helped me foster a deeper connection to JMU, student engagement, and to myself. He is much more than a boss; he is a mentor and guiding light through what may sometimes be dark woods. He values transpar-

ency, overcoming barriers, and accommodating needs. I want to be like Matt when I grow up.

He's a very passionate person and I think he has an amazing ability to uplift people while also giving good feedback. I think he is an amazing motivator and I really appreciated having him as a mentor for PASS.

He has an innate ability to make someone feel valued. I know he will say he doesn't do much, but Matt is a fortifying glue.

A STORY

To more richly illustrate the type of affective labor that Matt performs in the Learning Centers, relating to and encouraging his students, we want to share a story about an encounter he had with one of his PASS leaders, Alyssa. (We asked Alyssa, and she gave us the okay to share.) Alyssa was in her final year at our university, after working with Matt as a PASS leader for two years. One of her personal and professional goals was to be more present and a better listener. As a nursing student at the time, part of her philosophy was that in order to help people heal, listening is an important skill. Alyssa was sick that day, but it didn't seem to Matt like she wasn't listening to *herself* very well.

In the past, Matt had shared with Alyssa the children's book *Three Questions* by Jon Muth, which is based upon a parable by Leo Tolstoy. In it, the main character asks, "When is the best time to do things?" "Who is the most important one?" "What is the right thing to do?" (The ultimate lesson is: "Remember then that there is only one important time, and that time is now. The most important one is always the one you are with. And the most important thing is to do good for the one who is standing at your side. For these, my dear boy, are the answers to what is most important in this world. . . . This is why we are here."[27]) Matt appreciates simple remedies like this to quiet the mind. He and Alyssa had been meeting with another student during the semester who was interested in practicing silent meditation and, though that student wasn't with them that day, Matt asked Alyssa if she wanted to do a meditation anyway. Instead of sitting quietly together, he offered that they could listen to something. Sometimes Matt has an uncanny ability to predict what's best in certain moments. Sometimes he thinks of it as intuition, but after spending thousands of hours in one-on-one conversations with students over the years, he has also acquired an ability to know, in a short amount of time, just where people's challenges are and just what they might need. He knew that Alyssa needed some quiet time and space right then.

Matt offered Alyssa a choice of five episodes from a *Live Awake* podcast, by Sarah Blondin (n.d.), that he loves. Alyssa wound up selecting the specific episode he had in mind for her, "Exploring the Wilderness of Your Discomfort." They listened to the entire episode quietly together. In it, Blondin asks questions such as: "[What] if we could learn to wander in instead of away?" and "What could it look like if we stayed put?" She encourages listeners to "adventure into the wilderness of your own discomfort," "step forward to your edge," "look into the face of what we usually turn from," "bring light to the unchartered territories of your own life," and "venture out into what life is offering you." This episode focuses on "the gift of being fully present."[28] As she was listening, Alyssa started to cry, just gentle tears running down her face. Healthy Alyssa might not have had the same reaction, but sick Alyssa had her defenses down. Sick Alyssa was receptive to the experience, to feeling her feelings. And Emily wants to note that there is also great emotional work required for Matt in moments such as this—to feel his own feelings and to not be afraid of the feelings of others.

Part of the lesson of this moment, for Alyssa and Matt, was: let's pause, let's practice empathy for ourselves, let's open ourselves up to whatever message life is giving us. How can you be a good nurse, a good healer, if you can't listen to yourself? Sometimes it's easier to have empathy and compassion for others than ourselves. We have all been where Alyssa was—when we're low and our minds are racing and we don't feel well and there is so much to be done—and then we have been given an important message, a gift, really. What Alyssa heard that day from the podcast, and from Matt, was to stay in her body, to give herself permission to be uncomfortable, that this thing that feels hard or horrible is maybe also good. And that's affective labor. To us, it seems like it's not a woman or a man thing, but a human thing.

CONCLUSION

Throughout this chapter, we have explored affective labor in the context of the complex intersections of various parts of Matt's identity and positionality: his job in an alt-ac space in our university, his gender identity as a man in a woman-dominated unit and profession, and, especially, his disability of ADHD. At times, the interrelations among these various parts were so complex that we didn't even know how to organize the different sections in this chapter! But life is messy, and an ADHD brain can sometimes be chaotic, so we simply decided to embrace it, in all of its beauty and hilarity and truth.

Matt's ADHD shows up in many ways, in both his personal and professional life. Although he certainly experiences numerous challenges in academia and in his alt-ac role as a result, readers may have also been surprised to learn from this chapter that he feels *better* able to perform affective labor—labor that is required of his alt-ac job, regardless of the particular gender of the person performing it—because of it. This is no deficit narrative of disability here. Rather, Matt brings an energy, enthusiasm, and empathy to his work that we know inspires and nourishes his students, not just intellectually, but emotionally too.

We have a hunch that these qualities and behaviors are a result of ADHD, either directly or indirectly, as he learned to navigate the world with it. In his specific role as PASS coordinator in the Learning Centers, Matt is able to be with the students, deeply and authentically, to move beyond supervision toward real relationship, to get into the arena with them and do the hard work of connecting and feeling and growing. His ADHD is not something to overcome, not some "despite . . . " that he and others must begrudgingly tolerate or work around. Rather, Matt's disability, and his lived experience of it, has become a tremendous resource in his pursuit of this type of affective labor and his ability to lean toward joy.

NOTES

1. For example, see Anne Ellen Geller and Harry Denny, "Of Ladybugs, Low Status, and Loving the Job: Writing Center Professionals Navigating Their Careers," *Writing Center Journal* 33, no. 1 (2013): 96–129.

2. There are exceptions, of course; see, for instance, Sherry Wynn Perdue, Dana Lynn Driscoll, and Andrew Petrykowski, "Centering Institutional Status and Scholarly Identity: An Analysis of Writing Center Administration Position Advertisements, 2004–2014," *Writing Center Journal* 36, no. 2 (2017): 265–293.

3. Lisa Ede and Andrea Lunsford, *Singular Texts/Plural Authors: Perspectives on Collaborative Writing* (Carbondale: Southern Illinois University Press, 1990).

4. Matthew J. Trybus, Daisy L. Breneman, and Emily O. Gravett, "Ableism, Accessibility, and Educational Development: A Disability Studies Perspective," *New Directions for Teaching and Learning*, no. 158 (2019): 59–68.

5. M. Mingus, "Access Intimacy: The Missing Link. Leaving Evidence, May

5, 2011. https://leavingevidence.wordpress.com/2011/05/05/access-intimacy-the-missing-link/.

6. See, for example, John Gravois, "You're Not Fooling Anyone," Chronicle of Higher Education, November 9, 2007. https://www.chronicle.com/article/Youre-Not-Fooling-Anyone/28069; and Joseph Kasper, "An Academic with Impostor Syndrome," Chronicle of Higher Education, April 2, 2013. https://www.chronicle.com/article/An-Academic-With-Impostor/138231.

7. Thomas Brown, *Attention Deficit Disorder: The Unfocused Mind in Children and Adults* (New Haven, CT: Yale University Press, 2006), viii.

8. Brown, *Attention Deficit Disorder*, v.

9. Brown, 23.

10. Brown, 31.

11. Brown, 34.

12. Brown, 40.

13. Donald F. Dansereau, "Learning Strategy Research," in Judith W. Segal, Susan F. Chipman, and Robert Glaser, eds., *Thinking and Learning Skills* (Hillsdale, NJ: Erlbaum, 1985).

14. P. L. Thomas, "Power, Responsibility, and the White Men of Academia," HuffPost, May 30. 2017. https://www.huffpost.com/entry/power-responsibility-and-the-white-men-of-academia_b_592d58bce4b08861edoccbce.

15. Michael S. Kimmel and Bethany M. Coston, "Seeing Privilege Where It Isn't: Marginalized Masculinities and the Intersectionality of Privilege," in Michael S. Kimmel and Abby L. Ferber, eds., *Privilege: A Reader*, 4th ed. (Boulder, CO: Westview Press, 2017), 169.

16. Kimmel and Coston, "Seeing Privilege Where It Isn't," 161.

17. Kimmel and Coston, 167.

18. Mary Lee Vance, ed., *Disabled Faculty and Staff in a Disabling Society: Multiple Identities in Higher Education* (Huntersville, NC: AHEAD, 2007); Margaret Price, *Mad at School: Rhetorics of Mental Disability and Academic Life* (Ann Arbor: University of Michigan Press, 2011); Jay Timothy Dolmage, *Academic Ableism: Disability and Higher Education* (Ann Arbor: University of Michigan Press, 2017).

19. Beverly Daniel Tatum, "The Complexity of Identity: 'Who Am I?,'" in Maurianne Adams et al., eds., *Readings for Diversity and Social Justice: An Anthology on Racism, Anti-Semitism, Sexism, Heterosexism, Ableism, and Classism*, 1st ed. (New York: Routledge, 2000), 9–14.

20. Brown, *Attention Deficit Disorder*, 145.

21. Matthew John Trybus, *Charting the Course: Reframing Disability Services in Higher Education*, master's thesis, University of Vermont, 2007.

22. See, for instance, Additude Editors, "What I Would Never Trade Away," *ADDITUDE: Inside the ADHD Mind*, https://www.additudemag.com/slideshows/positives-of-adhd/ (accessed September 2, 2021); Scott Barry

Kaufman, "The Creative Gifts of ADHD," *Scientific American* (blog), October 21, 2014, https://blogs.scientificamerican.com/beautiful-minds/the-creative-gifts-of-adhd/; and Healthline, "The Benefits of ADHD," https://www.healthline.com/health/adhd/benefits-of-adhd#1. Accessed September 2, 2021.

23. Thich Nhat Hanh, *Peace Is Every Step: The Path of Mindfulness in Everyday Life* (New York: Bantam, 1991), 96–97.

24. Mary Ellen Guy and Meredith A. Newman, "Women's Jobs, Men's Jobs: Sex Segregation and Emotional Labor," *Public Administration Review* 64, no. 3 (2004): 289–298.

25. Sarah Rose Cavanagh, *The Spark of Learning: Energizing the College Classroom with the Science of Emotion* (Morgantown: West Virginia University Press, 2016), 32.

26. Cavanagh, *The Spark of Learning*, 32–110.

27. Jon J. Muth, *The Three Questions: Based on a Story by Leo Tolstoy* (New York: Scholastic, 2002).

28. Sarah Blondin, "Exploring the Wilderness of Your Discomfort." *Live Awake* (podcast). N.d. https://soundcloud.com/liveawakepodcast/podcast-exploring-the-wilderness-of-your-discomfort.

BIBLIOGRAPHY

Additude Editors. "What I Would Never Trade Away." ADDITUDE: Inside the ADHD Mind. n.d. https://www.additudemag.com/slideshows/positives-of-adhd/.

Blondin, Sarah. "Exploring the Wilderness of Your Discomfort." *Live Awake* (podcast). n.d. https://soundcloud.com/liveawakepodcast/podcast-exploring-the-wilderness-of-your-discomfort.

Brown, Thomas. *Attention Deficit Disorder: The Unfocused Mind in Children and Adults*. New Haven, CT: Yale University Press, 2006.

Cavanagh, Sarah Rose. *The Spark of Learning: Energizing the College Classroom with the Science of Emotion*. Morgantown: West Virginia University Press, 2016.

Dansereau, Donald F. "Learning Strategy Research." In Judith W. Segal, Susan F. Chipman, and Robert Glaser, eds., *Thinking and Learning Skills*. Hillsdale, NJ: Erlbaum, 1985.

Dolmage, Jay Timothy. *Academic Ableism: Disability and Higher Education*. Ann Arbor: University of Michigan Press, 2017.

Ede, Lisa, and Andrea Lunsford. *Singular Texts/Plural Authors: Perspectives on Collaborative Writing*. Carbondale: Southern Illinois University Press, 1990.

Geller, Anne Ellen, and Harry Denny. "Of Ladybugs, Low Status, and Loving the Job: Writing Center Professionals Navigating Their Careers." *Writing Center Journal* 33, no. 1 (2013): 96–129.

Gravois, John. "You're Not Fooling Anyone." Chronicle of Higher Education. November 9, 2007. https://www.chronicle.com/article/Youre-Not-Fooling-Anyone/28069.

Guy, Mary Ellen, and Meredith A. Newman. "Women's Jobs, Men's Jobs: Sex Segregation and Emotional Labor." *Public Administration Review* 64, no. 3 (2004): 289–298.

Hanh, Thich Nhat. *Peace Is Every Step: The Path of Mindfulness in Everyday Life*. New York: Bantam, 1991.

Healthline. "The Benefits of ADHD." n.d. https://www.healthline.com/health/adhd/benefits-of-adhd#1. Accessed September 2, 2021.

Kasper, Joseph. "An Academic with Impostor Syndrome." Chronicle of Higher Education. April 2, 2013. https://www.chronicle.com/article/An-Academic-With-Impostor/138231.

Kaufman, Scott Barry. "The Creative Gifts of ADHD." *Scientific American* (blog). October 21, 2014. https://blogs.scientificamerican.com/beautiful-minds/the-creative-gifts-of-adhd/.

Kimmel, Michael S., and Bethany M. Coston. "Seeing Privilege Where It Isn't: Marginalized Masculinities and the Intersectionality of Privilege." In Michael S. Kimmel and Abby L. Ferber, eds., *Privilege: A Reader*, 4th ed. Boulder, CO: Westview Press, 2017.

Mingus, M. "Access Intimacy: The Missing Link." Leaving Evidence. May 5, 2011. https://leavingevidence.wordpress.com/2011/05/05/access-intimacy-the-missing-link/.

Muth, Jon J. *The Three Questions: Based on a Story by Leo Tolstoy*. New York: Scholastic, 2002.

Perdue, Sherry Wynn, Dana Lynn Driscoll, and Andrew Petrykowski. "Centering Institutional Status and Scholarly Identity: An Analysis of Writing Center Administration Position Advertisements, 2004–2014." *Writing Center Journal* 36, no. 2 (2017): 265–293.

Price, Margaret. *Mad at School: Rhetorics of Mental Disability and Academic Life*. Ann Arbor: University of Michigan Press, 2011.

Tatum, Beverly Daniel. "The Complexity of Identity: 'Who Am I?'" In Maurianne Adams, Warren J. Blumenfeld, Heather W. Hackman, Madelin L. Peters, and Zimena Zúñiga, eds., *Readings for Diversity and Social Justice: An Anthology on Racism, Anti-Semitism, Sexism, Heterosexism, Ableism, and Classism*, 1st ed., 9–14). New York: Routledge, 2000.

Thomas, P. L. "Power, Responsibility, and the White Men of Academia." Huff Post. May 30, 2017. https://www.huffpost.com/entry/power-responsibility-and-the-white-men-of-academia_b_592d58bce4b08861ed0ccbce.

Trybus, Matthew John. *Charting the Course: Reframing Disability Services in Higher Education*. Master's thesis. University of Vermont, 2007.

Trybus, Matthew J., Daisy L. Breneman, and Emily O. Gravett. "Ableism, Accessibility, and Educational Development: A Disability Studies Perspective." *New Directions for Teaching and Learning*, no. 158 (2019): 59–68.

Vance, Mary Lee, ed. *Disabled Faculty and Staff in a Disabling Society: Multiple Identities in Higher Education*. Huntersville, NC: AHEAD, 2007.

13

Honoring Others by Honoring Ourselves

Affective Labor and Mentoring Programs

LEEANN HUNTER

I launched a professional development and mentoring program—called the Passport Program—at Washington State University (WSU) in spring 2016 to provide a creative and supportive space where students could grow personally and professionally. On the surface, the program provides much-needed services to our students in mentoring and professional development. In practice, the program runs much deeper, providing a nurturant space where students are received, supported, and honored. An early breakthrough in the program occurred when I invested over a dozen hours meeting with new students enrolled in the program to discuss their goals and obstacles, broadly framed. I was unprepared for the deeply personal turn these conversations would take, and over the course of two weeks, this practice fundamentally changed who I was as a teacher and community member, as my students broke my heart, infused me with life, and transformed my way of being in the university system. These meetings taught me that I had found my calling in supporting our students, that I had identified a crucial need in the university system, and that I would never survive if I tried to replicate this experiment even once. The emotional labor that I had invested in this project was enormous.

Around that same time, I was introduced to the science and art of self-compassion. The practice caught me by surprise. I hadn't realized that I was practicing more kindness toward others than I was for myself. The small shift I had been invited to take—to talk to myself as if I were my best friend—was a radical notion for me. This small practice launched me onto a journey of self-compassion that included the cultivation of my inner mentor—a voice that would send me words of loving-kindness, forgiveness, and support as I continued to tackle life's challenges. As I learned new tools to support myself, I became more interested in learning how to better support my students, without sacrificing my own well-being.

In this chapter I chronicle the profound experiences and insights I have accumulated in this heart-centered and student-centered mentoring practice, which largely revolve around mental health concerns. The challenges I have faced in meeting these expectations over multiple semesters has led to the development of structural innovations as well as insights from life-coaching practices (which I received training in through Tara Mohr's Playing Big facilitators training program, based on her book).[1] In the end, I hope to present a process for mentoring that honors both the student and the mentor, leading entirely from the heart but also from a disciplined and boundary-driven practice.

I draw upon the conceptual framework proposed in *Mentoring Undergraduate Students*, a 2017 report by the Association for the Study of Higher Education (ASHE).[2] In this framework, the authors outline the following forms of support that are provided in the mentoring literature they surveyed:

> (a) psychological and emotional support such as interacting in an authentic and caring manner, encouraging, motivating students, relating to their worldview, affirming, and befriending; (b) degree completion support such as advising, providing feedback, and helping students navigate academic policy and degree requirements; (c) academic subject knowledge support such as teaching, sharing information, involving students in research, and creating awareness of resources; and (d) career development support such as networking, internships and apprenticeships, career goal and aspiration setting, and role modeling.[3]

While the Passport Program addresses each form of support identified here, the kind of mentoring that I'm writing about is primarily the psychological and emotional support, focused on helping students develop a self-compassionate voice in the world—especially for those who are suffering from unrealistically high expectations of themselves, or from a fear of not understanding knowledge in the way that social class has constructed it to be. As I share my own experiences with mentoring, I acknowledge that I fall under the latter category—often feeling less socially educated and cultivated, and having to coach myself to believe that my different ways of experiencing the world, of creating new knowledge, of understanding deeply, all have tremendous value to add to the world. Over time, I have learned that my value is enormous precisely because of my experiences in the world, and because of my struggles, and because I have found support in launching forward on this journey. I aim to share these lessons with the students I mentor and in the program I have developed.

EDUCATIONAL CONTEXT: WHY I CREATED THE PASSPORT PROGRAM

I write from the perspective of someone who struggled to navigate the educational system and who benefited enormously from the support of mentors. My own story is one of transformation, from that of a shy, traumatized, noncommunicative young girl to the English professor, campus leader, and innovator in higher education that I am today. Over the course of my entire education, from early childhood to graduate school, I suffered from major episodes of depression, saddled by self-destructive thoughts and maladaptive behaviors. My first experiences with therapeutic treatments were in graduate school. What this means is that my entire education and much of my work experience before age forty were constrained and debilitated by forces invisible even to me. If they were invisible to me, then it is no wonder that so few people stepped in to offer me the support that I needed.

Most of my teachers were unremarkable signposts in the passage of my education as I drifted alongside the other blank-faced souls in the classroom. A select few were either additional perpetrators or life-changing mentors. More than anything else, what I needed were teachers and mentors who could see me and support me. I needed people to recognize that my quiet demeanor and my reluctance to communicate or make eye contact were signs that I needed external support. One teacher stands out as a mentor who facilitated my transformation, my growth, and my sense of self-worth. My high school English teacher

Bruce Kutney was able to see me as a young woman full of potential. He supported me, recognized my value, and offered me an unconditional supportive hand. I don't believe I'd be where I am today without his mentorship.

At my Research Doctoral I institution, I am described as a scholarly associate professor on what is called the career track, as opposed to the tenure track. In my department, my workload consists of a 60 percent teaching load (three courses per semester), 20 percent research or scholarly activity, and 20 percent service. In 2015 my department made an investment in me that reduced my teaching load by one course per semester and gave me freedom to explore new directions in undergraduate studies in English. For me, this experience was very much an alternative-academic appointment—I was not teaching, doing formal scholarship, or doing run-of-the mill service. I was afforded the opportunity to devise new initiatives. Out of this investment I developed the Passport Program, a mentoring and professional development program that has since taken on various shapes since its pilot in spring 2016. The pilot was developed in conjunction with two other career-track faculty who were donating their time to this special project.

STUDENT CHARACTERISTICS: SOCIAL CAPITAL AND CONFIDENCE

The Passport Program is open to all undergraduate students at WSU, but it targets English majors who are open to personal growth and professional development, and enrollment was initially only available by permission from me or our professional advisor. The program tends to draw a wide range of students, from those who are high-risk for retention to those who are high performing. Since the program began, all of the recipients of our annual department award for outstanding senior have been alumni from the Passport Program.

One of the reasons I do the work of mentoring is that I see myself reflected in many of my students. Much of this awareness about the range in social capital that our students possess became visible to me when I taught our Professional and Technical Writing course, which drew students from all majors from across the university. As I prepared them for their lives after college in this course, I witnessed a range of access to this social capital. As an English professor, I had cultivated this capital over the course of my postdoctoral years and first years as an assistant professor. I could suddenly see that there were students who feel confident—others might pejoratively describe them as entitled; students who know they can look me in the eye, smile, and affably ask me for an extension, an excused absence, or some other accommodation. Then there were those students who either didn't know they could ask for those things or had been taught by their teachers that it was inappropriate to ask—even in their most extenuating circumstances, such as the death of a close friend or relative, the wildfire destruction of their family home, or the loss of financial support. I made it my commitment to serve these students who don't know that they have a right to be here at this university and communicate openly and honestly with their professors about their academic needs and circumstances.

Because I was a student who suffered from invisible barriers to success or less easily defined obstacles, I am especially keen to identify the behaviors that express these barriers, which may include multiple forms of hiding or coping behaviors: missing class, not responding to emails, not showing up for appointments, not making eye contact with the professor, not submitting work for review, following rules even if they are harmful to the student's growth, not raising their hands, not journaling in class, or not speaking in small groups. At the same time, there are students who hide in plain sight. They contribute to class discussion, they complete their assignments on time, they never miss class, and they never miss a beat—because any deviation from the rules, and any failure, presents the terrifying possibility for vulnerability. They are unable to be vulnerable. They are unable to acknowledge what they don't already know. They are unable to share their fears, their insecurities, their empty vessels. Many of our students are hiding, and they are learning to be invisible, because if they are invisible, we won't make them uncomfortable, we won't notice them, we won't call on them, and we won't make them have to be vulnerable and brave.

The affective labor that I engage in on a regular basis in my own teaching, and in my own work as a campus leader and a program leader in my department, is that of seeing our students, and helping them to see themselves, helping them to stand in the light with their raw material and their undeveloped selves. My mission is to provide our students with the tools to help build themselves up and to help them to be brave. Their education means little on their paths toward defining their vocation if they don't believe in themselves and their ability to contribute to an organization or to society as a whole.

RELATIONSHIP FEATURES: PROFESSOR OR MENTOR?

Where does mentoring fit into the career of an academic in higher ed? The clearest kind of mentoring is that which happens within the context of disciplinary advising—of a lab, a research project, or a thesis. When it comes to classifying that activity, do we count it as teaching, or service? As the nature of the mentoring shifts, it appears to fall in different categories. When mentoring involves empowerment, inspiration, interpersonal communication, academic goal-setting, navigating personal obstacles, and other life-oriented skills, the mentoring falls more under the category of service, or what the institution may provide outside of academic departments—in career services, student services, and student life.

Students know that once they join the Passport Program, they will have me as a resource and a mentor for as long as they choose. This mentorship takes on many forms, including continued mentoring for the duration of their undergraduate studies—which might include academic and career advising, emotional and psychological support, and additional sponsorship. After they graduate, I invite them to connect with me on social media (especially Facebook and LinkedIn) so that I can continue to follow their journeys. Some of these mentoring relationships have evolved into more personal or familial relationships during the years after graduation. In any case, students are in no way obligated to maintain contact, but I check in with them periodically. I teach students how to integrate the disciplinary methods of English studies into their personal and professional lives. This view always treats the discipline, and my training in this discipline, as my core tool. While the work I do with students may appear to be emotional and consuming, it is instead grounded in the tools of my discipline and the tenets of my academic study. At my core is the power of the belief in stories, and that every story can be rewritten.

The added benefit of me being a faculty member in their discipline is that I intimately understand their workload and academic challenges. I personally know their professors and fellow classmates. I am also often their professor in a different context, where it is important that I make explicit the difference between my role as mentor and role as professor—often specifically identifying myself prior to making a statement or question: "As your mentor . . . " or "As your professor. . . . " These roles have been important to tease out. The mentor in me is more concerned with the students' well-being in all contexts, and specifically asks questions that target those contexts. The professor in me, while also concerned with their well-being, specifically targets the academic contexts of the course in question. In other words, if I begin as their professor and our relationship naturally evolves into questions of their well-being in all contexts, that relationship assumes a mentoring quality. It is easy to see, then, how mentoring can take the form of unsupported emotional labor, because it occurs outside the bounds of specific coursework and outside the bounds of the professional student services across campus.

FORMS OF SUPPORT: A MENTORING BLUEPRINT

Our students benefit most from a multifaceted approach to mentoring—one that provides various levels of external support while also educating them on a variety of internal tools they may cultivate and draw upon. They all need a better sense of what the university provides; it's not enough to teach students basic skills and content. They need to learn to be more agile in their approach to life, careers, and a vision for the future. One of the ways we help students develop this agility is by serving as a creative partner in helping to facilitate their own vision of the world (not our vision). The larger the network of support we can build for our students, the greater impact we can have on just that small group of students each semester. The Passport Program is designed to offer students five levels of support:

- University-wide: education about and access to the services the department and university provide
- Program-wide: weekly workshops led by guest speakers in a supportive and consistent environment
- Mentoring in small groups: activities facilitated by program fellows in groups of 2–3 program students
- Mentoring one-on-one: meetings with 2–3 designated mentors required during the semester
- Mentoring oneself: education in the tools needed to access their inner wisdom

The Passport Program is driven by the vision that every student deserves at least three designated mentors. I also do the work of cultivating natural mentoring relationships by bringing in a range of graduate students and faculty to lead and/or facilitate workshops. We practice open pedagogy in the public meeting room, where anyone is encouraged to drop in—during future iterations of the program, I will begin providing spaces for developing and fine-tuning our approaches to mentoring. The Passport Program creates a vehicle for formally delivering mentoring support in all of the areas recommended by the 2017 ASHE report *Mentoring Undergraduate Students*. To highlight features of the Passport Program and how this mentoring support might look in practice, I will briefly describe one of the workshops I deliver in the program, and how its ideals are supported in one-on-one mentoring and the development of inner wisdom.

At the heart of the Passport Program is a Transformational Storytelling workshop that I deliver to students each spring. In this workshop, we look backward at pivotal memories in our lives, capture them, convert them into elaborate texts, and identify patterns in them that we can interpret. In other words, we utilize key methods students develop as English majors to analyze their lives. It is this disciplinary intervention that best distinguishes the work we do in the Passport Program versus the work, for example, of an advisor or counselor. One of the powerful insights that we all gain from this process is that our narratives can be reframed when we look back at our memories more compassionately, looking for contexts and lessons learned. The close reading method I have developed for this workshop specifically guides students toward a more tangible and progressive representation of their significant memories leading up to who they are now as students at WSU.

I begin by sharing my own stories about how I got to where I am. When we examine our lives and see how we got to where we are, we can have more trust that our paths, including surprise pitfalls and push-backs, are an important part of our story moving forward: we become capable of integrating these experiences into who we are and who we will become. One of the most beautiful insights of looking backward, detecting patterns, and reframing our life narratives is that we begin to see how the most exceptional disappointments, obstacles, and deviations from our dreams inevitably led us to the present moment. When we view those moments as growth moments, we accept them as integral pieces of our identity. We are able to take these experiences and project them forward. And now, as new barriers arise and new paths emerge, and my life blossoms, but also shrinks, I trust that my life will work out. I trust that a lesson will emerge from these experiences. I trust in the power of stories to carry me forward.

We apply this reframing of our narratives, for example, in the most common of ways, such as when a student becomes unable to pursue their desired path of becoming a teacher—perhaps they don't meet the criteria for the College of Education, or they are simply not accepted into the program the first time they apply. The problem is common enough to have upset many of our students. Calling it an upset is an understatement. Suddenly they are faced with the dilemma of what they want to do with their degree in English. I reframe the discussion in terms of the student's love of teaching. While they may have been denied—perhaps temporarily—access to teaching certification, it's important that they become aware of the other ways to fulfill a mission dedicated to teaching. That teaching is not just about delivering a curriculum to school-age children. It can be about learning, growing, evolving, at any age, in any organization, in any part of our lives. When we frame higher education in terms of "what" students will do when they graduate, we set them up not only for failure in school but also for a crisis of faith. We teach them that there is only one destination and only one path to follow to get there. The reality is that they must learn to move all around the map, exploring, adapting, acting nimbly, and opening their hearts to new inspirations, new tangible contributions to their path. In one-on-one mentoring, I draw these students a tree with many branches. The trunk consists of the skills and interests they have been accumulating over time. Each branch represents a different sector of society—academic, nonprofit, private. I show that a love of teaching, for example, can take place in all three branches, or a love of creative writing can take place in all three. Within a branch, then, are a plethora of possibilities for nurturing their interests. If one branch doesn't work out, they can move to another. The tree is still intact; the tree is still rooted and can grow in many different directions. What's important is to understand what makes the tree grow.

Thinking more globally about our students' experiences in the undergraduate major, it's important for students to see that it's not always just about how their specific actions lead to desirable or undesirable outcomes. Education is not just about the curriculum, and it's not just about the test scores. Education is much more complex—students learn when they fall in love, when they are rejected, when they skip class, when they pull an all-nighter, when they fail an exam. These are all lessons in conduct, in character, and in good action. They make choices every day, and sometimes they choose self-care over class, or they choose friendship and connection over study. One is not better than the other; they are experimenting, finding themselves, expanding outward in all directions. We are not always in control of our outcomes. They do everything right—they make study their number-one priority—and yet the universe will conspire to bring them illness, death, accidents, social injustice, or heartbreak. They cannot control for these external factors. Their lives are more complex than a textbook, and so is their education. To grow into beautiful citizens and professionals, they need to learn their values beyond the template of a course map. Life is messy, people are messy, and to prepare students for the challenges they will face as human beings in the twenty-first century, they need to be seen and respected as human beings. Thus, an integrative educational experience means that students are learning to navigate the choices they make every day alongside their directed academic choices.

When we practice mentoring, we do not need to be emotionally invested in our students, but we do need to listen, and we need to be curious, and we need to take interest in our subjects. It's an act of conscious exploration. And instead of delivering our wisdom to select students whom we care about, we practice conscious inquiry in our relationships with students. Instead of saying, here's what you need to do, and here's how to get here (as we might in academic advising, most explicitly, or in formal research mentoring), we ask the student: who do you want to be? And if the answer is a novelist, a high school English teacher, or something else that is defined by a specific destination, we need to ask: Why? What do you want your full life to look like? What compromises are you willing to make? What parts of your life are most important to you? What do you value? What are some steps that will move you in that direction? It's rare that we acknowledge that careers are more complex than a single job destination.

For those of us who tend toward a more exhausting investment in mentoring our students, I will provide some frameworks for thinking about mentoring as an interactive process of inquiry, rather than a depositing approach. The key method that I learned in Tara Mohr's Playing Big facilitators training program was that to create the biggest impact on someone, we must lead them to their own inner wisdom, their own solutions, and their own answers. Providing a litany of tools and solutions that worked for us is not a good solution, and much like in the banking concept, filling our students like containers with resources is not going to change their life or the way they think about their life. The key is to ask good short, strong questions that lead them to their own inner wisdom.

I experienced this coaching myself during the training, and it was my experience of finding my own inner wisdom that forever changed how I think about mentoring. My coach was helping me to unpack some of my feelings about wanting to "hide" or "huddle" during a difficult episode in my life. She asked me what voices were contributing to this feeling—what "inner critic" persona in Tara Mohr's Playing Big toolbox. While I've often thought there was just one inner critic who was hounding me, I realized there was another one that was not so much of what I'd think of as a critic, but as a halting force in my life. My coach asked me questions that led me to deep realizations about the stories I was telling myself, and the stories that I could change. As the coaching recipient, I really was being asked to do all the hard work of reframing my narratives and analyzing the stories I was telling myself. In these ways, my cognitive landscape altered, and I found growth. For the coach—which I also experienced the practice of serving as—the greatest efforts were made in listening, observing, and asking pointed questions. While these efforts are significant, they are not the same kind of emotional labor that I once took on as a mentor: that feeling that I needed to stay with a student until all of their problems were solved.

We cannot make students believe in themselves in a matter of thirty minutes. We cannot make them feel and practice self-compassion. We can, however, lead them to discover where these feelings might lie inside themselves—we may lead them to discovering a glimpse of beauty in themselves. We may rewire their brains in tiny subtle ways. Ultimately, it is up to them to do the hard work of self-reflection and transformation. We cannot save them ourselves. Just as depositing lacks efficacy in the classroom, it is equally inefficient outside the classroom on more consequential issues regarding student growth. When you as a potential mentor consider your own growth, and your own difficult journeys, how were you mobilized? How was your movement made possible? Others—including mentors—can fill us with advice, but this is not how mentors are most effective. It is the unconditional support and the power they have to help us believe in ourselves. So while it's valuable to facilitate our students' discovery of their inner wisdom, as educators, we provide them with additional tools, resources, and strategies for reframing their narratives.

CONCLUSION

Kelly Ward, who was the series editor of the 2017 ASHE report *Mentoring Undergraduate Students*, was a mentor to scores of women inside and outside of the academy and all over the world, before her accidental death at age fifty-four in the summer of 2018. At the faculty women memorial I presided over, women shared their testimonials of Ward—testimonials that had little to do with her scholarly expertise or professional networks. It was the small personal interventions she made in our lives that made a difference: she made us feel seen, she knew that small signs of support made a big difference, and over and over again, women showed that she taught us to believe in ourselves. Her powerful mentoring style had little and everything to do with her job description—and it went far beyond her service to the institution or the discipline. Her mentorship promoted individual strength and a celebration of women's professional lives, integrating our personal relationships into our professional contexts. She knew that the two could never be separate, or balanced, but that they irrevocably overlapped, one informing the other. As I remember her, it's not the books she wrote, it's the care and support she provided me. On me, she left a fingerprint, not in the way that we often think of advisors shaping their intellectual disciples, but as a human being in this world with other human beings, all of whom need support, in the way she supported me and hundreds of other women. We leave fingerprints on the world, often through our relationships. Those prints ripple over the course of time and generations, to carry us on forever. We think so much of the legacies we leave in the form of books, art, physical creations, awards, and then even our own children. I accept, much in the way of Virginia Woolf's Clarissa Dalloway, that I am not just here, here, here, but everywhere, and everyone who I have ever come into contact with.

A student once reminded me of the impact I made on her when I was lamenting the fact that I had made little to no progress on my book project. Universities measure impact in terms of publications. Without a book under my belt, I felt that my value was zero. As my student sat before me, listening to my brief lamentation, she showed me one of the ways I had made a positive impact on her. On her laptop next to her keyboard was a summary of her mission statement—her purpose; her intention to make an impact on the universe. It was a statement that I had helped her craft in the Passport Program. As this beautiful, blossoming human being sat before me, she reminded me that I had made a difference in her life. That her life was ever so much more valuable than any book I could ever write. That while my impact on her could not be quantified and significantly captured immediately in the institutional or disciplinary statistics, what I could see was a significant impact on her personal and professional identity. Our relationship—and my investment in her growth, and that of so many other students I have mentored—was more significant than any book. We create through our relationships—through the stories we share, the listening we provide, and the space we hold for one another.

A friend recently told me a story of a tree he visited in a park, a tree to which he gave an offering every time he sat to meditate under it. One time, he forgot to give the tree an offering, and instead of feeling neglectful, he awakened to the idea that his offering was just him sitting there with the tree, noticing the tree, and seeing the tree. I've thought often of the power of this offering: the power of simply sitting with and receiving one another. Yes, this is emotional labor, yes, this is mentoring, and yes, we create and leave fingerprints on the lives of everyone we touch through this simple act.

We are called to serve our students in higher education. Our job as educators, and as workers in higher ed, is to help build a future where knowledge discovery, creation, and dissemination has fertile ground to grow from. While the institution itself forms part of that ground, the most dynamic territory is that of the students themselves. When we invest in our students, we invest in the future of higher education, as they move into positions of power as legislators, business owners, active community members, and voters. And so we serve and transform this global community. We make our impact in more ways than one. We leave metaphorical fingerprints on each student and colleague we touch. Mentorship and teaching comes from a place of helping others to find their best selves. The goal is to help them identify the light, the curiosity, the flame, the self-compassion, that will enable them to direct their own learning with openness and curiosity and inquiry.

NOTES

1. Tara Mohr, *Playing Big: Practical Wisdom for Women Who Want to Speak Up, Create, or Lead* (New York: Avery, 2014).

2. Gloria Crisp et al., *Mentoring Undergraduate Students: ASHE Higher Education Report, Vol. 43, No. 1* (San Francisco, CA: Jossey-Bass, 2017).

3. Crisp et al., *Mentoring Undergraduate Students*, 84.

BIBLIOGRAPHY

Crisp, Gloria, Vicki L. Baker, Kimberly A. Griffin, Laura Gail Lunsford, and Meghan J. Pifer. *Mentoring Undergraduate Students: ASHE Higher Education Report, Vol. 43, No. 1.* San Francisco, CA: Jossey-Bass, 2017.

Mohr, Tara. *Playing Big: Practical Wisdom for Women Who Want to Speak Up, Create, or Lead.* New York: Avery, 2014.

14

More Denial, More Problems

DEBORAH MARON

To admit that I am a white problem is simply to state a fact. Yet asserting it makes me uncomfortable, in seemingly paradoxical ways: I am embarrassed to be a problem, yet admitting it feels like boasting. (Isn't it wonderful that I've recognized that I am a problem by virtue of being white?) In beginning to write about how it feels to be a white problem, I have felt much as I often do in the face of my own and others' racism: paralyzed, uncertain how to begin. . . . To perform antiracism, I have to decisively act, drawing critical attention to myself.

—Karen Teel, "Feeling White, Feeling Good: 'Antiracist' White Sensibilities"

I planned to do a dissertation project that explored the relationship between a librarian's marginalized identity and their propensity to organize library collections in particular ways. My dissertation committee of white individuals pressed me at my proposal defense about why I felt it necessary to ask participants about how race, in particular, plays a role in their work. Because I never had a frank conversation about race with these individuals (unlike with close friends of mine), I did not know how they personally regarded issues of racism and pervasive whiteness in the United States, especially in libraries. Trying to avoid what I feared would be a difficult discussion, I did not adequately defend my decision and instead welcomed a change of topic, with a huge sense of relief.

A Southern university saw an uptick in racist occurrences, which spurred a heated conversation among students and faculty about white racism and the responsibility of a historically white academic department to speak up. On a listserv discussion about it, a white student invalidated the experiences of his fellow Black students. Horrified, I wanted to shut down the ignorant and hurtful remarks to show solidarity with the Black students. However, after considering that it might jeopardize my own standing within the department, I did nothing.

I organized and moderated a high-profile conference panel in which I talked with librarians who organize material related to marginalized groups. I did not, on that stage, ask the Black and queer panelists what it felt like for me, a white woman, to be driving the narration of their experience in front of a mostly white audience. I sensed disappointment and perhaps anger from some of them in how it went, but paralyzed by my own failure on that stage, I lacked the courage to follow up.

A graphic video circulated earlier this year of George Floyd, a Black man, crying out as his body was literally crushed to death on the street by white police officers in Minneapolis, Minnesota. Despite the fact that numerous other murders of Black adults and children resided somewhere in the shared consciousness of white Americans, it was Floyd's murder in particular that shook the souls of many whites, provoking in many of us a horror, fury, and a professed desire for justice that we had delayed and deferred. The show of support by whites was unprecedented. Floyd's murder galvanized thousands of whites across the United States to organize protests advocating for Black lives. Whites began professing their support on social media. Photographs of murals and infographics commemorating the loss of Black lives were posted on Instagram. So were links to articles with statistics enumerating murders of other Black individuals whose deaths had been ignored. Book sales of antiracist literature authored by scholar-writers such as Ibram X. Kendi and Robin DiAngelo spiked.

"WILL WE CARE IN THREE WEEKS WHEN IT'S NO LONGER A SOCIAL MEDIA TREND?" PERFORMATIVE AND MUNDANE ANTIRACISM

I saw something a BIPOC (Black, Indigenous, and People of Color) activist wrote on Twitter after George Floyd's death and in the midst of Black Lives Matter protests, to the effect of ,"Will White people care in three weeks when fights for Black lives are no longer a social media trend?" Some Black activists express concern that with Floyd's murder we might be engaging in *performative antiracism,* wherein whites do not genuinely embrace the antiracist virtues we espouse and claim to believe in. Though we might tweet what could be at worst considered platitudes ripped from the pages of *White Fragility* (saying *I am part of the problem, I am privileged),* or statistics of Black deaths, or retweet prominent Black activists and writers, are we okay with being more specific about how we ourselves contribute to white supremacy on a day-to-day basis?

People who don white KKK robes or give Nazi salutes are easy to condemn, because their racism is conspicuous. Typically what is unforgivable is the exceptional, overtly egregious, unusual, viral, not the "ordinary."

The readers of this book probably work in an academic library, a public library, or in a library-adjacent workplace like a library school. (I'm in the latter, a researcher and former practitioner.) Like me, you may be white but do not identify as a Nazi. You are a person who, measured against someone like a Nazi, is not evil, or particularly racist, but are rather "ordinary." You are an "ordinary" professional whose everyday behavior corresponds to what is expected in the workplace. You might believe that if you behave professionally and don't do anything "egregious," you are doing well. You might already question if your library workplace does enough, and so you go the extra mile. You might have already instituted organizations in person or on social media that help cultivate an antiracist library. Unaware of your particular context, I can't say how much you as individual readers will feel this chapter is helpful to you, based on the degree of effort you already put into antiracism in the library.

I can say, however, that when we as white professionals scrutinize our ordinary or unexceptional behaviors—among them, how and with whom we converse at work, how we write and enforce policy, and how and whom we hire—we might begin to question our individual commitment to the virtues of antiracism. For example, if you shut down overt racism but let certain microaggressions you witness slide, does that mean you're doing enough? And is it enough, once you know yourself, to pick and choose when to act? If we fail to analyze our own subjectivity, are we doing enough for our workplaces?

In this chapter I add to growing antiracist discourse among antiracist white and BIPOC librarians by considering the problem of *ordinary and mundane racism*. Using primarily Black- and Brown-authored literature, I incorporate the work of philosopher George Yancy to define ordinary and mundane racism as a white person professing, posturing, avoiding, or not recognizing how to make a material change in the local library in order to improve it. I provide examples of ordinary racism in the library and the effects it has had on groups and individual BIPOC librarians. I conclude that a mitigating or preventive measure is acting in accordance with the feminist, psychosocial, and antiracist principle of *reflexivity*. Whereas *reflection* focuses on how we observe an environment apart from ourselves, *reflexivity* focuses on how a person processes information about their actions within the everyday environment and subsequently alters their thoughts and behaviors based on that process.[1] While the person with low reflexivity helps to maintain the status quo in their environment, the highly reflexive person challenges their norms and past behavior and alters future actions based on negative responses. Here, I suggest activities and exercises wherein white librarians can challenge their biases and positively alter their everyday activities. I posit that high individual reflexivity can contribute to positive material change in the library.

I acknowledge that the more *reflexive* a white person becomes about the racism they perpetuate individually on a day-to-day basis, the more insecure they might become about themselves because they realize their racism is not wholly curable. Imbricated as we are into a system of inequality, we cannot wholly obliterate racism from our mind and actions.[2] This is a frustrating reality. *Can we still be better in a way that materially and effectively supports the people of color with whom we work? How do we start talking frankly about the many guises that our own "work racism" takes?*

What We Think

Do the BIPOC librarians we work with believe our actions to be useful or performative? The majority library institution perpetuates a tidy narrative of what the library is about, which we might, as whites, buy into in varying degrees. In the lore, the library is a place that champions equality and freedom; it is a place that in its magnanimity is relatively unproblematic and transcends some of the problems that undergird other economic, social, and educational structures.

What We're Attempting to Do

What happens when we remain unaware of the role our whiteness plays in the library? The belief that we can ably challenge whiteness in the library is predicated on the belief that we know ourselves, and that we are okay with challenging the status quo. In actuality, whites are conditioned in such a way that we do things so as not to relinquish our positions of power. Charles Mills writes that despite our claiming to believe in the social contract (do unto all others as you would have them do unto you), we operate via a *racial contract*—the tacit agreement among whites to permit and perpetuate the mundane forms of racism so that things remain the same.[3] The truth of this claim might not seem obvious in the view of those readers who—like me—feel like they have helped cultivate a workplace that is safe and equitable for people of all races. We have, for example, at some predominantly white institution (PWI) libraries seen an uptick in the removal of white library portraiture or historical busts, "queering" of the architecture, collecting objects related to racially marginalized groups, and multicultural programming.[4] We have seen this type of work performed well in some public libraries, with measurable success.[5] We are also affirmed in our antiracism as white majority libraries to write mandates that profess moral values such as diversity, inclusivity, social justice, and cultural resonance—values that undergird antiracist causes. However, when we in the dominant majority measure our understanding of "antiracism" and "diversity" and "inclusivity" and "resonance" against what we actually do in many libraries and library adjacent workplaces, we see a problem.

What Is Actually Happening: Discrimination in Hiring, Recruitment, and Retention

It isn't enough that diversity as a concept is now being explored at individual libraries. Racial inequality is not just part of a problem. It is *the* problem and an institution of its own, a force that guides our decisions, our choices, and our perceptions of ourselves as professionals. We must consider that it is difficult to deploy and actualize racial justice when the whole system of libraries is built on racial inequality. Racism is not part of but rather created the library system from its inception. By dint of how they were founded, *predominantly white libraries are undergirded by a racist framework, and they support a racialized reward system that sustains inequality.*

Although the racial reckoning of 2020 may have altered the library landscape in some ways and continues to do so, we might first consider historically entrenched aesthetic conventions as a form of oppression. Take our image of "the progressive librarian" and/or "quirky librarian" who goes unmarked by society because they are white. I am white, and my aesthetic choices often fall outside the norm. However, I have not historically been the object of scrutiny based on my race or my clothing while working in a library. As white librarians we may regard ourselves as well read, less *conventional* than other folks, and broad-thinking, and therefore we feel we are more appreciative of diversity in terms of what material the library offers to patrons and perhaps believe ourselves to (and do) value forms of diversity in ourselves and in others.[6] It is arguable, however, that the library institution as a whole, of which the workforce is 88 percent white and governance is majority white, does *not* actively appreciate and celebrate diversity or identity expressions in everyone, and this lack of appreciation might fall across racial lines and seep into the aesthetic code at work. In one recent publication celebrating diverse aesthetics, librarians of various cultural backgrounds were shown making bold aesthetic choices in their garb, body art, and hairstyles while at work.[7] However, although the bespectacled, boldly patterned librarian might embody a celebrated *geek chic*, authors such as Vani Natarajan argue that this type of chic (as well as other expressions of one's identity through clothing, hair, and adornment) is more often permissible for *white* librarians. Accordingly, a predominantly white library may legislate beauty within its physical environment similar to how institutions outside the library legislate it, in ways that center whiteness as "the ideal."[8] Jessica Macias explains that even if it is not articulated formally, our unspoken rule around the white librarian aesthetic seeks to justify the mundane racism of our institution, wherein people of color are not hired or promoted. In addition to being given fewer job opportunities for not looking "white enough," Macias argues that people of color might be punished in other (and to some, less "obvious") ways for their supposed transgressions. Citing her own experience, she writes:

> I have sat through numerous diversity initiatives, training sessions and workshops meant to increase diversity and help the staff better reflect on

> the communities we serve. All the while, the same institutions that rallied behind these initiatives for years created and maintained policies that reminded me and others never to wear our hair in an "unprofessional" or "unkempt" fashion. The underlying message was clear—do not wear your hair unruly or natural. . . . In 2015, a young Black staff member began wearing her hair in long, box braids. As her supervisor I was asked to remind her to wear her hair back so that it would not fall forward in her face, on the desk, or on the materials that library patrons were borrowing. Suddenly the library had turned into a restaurant, and our books were likened to food we could contaminate. There were multiple White women on my staff, none of whom had been asked to wear their hair back, so I was discouraged to see my coworkers rally in unison around the assertion that my Black colleague's hair made her unfit for her position.

Macias writes further that her own friendly relationship with the young Black woman became a "threat" and she began to receive complaints from white colleagues about her work and her own appearance (including her fingernails, which they said looked appropriate for a "rap video" but not a library).[9]

Prolific writer and former Princeton University archivist Jarrett Drake, in his article "I'm Leaving the Archival Profession: It's Better This Way," also critiques work standards, writing that "professionalism further asks that [BIPOC] remain content with the status quo, predictability, and propaganda. Professionalism asks us to believe the fiction that our fidelity, niceness, obedience, and servitude will save us and our jobs. They won't."[10] As a Black archivist, he recounts several racist experiences he himself endured in the library—including the time he was racially profiled in a "benign" way by a driver who was seemingly confused to be driving a Black man to a job interview at Princeton. And Drake is by no means the only librarian of color frustrated and disappointed enough to depart the library profession. A recent finding points to racism's egregiousness and extent: for example, librarian Theresa Byrd, who for many years helmed the Spectrum Scholar Initiative, which provided mentorship opportunities and scholarships to numerous students of color in library schools, reported at a conference talk in July 2018 that 20 percent of former Spectrum Scholars—BIPOC library students who are mentored and supported during library school and early career—are leaving the library profession due to racial trauma in the workplace (librarian Danielle RaPue first tweeted this number out).

In another article Byrd argues that in addition to the blatant abuse that many librarians of color withstand, we "have failed miserably at diversifying the profession" because of the predominantly white institution's tendency to "token hire":

> I'm so sick of [diversity fellowships]. . . . You're putting a target on someone's back: "You're the diversity fellow." It says: "You're not really part of the organization. We'll keep you for three years." What I don't understand is, why can't you just recruit and hire people into these jobs, rather than have these revolving doors? I don't know that people in the organization take them [diversity fellows] that seriously, because they know many of them are going to be gone. I think it's a way for predominantly white institutions (PWIs) to say, "Look how great we are. We're helping people." No, you aren't. If you really want to help a POC, just give them a job through the regular process.[11]

In alternative press Library Juice's *Journal of Critical LIS,* David James Hudson has documented the ways in which diversity mandates, penned by a majority, use clumsy language to avoid mandating the kind of equality we as whites claim to espouse.[12] Additionally, Black individuals detail discomfiting personal experiences they have had, not just as professionals but also as library patrons of color. In her article "Archiving While Black," Ashley Farmer—a Black woman professor at the University of Texas–Austin—shares the following:

> I can recall multiple instances in which both archivists and patrons looked surprised and worried when I brought my majority-black classes into the archive for a lesson. Moreover, one has to only consider other incidents—police accosting a black student at gunpoint outside a Yale library; a white graduate student calling campus police on a black graduate student who was napping in a common room of their dormitory, also at Yale—to know that the presence of black people still incites panic on campuses across the country.[13]

Some egregious displays have garnered relatively more publicity: at a predominantly white library conference in the Pacific Northwest, April Hathcock, a Black woman archivist and revered writer, endured what she considered to be ad hominem, racially motivated attacks from a white male colleague on a public panel. In her blog *At the Intersection,* she informed readers that as her colleague attacked her, a white audience just stared and did nothing.

Unfortunately, this is just the tip of the iceberg. There are many other first-person accounts, surveys, and other data to support claims of racial abuse. Such evidence suggests that many white librarians might care about antiracism in theory but do not practice their theory. What Mustafa Emirbayer and Matthew Desmond call a *genuine* commitment to reflexivity and antiracism would not permit these injustices.[14]

RACISM IN ACADEMIC LIBRARIES AND THE ROLE OF WHITE ACADEMICS

White librarians might not describe the academic library as "white" or live consciously as they play out whiteness, instead claiming that certain "aspects" of their place of hire are racially inhospitable. This, however, downplays not just how much the racial contract shapes the emotional machinery of the library but also how it has shaped its macrocosm, the college or university. The university undeniably played a role in shaping our sensitivity and propensity for excellence as students, and it still shapes our ability to succeed as professionals in the greater university system. In her seminal article "Your Worries Ain't Like Mine," librarian and professor Deborah Curry writes that "persistence of systemic and individual racism both within society and higher education influences the behavior and attitudes of librarians of color and their white colleagues" and that "racism, prejudice and discrimination in academe often have a direct impact on the recruitment and retention of African American librarians and other librarians of color."[15] Curry's indictment speaks to other things we know to be true in predominantly white colleges: the overarching absence of academic and emotional support for students of color, the absence of resonant educational practice that elevates marginalized rhetorical style in the classroom, and other forms of racial hostility from white individuals in higher education. All of these factors have effectively contributed to academic struggles among individuals of color that is higher on average than that of white students and faculty at some universities.[16]

READING MATERIAL AND THEORETICAL TRANSCENDENCE

In the spirit of understanding the limits of our own reflexivity at the university library, white academics might ask themselves: what authors do we read to understand the concept of self-criticality? As academics from different fields, with many of us educated at PWIs, we can consider the way theoretical literature has given us racial myopia. For example, after my proposal defense, a professor of color I have a friendly relationship with offered to read my dissertation proposal and provide notes over coffee. Overall, she liked the work, but she had one significant question for me: *Why did I not cite more people of color in a study about race?* When I was made aware of this significant oversight in my own corpus, it brought to mind the kinds of things I learned—and did not learn—in courses I'd taken. At the start of my academic career I was a newcomer to the Marxist critical theory canon. In my survey course on critical theory, taught by a well-respected white male professor, I read a *lot* of literature about oppression and surveillance that centered gender or class difference as the point of departure, but *not* racial difference, or intersectionality, as a means of understanding oppression and surveilling. Not incidentally, many of the authors I read were also white men and women, writing the experience of oppression from their (unmarked, default, unspoken) white subjectivity. This kind of material—white material—shaped my consciousness and my own unmarked and default sense of subjectivity.

In terms of my own experience as a library science academic who tries to engage with counternarratives and revisions of common history, I never read excellent, counternarrative-rich books like *Topographies of Whiteness*, nor do I recall reading in any of my library school courses other counternarrative that examined in depth the racial history of the library. This is not to say that white academics in library science do not attempt to educate majority librarians about whiteness in the field. On the contrary, many white authors have written about race and racism and have done so in my own field of classification studies. However, they often shine the light of accountability away from themselves and lean on jargon, which gives the illusion that they are whites who have managed to *transcend* racism. Yancy has counted this all-too-common academic practice among some of the most egregious violations of antiracism, writing that whites "deploy theory as a way of not being forced to examine aspects of their own white subject position." He says that "the deployment of theory can function as a form of bad faith."[17]

Interventions

Habituated as we are not to think about race, we fail to consider how the manifestation of it within and outside ourselves affects the lives of those around us. White people who are interested in social justice might therefore underestimate the degree to which racial injustice is perpetrated not just by our silence but by other kinds of everyday actions. We might therefore do well to interrogate ourselves about our everyday actions to evaluate how committed we actually are to antiracism. As readers of affect theory and as people interested in emotional labor, we concern ourselves with the kind of interactions that happen between humans and nonhumans that might cultivate positive, negative, or neutral experiences for the actors in that environment. I believe that white academics can use conceptual tools—some of which we acquired pursuing our postgraduate education—in order to better understand the harmfulness of some of these interactions and our own role in fostering them.

Questioning Our Subjectivity in Everyday Actions

We perpetuate everyday racism when we do not understand or evaluate our own *personal* commitment to making better choices in our daily lives.[18] Revisiting critical theory as well as antiracist handbooks, and the idea of reflexivity, can be illuminating for understanding ourselves as white subjects who are *also* trying to be good allies, every day. To better understand how we can improve our actions, we can begin to be self-critical about the following aspects or *facets* of our subjectivity. Antiracism handbooks, such as those on the Museum for African-American History's website, as well as Ibram X. Kendi's book *How to Be an Antiracist*, are a good place to start. I suggest an exercise for library scholars and practitioners based on my own thoughts along with literature and discussions I have come across in the community: write down a general question to ask yourself under each of the following facets to better understand your own commitment to antiracism in the library. You can then elaborate with a more specific example of each. Here are five facets to reflexive self-questioning, provided by Wikipedia under the since-disappeared entry "Subjectivity":

- *Our consciousness:* How self-aware we are about our perspectives and beliefs—including the truth about how we act on them.
- *Our agency,* or our capacity to engage with a social structure per the reflexivity we possess, that gives us the ability to question and look at ourselves.
- *Personhood of the self and others:* How society confers on us (or how we establish) our status of "being a person."

- *Truth:* How we establish what we know to be true (or the privilege conferred on us to call something true).
- *Reality:* How we establish what is real (or the privilege we might have to create or call something real)

And here are some examples of facets with questions:

- *Our consciousness:* How self-aware we are about our perspectives and beliefs—including the truth about how we act on them.

Question: Do you think about your privilege in the choices you make that relate to collaborations with librarians of color, or how your choices and privilege affect outcomes for patrons of color at the library?

Example: I count cultural resonance as an important factor in my work. Who helmed the decisions on our recent library project where I helped to create descriptors for photos related to African American history at the university? Were my decisions culturally resonant, and how did I evaluate and justify the outcome of my choices?

- *Our agency,* or our capacity to engage with a social structure per the reflexivity we possess, that gives us the ability to question and look at ourselves.

Question: How do I exercise my agency at work as it relates to equality at work/what does it look like?

Example: We have demonstrated a tendency to token hire at our workplace, instead of seeking out qualified individuals of color on their own merits for regular hire. I am part of a diversity committee as well as a hiring committee. What latitude do I have and what have I attempted to do, to challenge the status quo as far as representation at work goes?

Sociolinguistics

How we regard aesthetic and language norms—and the level of credence we give these norms in our daily lives—matter. This is especially true as we consider language as a tool we use to elevate or oppress others. We might turn to *sociolinguistics*—which examines how language happens in the social context—to frame our overarching problem of how white librarians might be abusing language and social presentations in their job, in ways that maintain the status quo.

Register, a sociolinguistics term, refers to how a particular cultural group formalizes conventions of language and its accompanying aesthetic/way of being. In our case, the most relevant concept is what formal linguist and metadata librarian Mary Bolin calls the *occupational register* of library science. As Bolin explains, the occupational register in library science—the proper procedures and scripts for writing and interacting with documents, such as those used for doing everyday library work, or for hiring, retention, and promotion—rewards and punishes individuals in ways that maintain a status quo (for instance, the favoring of men over women).[19] This concept can help us understand how the interactions between white individuals and their colleagues in a diverse workplace foster a white occupational register—a thing that formalizes white aesthetics, norms, and conventions (that are rewarded) and designates anything diverse as being "informal" and therefore deserving of punishment or dismissal. (Relatedly, Samy Alim discusses how Black Americans "styleswitch" in formal and informal scenarios, e.g., switching from Black grammar and affect to white grammar and affect to adapt or be more favorable to a predominantly white environment or audience. It can be argued that when people cannot adequately styleswitch to suit the professional norms, they are punished.[20]) Accompanying this notion of a white occupational register is the concept of white affect, or how I refer to the oppressive work atmosphere and subsequent emotional responses that are predicated on white racist interactions that contribute to a formalized register.

In this chapter, I use (and highly recommend) the corpuses of *critical whiteness studies*, a field of inquiry designed to function as an activist intervention that shines a light on the many insidious forms of white racism.[21] We can also investigate more of what linguistics and philosophy of language has to offer. For example, when a white librarian speaks with a colleague of color, they can consider what message they are conveying through the interaction. Is it truly neutral, or does it—in its myriad conventions—have a negative effect on the listener? For this we might consult continuing educational modules that incorporate speech act theory, which focuses on the ways in which instances of speech can be perceived as positive or negative actions with consequences for the recipient.[22] We can also put the core tenets of speech act in conversation with Judith Butler's notion of performativity.[23] White people's tendency to profess their antiracism for attention, known as "white performative guilt," has recently come under scrutiny.[24] Therefore, instead of simply verbally affirming our faith in our own antiracism, we as whites might analyze the *outcomes* of our words and communication style in the projects and collaborations in which we partake.

In terms of educational interventions that offer us the cultivation of positivities, we might also consider using culturally sustaining pedagogy, an approach to teaching from linguistic studies that emphasizes active engagement with and elevation of marginalized cultural rhetorical style, rather than simply "tolerating" or "respecting" it.[25]

Finally, we have the concept of testimony from social epistemology, in which theorists believe that a justified belief can be acquired by hearing (validating) what others say or write, even if you do not "agree with" or understand it off the bat.[26] Via credence to testimony, we can justify the reality of the library as a composite of our and others' perceptions of particular (raciated) events that we record. We as whites might look to testimony (testifying) as a mode of documenting our awareness about our own white racism in our previous and current library work that happens alone and with others. To testify to our actions, we might create inventories of our projects and analyze them through the lens of critical whiteness, and then meet with other white colleagues to discuss them for their marginalizing effects and how we might improve. We might think about how the documents can be preserved in what scholar Joe Tennis calls an ontogeny (or documentary trail)—in this case, an ontogeny of temporal progress, or effort to address, mitigate, and prevent trauma in the library, in a way that does not seek to obfuscate past shortcomings but, rather, to encourage us to learn from them.

As a highly sensitive person, I cringed while writing the beginning portion of this chapter, where I admitted things that I felt too ashamed to acknowledge to myself for a long time. I also realize that white people might criticize me for my views. However, any embarrassment and shame I feel about things I've done or concern about what other people might say or think about me is trumped by the feeling that racism is important to talk about. Hence, this chapter.

It is a fact that our professional decisions in a moment can have profound, unintended negative effects that last beyond that moment alone. It can be the moment I decide not to stand up for what is right because I lack the courage, or the time I decide not to take accountability for my prior actions because I'm too embarrassed, or the time I vocalize my antiracism as a gesture on social media instead of doing something more productive with my awareness.

Some effects of your actions you can see immediately, and some you see eventually. Sometimes you think a lot about the ripple effects that you won't ever see.

Racism in general comes to seem almost monolithic—something we can never hope to fix.[27] The truth is that the monolith is built of all the littler stuff we don't account for. *That's* why it seems impossible.

Regardless of what our intentions are and what we have done in the past, we need to talk.

NOTES

1. Gillie Bolton and Russell Delderfield, *Reflective Practice: Writing and Professional Development* (London: Sage, 2018), 12–14.

2. George Yancy, *White Self-Criticality beyond Anti-Racism: How Does It Feel to Be a White Problem?* (Washington, DC: Lexington Books, 2014), xvii.

3. Charles Mills, *The Racial Contract* (Ithaca: Cornell University Press, 2014).

4. Dave Beech, *After the Educational Turn: Critical Art Pedagogies and Decolonialism* (London: Black Dog Publishing, 2018); Kirsten Thorpe, "Transformative Praxis—Building Spaces for Indigenous Self-Determination in Libraries and Archives," *In the Library with the Leadpipe*, January 23, 2019, http://www.inthelibrarywiththeleadpipe.org/2019/transformative-praxis.

5. Cikeithia Pugh and Brooke Doyle, "Equity, Diversity, Inclusion: Seattle's 'Loud at the Library' Collaboration," *Children and Libraries* (Fall 2019): 27–29.

6. See Sarah Hannah Gómez, "The Weight of Being a Mirror: A Librarian's Short Autobiography"; Jessica Macias, "Looking the Part"; Vani Natarajan, "Nostalgia, Cuteness, and Geek Chic: Whiteness in Orla Kiely's Library"; and Megan Watson, "White Feminism and Distributions of Power in Academic Libraries," all in Gina Schlesselman-Tarango, ed., *Topographies of Whiteness: Mapping Whiteness in Library and Information Science* (Sacramento, CA: Litwin Books, 2017).

7. Kyle Cassidy, *This Is What a Librarian Looks Like: A Celebration of Libraries, Communities, and Access to Information* (New York: Black Dog & Leventhal Publishers, 2017).

8. Natarajan, "Nostalgia, Cuteness, and Geek Chic."

9. Macias, "Looking the Part," 116–117.

10. Jarrett Drake, "I'm Leaving the Archival Profession: It's Better This Way," *Medium. On Archivy*, June 26, 2017, https://medium.com/on-archivy/im-leaving-the-archival-profession-it-s-better-this-way-ed631c6d72fe.

11. Anne Ford, "Underrepresented, Underemployed: In the Library-Job Search, Some Face Special Barriers," *American Libraries*, November 1, 2018, https://americanlibrariesmagazine.org/2018/11/01/underrepresented-underemployed/.

12. David James Hudson, "On 'Diversity' as Anti-Racism in Library and Information Studies: A Critique," *Journal of Critical Library and Information Studies* 1, no. 1 (2017), https://journals.litwinbooks.com/index.php/jclis/article/view/6.

13. Ashley Farmer, "Archiving While Black," Chronicle of Higher Education, July 22, 2018, https://www.chronicle.com/article/Archiving-While-Black/.

14. Emirbayer and Desmond, "Race and Reflexivity."

15. Deborah A. Curry, "Your Worries Ain't Like Mine: African American Librarians and the Pervasiveness of Racism, Prejudice and Discrimination in Academe," *Reference Librarian* 21, no. 45–46 (1994): 299–311.

16. Chris Piotrowski and Bob Perdue, "Factors in Attrition of Black Students at a Predominantly Euro-American University," *Psychological Reports* 83, no. 1 (1998): 113–114; Terrence Blackman and John Belcher, "Using a Mathematics Cultural Resonance Approach for Building Capacity in the Mathematical Sciences for African American Communities," in Limin Jao and Nenad Radakovic, eds., *Transdisciplinarity in Mathematics Education: Blurring Disciplinary Boundaries* (New York: Springer, 2018); Jacqueline F. Rowser, "Do African American Students' Perceptions of Their Needs Have Implications for Retention?" *Journal of Black Studies* 27, no. 5 (1997): 718–726; Ted Ingram et al., "The Motivational Factors of African American Men Enrolled at Selected Community Colleges," *Journal of Research Initiatives* 2, no. 1 (2016): 1–17; Kelly A. Rodgers and Jessica J. Summers, "African American Students at Predominantly White Institutions: A Motivational and Self-Systems Approach to Understanding Retention," *Educational Psychology Review* 20, no. 2 (2008): 171–190; Django Paris and H. Samy Alim, *Culturally Sustaining Pedagogies* (New York: Teachers College Press, 2017).

17. George Yancy, *Black Bodies, White Gazes: The Continuing Significance of Race* (Lanham, MD: Rowman & Littlefield, 2008), 229.

18. Yancy, "White Self-Criticality."

19. Mary K. Bolin, "The Library and the Computer Center: Organizational Patterns at Land Grant Universities," *Journal of Academic Librarianship* 31, no. 1 (2005): 3–11.

20. H. Samy Alim and Geneva Smitherman, *Articulate While Black: Barack Obama, Language, and Race in the U.S.* (New York: Oxford University Press, 2012); John McWhorter, *Talking Back, Talking Black: Truths about America's Lingua Franca* (New York: Bellevue Literary Press, 2016).

21. Zeus Leonardo, "The Souls of White Folk: Critical Pedagogy, Whiteness Studies, and Globalization Discourse," *Race Ethnicity and Education* 5, no. 1 (2002): 29–50.

22. Frederik Droste, *Locution, Illocution, and Perlocution* (Munich: GRIN Verlag, 2013).

23. Judith Butler, "Performative Agency," *Journal of Cultural Economy* 3, no. 2 (2010): 147–161.

24. Heven Haile, "Hey Hey, Ho Ho, White Performative Allyship Has Got to Go," *Columbia Spectator Daily*, October 16, 2017. https://www.columbiaspectator

.com/opinion/2017/10/17/hey-hey-ho-ho-white-performative-allyship-has-got-to-go/.

25. Paris and Alim, *Culturally Sustaining Pedagogies.*

26. Alvin Goldman and Cailin O'Connor, "Social Epistemology." *Stanford Encyclopedia of Philosophy,* accessed January 30, 2020, https://plato.stanford.edu/entries/epistemology-social/; Joe Tennis, "Intellectual History, History of Ideas, and Subject Ontogeny," in Fernanda Ribeiro and Maria Elisa Cerveira, eds., *Challenges and Opportunities for Knowledge Organization in the Digital Age,* 308–313 (Wurzburg, Germany: Ergon Verlag, 2018).

27. Jessie Daniels, "Race and Racism in Internet Studies: A Review and Critique," *New Media and Society* 15, no. 5 (2013): 695–719.

BIBLIOGRAPHY

Alim, H. Samy, and Geneva Smitherman. *Articulate While Black: Barack Obama, Language, and Race in the U.S.* New York: Oxford University Press, 2012.

Beech, Dave. *After the Educational Turn: Critical Art Pedagogies and Decolonialism.* London: Black Dog Publishing, 2018.

Blackman, Terrence, and John Belcher. "Using a Mathematics Cultural Resonance Approach for Building Capacity in the Mathematical Sciences for African American Communities." In *Transdisciplinarity in Mathematics Education: Blurring Disciplinary Boundaries,* edited by Terrence Blackman and John Belcher. New York: Springer, 2018.

Bolin, Mary K. "The Library and the Computer Center: Organizational Patterns at Land Grant Universities." *Journal of Academic Librarianship* 31, no. 1 (2005): 3–11.

Bolton, Gillie, and Russell Delderfield. *Reflective Practice: Writing and Professional Development.* London: Sage, 2018.

Butler, Judith. "Performative Agency." *Journal of Cultural Economy* 3, no. 2 (2010): 147–161.

Cassidy, Kyle. *This Is What a Librarian Looks Like: A Celebration of Libraries, Communities, and Access to Information.* New York: Black Dog & Leventhal Publishers, 2017.

Curry, Deborah A. "Your Worries Ain't Like Mine: African American Librarians and the Pervasiveness of Racism, Prejudice and Discrimination in Academe." *Reference Librarian* 21, no. 45–46 (1994): 299–311.

Daniels, Jessie. "Race and Racism in Internet Studies: A Review and Critique." *New Media and Society* 15, no. 5 (2013): 695–719.

Drake, Jarrett M. "I'm Leaving the Archival Profession: It's Better This Way." *Medium. On Archivy.* June 26, 2017. https://medium.com/on-archivy/im-leaving-the-archival-profession-it-s-better-this-way-ed631c6d72fe.

Droste, Frederik. *Locution, Illocution, and Perlocution*. Munich: GRIN Verlag, 2013.

Emirbayer, Mustafa, and Matthew Desmond. "Race and Reflexivity." *Ethnic and Racial Studies* 35, no. 4 (2012): 574–599.

Farmer, Ashley. "Archiving While Black." Chronicle of Higher Education. July 22, 2018. https://www.chronicle.com/article/Archiving-While-Black/243981.

Ford, Anne. "Underrepresented, Underemployed: In the Library-Job Search, Some Face Special Barriers." *American Libraries*. November 1, 2018. https://americanlibrariesmagazine.org/2018/11/01/underrepresented-underemployed/.

Goldman, Alvin, and Cailin O'Connor. "Social Epistemology." *The Stanford Encyclopedia of Philosophy*. Summer 2018. https://plato.stanford.edu/archives/sum2018/entries/epistemology-social/.

Gómez, Sarah Hannah. "The Weight of Being a Mirror: A Librarian's Short Autobiography." In *Topographies of Whiteness*, edited by Gina Schlesselman-Tarango. Sacramento, CA: Litwin Books, 2017.

Haile, Heven. "Hey Hey, Ho Ho, White Performative Allyship Has Got to Go." *Columbia Spectator Daily*. October 16, 2017. https://www.columbiaspectator.com/opinion/2017/10/17/hey-hey-ho-ho-white-performative-allyship-has-got-to-go/.

Hathcock, April. "ALAMW: What Happened and What Should Happen Next." *At the Intersection* (blog). January 30, 2019 https://aprilhathcock.wordpress.com/2019/01/30/alamw-what-happened-and-what-should-happen-next/.

Hudson, David James. "On 'Diversity' as Anti-Racism in Library and Information Studies: A Critique." *Journal of Critical Library and Information Studies* 1, no. 1 (2017). https://journals.litwinbooks.com/index.php/jclis/article/view/6.

Ingram, Ted N., Lavon Williams, James Coaxum III, Adriel A. Hilton, and Ivan Harrell. "The Motivational Factors of African American Men Enrolled at Selected Community Colleges." *Journal of Research Initiatives* 2, no. 1 (2016): 1–17.

Jao, Limin, and Nenad Radakovic, eds. *Transdisciplinarity in Mathematics Education: Blurring Disciplinary Boundaries*. New York: Springer, 2018.

Leonardo, Zeus. "The Souls of White Folk: Critical Pedagogy, Whiteness Studies, and Globalization Discourse." *Race Ethnicity and Education* 5, no. 1 (2002): 29–50.

McWhorter, John. *Talking Back, Talking Black: Truths about America's Lingua Franca*. New York: Bellevue Literary Press, 2016.

Mills, Charles. *The Racial Contract*. Ithaca, NY: Cornell University Press, 2014.

Paris, Django, and H. Samy Alim. *Culturally Sustaining Pedagogies*. New York: Teachers College Press, 2017.

Piotrowski, Chris, and Bob Perdue. "Factors in Attrition of Black Students at a Predominantly Euro-American University." *Psychological Reports* 83, no. 1 (1998): 113–114.

Pugh, Cikeithia, and Brooke Doyle. "Equity, Diversity, Inclusion: Seattle's 'Loud at the Library' Collaboration." *Children and Libraries* (Fall 2019): 27–29.

Rodgers, Kelly A., and Jessica J. Summers. "African American Students at Predominantly White Institutions: A Motivational and Self-Systems Approach to Understanding Retention." *Educational Psychology Review* 20, no. 2 (2008): 171–190.

Rowser, Jacqueline F. "Do African American Students' Perceptions of Their Needs Have Implications for Retention?" *Journal of Black Studies* 27, no. 5 (1997): 718–726.

Schlesselman-Tarango, G., ed. *Topographies of Whiteness: Mapping Whiteness in Library and Information Science*. Sacramento, CA: Litwin Books, 2017.

Teel, Karen. "Feeling White, Feeling Good: 'Antiracist' White Sensibilities." In *White Self-Criticality beyond Anti-Racism: How Does It Feel to Be a White Problem?*, edited by George Yancy. Lanham, MD: Rowman & Littlefield, 2015.

Tennis, Joseph T. "Intellectual History, History of Ideas, and Subject Ontogeny." In *Challenges and Opportunities for Knowledge Organization in the Digital Age*, edited by Fernanda Ribeiro and Maria Elisa Cerveira, 308–313. Wurzburg, Germany: Ergon Verlag, 2018.

Thorpe, Kirsten. "Transformative Praxis—Building Spaces for Indigenous Self-Determination in Libraries and Archives." *In the Library with the Leadpipe*. January 23, 2019. http://www.inthelibrarywiththeleadpipe.org/2019/transformative-praxis.

Yancy, George. *White Self-Criticality beyond Anti-Racism: How Does It Feel to Be a White Problem?* Washington, DC: Lexington Books, 2014.

Conclusion

LEE SKALLERUP BESSETTE

The work we study is rarely accidental. We do not stumble upon a subject and decide, willy-nilly, to study it.

—Amy E. Robillard, *We Find Ourselves in Other People's Stories* (2019)

❖ ❖ ❖ ❖ ❖ ❖ ❖

The world is literally in the process of burning. As I write this, Australia is engulfed in flames on the other side of the world from me, while up the road white supremacists are protesting and exercising their right to bear arms, and I am too afraid to check social media to see if anyone has yet died from a confrontation. But it is my privilege to be able to look away and write these words instead, or to watch safely from my own vantage point, relatively untouched, except to become increasingly numb to the news that can seem to get worse every day.

I start this conclusion with this grim predicament because I am sitting, looking at a blank screen, wondering what I can say that will make any sort of difference. But then I remember that this book is ultimately about relationships, and perhaps, probably, I hope that it is relationships—positive, nourishing, productive relationships among individuals—that will help us move forward to somewhere better than where we are right now in the early months of 2020.

Little did I know when first writing these words just how bad it was about to get.

We are all academics in this volume, even if not in title anymore. We step back to examine our positions, our institutions, and our relationships. We develop theories, produce strategies, and propose changes. Sometimes, it is enough just to name and acknowledge the things that we knew existed but weren't sure if anyone else did. We write to be seen, but also to let others know that they are, too, seen. That they are not alone. And that we are trying to forge a path forward.

Even the format of this book posed concerns about whose voices would be represented on that path. When I sent out the initial call for proposals for this collection, I knew that I was already making choices that would limit who would be able or willing to contribute; I had to balance the legitimacy that a traditional academic press would bring to a collection like this versus being unable to compensate authors for their affective labor in writing their contributions. I answered more than one interested and excited potential contributor with the news that I could not pay them for their contributions, and they replied that they no longer wrote without compensation, either for ethical reasons or plain economic ones, and often a mixture of both.

Please mine your feelings for free, I was asking. For a book about affective labor.

Others found themselves in precarious employment conditions, limiting their ability to speak openly about their workplaces, their challenges, their limitations. I remember when I would write publicly and visibly about being an adjunct or a contingent faculty member, receiving emails and messages from others in far more precarious positions than mine, telling me to keep writing, feeding me leads to write about or to forward to editors at my publication. Part of me feels a heavy responsibility to remember and write—as much for those who can't as for those who can.

And so this collection is made up of contributors who could afford to take the time and commit the labor to write through their affective and emotional states and who also have the job security to write about labor conditions, affective or otherwise. I was relying not only on their privilege and my privilege but also on our collective affective investment in the topic at hand. Fittingly, the concept of *affective investment* was coined by researchers Lisa Meloncon, Laura Wilson, and Mahli Mechenbier for their forthcoming book, *Investigating Contingent Labor Conditions.* Affective investment is partially what drives adjuncts to keep teaching in less-than-ideal labor conditions. More than the psychic wage, it is a "highly contextualized (depending on time and place) personal commitment to and participation in the relational configuration and interaction between material bodies, imbued with various emotions and physical and physiological characteristics; institutional and organizational infrastructures, embedded with their own cultural orientations; and the political and social aspects of decision making."[1] While going through the process of writing that book, Melançon began to theorize how affective investment is also a factor in the research process:

> Researchers who have to deal with difficult topics of all sorts experience a form of affective investment. If I were to alter this definition for research practice I would do it in this way. I would add that affective investment presses on both researcher and at times the research participants[,] and a reflexive component must be included in research practice to continually process the role of affective investment on the research project itself. In other words, the definition itself holds but the explanation of what it may mean and how to address it, deal with it, understand it shifts when you view it through the lens of research practice. To theorize research practice would mean to give terminology to existing practices and dilemmas faced by researchers while conducting research.[2]

My own affective investment in this project ran deep. Here it was less about the research itself and more about the editing of others' affective labor and investment. It nonetheless resonated with me and the work I was asking my contributors to do, which added to my own desire to get things "right."

I was overwhelmed when I received the abstracts, excited by the directions that the contributors wanted to take, the care they took with their contributions, the excitement expressed about the opportunity to write about affective and emotional labor as it relates to their varied alt-ac roles. What also surprised me, but probably shouldn't have, is how connected I am to almost all of the contributors. I am disappointed by the lack of some forms of diversity in the submissions, but I remember that just because one says they are open to diverse contributions, it doesn't immediately mean that everyone feels welcome to contribute.

Nancy K. Baym's theory of relational labor was helpful to me to better understand the network of contributions I received, and it represents a way to think about diversity and truly inclusive institutions and networks. In her book *Playing to the Crowd: Musicians, Audiences, and the Intimate Work of Connection* (2018), Baym defines relational labor as "the ongoing, interactive, affective, material, and cognitive work of communicating with people over time to create structures that can support continued work."[3] She goes on to enumerate a number of elements that compose relational labor, but most importantly, for me, "the ongoing sense making needed to understand yourself, others, and the relationships you are building."[4]

While Baym is primarily interested in musicians using relational labor to ensure music sales, gigs, and other economic benefits that support musicians' ability to continue practicing their art and craft, one can see the benefits of this approach to understanding academic networks, particularly when you are in a position of relative privilege and power, in an effort to increase the diversity of said network. Think of it this way: where is the motivation for someone to buy what I am selling? Where is the evidence that I had done the appropriate relational labor that would convince someone to trust me with a difficult topic such as affective and emotional labor?

Clearly I have done better work in some areas than others. The relative whiteness of the contributors tells me that I have not done the relational labor in this area effectively. That others were willing to disclose their own disabilities shows me that my work in that area has borne fruit. And I could simply hide behind the assertion that faculty development is still "primarily white and female."[5] I do not want to let myself off the hook, or let our profession off the hook, for not doing the work. I offer the concept of relational labor as a way forward to approach making alt-ac work more inclusive.

When the chapters came in, I was confronted with contributors' intimate thoughts and feelings, and I, as the editor, experienced a new (for me) form of professional intimacy, tasked with the responsibility of editing and possibly guiding and reshaping the authors' words and feelings in potentially uncomfortable directions. I have already asked so much, and now I am in a position to try to ask for more.

Adrian Kelly explored the concept of professional intimacy in faculty development, borrowing the term from research and theorizing on nursing. She notes that "the intimacy of academic development encounters is not prominent in academic development theoretical literature and perhaps is viewed dichotomously with skill."[6] In other words, it is to our detriment to talk about best practices, what the research of good teaching and learning tells us, and about the technical skills needed for our jobs, if we also divorce them from the affective skills necessary to accomplish the job of being skilled faculty developers—erasing and negating an essential part of our jobs.

Certainly, I can read every book on editing, academic and otherwise (and I have read quite a few for other writing projects), but they do not ever address the professional intimacy that an editing project like this requires. This becomes all the more evident when working with authors on particularly difficult and fraught topics, trying to help them write the best chapters possible for themselves and for the volume. I edited the words and made technical suggestions, but I also reassured, listened, changed my mind based on our interactions, encouraged, and practiced exactly the kinds of emotional labor described here in this volume.

This isn't to complain; this is the kind of work I expected when taking on a project such as this one. I had my own affective investment, my own history of relational labor, and my own experiences with professional intimacy to draw on in order to navigate the terrain successfully. It was a challenge I was happy to engage with—one that was far from toxic, but instead productive, and professionally and personally satisfying.

The purpose of this reflection-as-conclusion is to name, to give language to the various forms of affective and emotional labor that is required of us, that we perform on a daily basis in order to be effective at our jobs. But once we name it, what comes next? One of the hardest questions to answer is, so what do we do about all of this? We talk about it, for one, but take those conversations to the organization and structures with the goal to change said structures: "We need to speak at more interdisciplinary tables and to write precisely about our labor issues, as well as about the politics of knowledge organization and how our work impacts the production culture of the academy."[7] One reason I wanted to include as many different "staff" or alt-ac roles as possible was not only to learn from one another and what our professions have been discussing around these issues, but also to try to create a sense of solidarity across roles on campus, to encourage us to start or continue working together on these issues to change the academy for the better.

This volume, then, is an extension of Brandi Lawless's call that we document our emotional labor and continue doing so through scholarly pursuit.[8] And while Lawless is speaking to academics whose primary roles are more "traditional," aka professors, her words nonetheless represent an important call to all of us who work within institutions supporting students and faculty. The work of editing this book is both affective and scholarly. I have spent this conclusion outlining the emotional and affective work that I underwent while editing this book in order to highlight how intertwined it is with the scholarly work that I performed simultaneously. I want to name it; I want to give it language and context; I want it to fuel further conversations, scholarship, and ultimately change within our institutions.

The pandemic of 2020 (and beyond) has brought greater attention to the issues of the affective and emotional labor that staff across the university have been asked to perform, on top of the already taxing usual amount. Patrice Prusko and Whitney Kilgore wrote about "compassion fatigue" in instructional designers[9] while the Chronicle of

Higher Education devoted a full feature piece on burnout in the student services ranks,[10] and although the piece doesn't name affective or emotional labor, the descriptions of the new roles and responsibilities of these higher educational professionals would have fit alongside any of the chapters included here. My own contribution on the Chronicle of Higher Education website, "The Staff Are Not OK,"[11] was well-received from colleagues and strangers alike, in part because the piece appeared in the Chronicle and thus now the issues I described around emotional labor were seen as valid in the eyes of their bosses and administrators. I had not only given them language but also legitimacy.

I hope that this book becomes an even more powerful tool for staff to be able to advocate more effectively for the work that we do to be recognized and rewarded. The emotional and affective labor isn't going away, but as this collection shows, we need to have more and better conversations about what that means to us and to our work. I don't know what our institutions are going to look like on the other side of this global health crisis, but I remain hopeful that we remember the humanity of our staff and students and move forward collaboratively with the goal of rebuilding something better.

NOTES

Thanks to Thomas J. Tobin for his feedback.

1. Lisa Melonçon, "Affective Investment," *Lisa Melonçon Personal Blog*, June 13, 2019, http://tek-ritr.com/affective-investment/.

2. Melonçon, "Affective Investment."

3. Nancy K. Baym, *Playing to the Crowd: Musicians, Audiences, and the Intimate Work of Connection* (New York: NYU Press, 2018): 19.

4. Baym, *Playing to the Crowd*, 19.

5. Kathryn M. Plank, "Intersections of Identity and Power in Educational Development," *New Directions for Teaching and Learning* 159 (2019): 92.

6. Adrian Kelly. "Intimacy and Emotional Labour in Academic Development," *International Journal for Academic Development* 20, no. 1 (2015): 100.

7. Lisa Sloniowski, "Affective Labor, Resistance, and the Academic Librarian." *Library Trends* 64, no. 4 (2016): 663.

8. Brandi Lawless, "Documenting a Labor of Love: Emotional Labor as Academic Labor," *Review of Communication* 18, no. 2 (2018): 92.

9. Patrice Prusko and Whitney Kilgore, "Burned Out: Stories of Compassion Fatigue," *Educause Review*, December 1, 2020, https://er.educause.edu/blogs/2020/12/burned-out-stories-of-compassion-fatigue.

10. Emma Pettit, "They're Called #TeamNoSleep," Chronicle of Higher Education, January 13, 2021, https://www.chronicle.com/article/theyre-called-teamnosleep.

11. Lee Skallerup Bessette, "The Staff Are Not OK," Chronicle of Higher Education, October 30, 2020, https://www.chronicle.com/article/the-staff-are-not-ok.

BIBLIOGRAPHY

Baym, Nancy K. *Playing to the Crowd: Musicians, Audiences, and the Intimate Work of Connection*. New York: NYU Press, 2018.

Bessette, Lee Skallerup. "The Staff Are Not OK." *Chronicle of Higher Education*. October 30, 2020. https://www.chronicle.com/article/the-staff-are-not-ok.

Kelly, Adrian. "Intimacy and Emotional Labour in Academic Development." *International Journal for Academic Development* 20, no. 1 (2015): 93–104.

Lawless, Brandi. "Documenting a Labor of Love: Emotional Labor as Academic Labor." *Review of Communication* 18, no. 2 (2018): 85–97.

Melonçon, Lisa. "Affective Investment." Lisa Melonçon [blog]. June 13, 2019. http://tek-ritr.com/affective-investment/.

Pettit, Emma. "They're Called #TeamNoSleep." *Chronicle of Higher Education*. January 13, 2021. https://www.chronicle.com/article/theyre-called-teamnosleep.

Plank, Kathryn M. "Intersections of Identity and Power in Educational Development." *New Directions for Teaching and Learning* 159 (2019): 85–96.

Prusko, Patrice, and Whitney Kilgore. "Burned Out: Stories of Compassion Fatigue." *Educause Review*. December 1, 2020. https://er.educause.edu/blogs/2020/12/burned-out-stories-of-compassion-fatigue.

Robillard, Amy E. *We Find Ourselves in Other People's Stories: On Narrative Collapse and a Lifetime Search for Story*. New York: Routledge, 2019.

Sloniowski, Lisa. "Affective Labor, Resistance, and the Academic Librarian." *Library Trends* 64, no. 4 (2016): 654–666.

Contributors

❖ ❖ ❖ ❖ ❖ ❖ ❖

LINDSAY BERNHAGEN is the director of the Center for Inclusive Teaching and Learning at the University of Wisconsin–Stevens Point, where she is deeply involved in university and community service. In addition to teaching undergraduate and graduate courses in women's and gender studies, sociology, and education, she serves as editor of *To Improve the Academy* and maintains an active research agenda on women in higher education. Her writing has appeared in *To Improve the Academy, Studies in Graduate and Professional Student Development, New Directions for Teaching and Learning*, and *Slate*. Lindsay has a PhD in comparative studies; an MA in women's, gender, and sexuality studies; and an MA in music, all from Ohio State University.

LEE SKALLERUP BESSETTE is the assistant director for digital learning at the Center for New Designs in Learning and Scholarship at Georgetown University. Previous to working in faculty development, learning design, and academic technology, she was a contingent faculty member primarily teaching writing to traditionally underserved student populations at regional comprehensive state universities. Her writing has appeared in the *Chronicle of Higher Education, Inside Higher Ed, Women in Higher Education, ProfHacker, National Teaching and Learning Forum*, and *Educause Review*, among other places. She also cohosts a podcast, *All the Things ADHD*. Her website, readywriting.org, has links to more of her writing and podcast work.

CARLY J. BORN is the academic technologist for digital learning experiences at Carleton College. She has experience teaching English in Japan, Japanese in the United States, and instructional technology training for both K–12 in-service teachers and university professors. She has given numerous presentations at academic conferences, including the Educause Learning Initiative annual meeting, the Computer-Assisted Language Instruction Consortium, and the National Humanities Alliance.

She holds an MA in teaching Japanese as a foreign language with a specialization in computer-assisted language learning from the Monterey Institute of International Studies and an instructional design graduate certificate from University of Wisconsin–Stout.

DANIEL DALE is an assistant director of the Center for the Enhancement of Teaching and Learning and adjunct professor at the University of Cincinnati. In his previous position, he oversaw the supplemental instruction and learning assistant peer education programs, where he managed a large staff of student workers. He received his PhD in literary and cultural studies from the University of Cincinnati.

MELISSA DALGLEISH manages the Research Training Centre in the Hospital for Sick Children Research Institute, which serves more than 1,500 undergraduate, graduate, and postdoctoral researchers. In addition, she is the president of the Graduate and Postdoctoral Development Network, a Canadian consortium of graduate and postdoctoral career and professional development providers. Prior to joining the institute, Melissa launched the Graduate and Postdoctoral Professional Skills program at York University, where she earned her PhD. Her writing has appeared in *Inside Higher Ed, Chronicle Vitae, University Affairs, Hook & Eye,* and elsewhere, and she speaks and teaches about graduate career and program development at universities across North America.

MARTHA DIEDE directs the Center for Teaching and Learning Excellence at Syracuse University. In previous positions, she ran initiatives such as the Chancellor's Leadership Academy and offered workshops for the So-Con Academic Conference Leadership Development Program. She was also a full professor of English. She has written one book, *Shakespeare's Knowledgeable Body,* and coedited two others, *The Spirit of Adoption* and *Bridges Not Blockades: Transcending University Politics.* Her writing has also appeared in *Journal of Faculty Development* and several edited collections. She earned a PhD and MA in Shakespeare from Baylor University.

TRACI FREEMAN is the dean of the Endicott Center for Teaching and Learning and an associate professor of English at Endicott College. She has a PhD in English, with a specialization in women, gender, and literature, from the University of Texas at Austin. Her publications focus on writing pedagogy, writing center administration, and teaching and learning in a variety of contexts.

EMILY O. GRAVETT is an assistant director in the Center for Faculty Innovation and an associate professor in the Department of Philosophy and Religion at James Madison University. Her writing has appeared in publications such as *To Improve the Academy, International Journal for Academic Development, College Teaching, New Directions for Teaching and Learning,* and *Journal of Faculty Development*. Emily has a PhD in religious studies from the University of Virginia.

LEEANN HUNTER is a scholarly associate professor of English at Washington State University. She previously served as the assistant director of Undergraduate Studies in English, where she created the Passport Program: a mentoring and development program dedicated to promoting long-term personal and professional well-being through community-oriented practices. She currently implements these practices in specially designed classes that focus on work, wellness, growth, and transformation. Her work has appeared in the *Journal of Interactive Technology and Pedagogy, ADE Bulletin, Composition Forum,* and *WSQ: Women's Studies Quarterly*. She received her PhD in Victorian literature from the University of Florida.

REBEKAH KATI is the institutional repository librarian at the University of North Carolina–Chapel Hill. In this capacity, she acts as the service manager and product owner for the Carolina Digital Repository. She is coeditor-in-chief of the *Journal of Librarianship and Scholarly Communication*. Her research interests include repositories, open access, labor, and equity in scholarly communications. She received her master of library science and master of information science from Indiana University–Bloomington.

ELIZABETH LUNDBERG is a senior academic advisor and adjunct professor at the University of Iowa. As an advisor, she works mainly with students seeking admission to competitive or selective programs. She has a PhD in English from the University of Iowa and teaches general education and first-year experience literature courses. Her work has appeared in *GLQ: A Journal of Lesbian and Gay Studies, Deletion: The Open Access Online Forum in Science Fiction Studies,* and *Science Fiction Studies*. She has presented a version of her contribution to this volume at the National Academic Advising Association's national conference.

DEBORAH MARON is a doctoral candidate at the School of Information and Library Science at the University of North Carolina–Chapel Hill.

Her work focuses on racial justice in cataloguing and metadata practice, which includes analyses about how librarians believe their racial identity relates to the work they do in the library. She worked previously as a librarian for digital archives. Her scholarly writing has appeared in the *Journal of Documentation* and conference proceedings for the Dublin Core Metadata Initiative.

NICOLE PAPAIOANNOU is an instructional design consultant focused on workplace learning and virtual business solutions. As the owner of Your Instructional Designer and its learning network, the Upskill Experience, she helps her clients achieve performance goals through human-centered learning design and coaching. While Nicole currently works predominantly in the B2B space, her career journey began in academia as an adjunct professor, writing center consultant, and cofounder of #FYCchat. She has a PhD in English from St. John's University, where her doctoral research focused on student engagement, writing across contexts, and transfer of learning.

GRACE POLLOCK is a research support facilitator at McMaster University in Canada and former vice-chair of the University President's Advisory Committee on Building an Inclusive Community. In her work, she aims to foster connections among students, faculty members, and community partners in ways that broaden their access to resources and opportunities while also advancing institutional priorities. As a feminist scholar and member of intersecting equity-seeking groups, she strives to be an ally and collaborator in social justice initiatives within and beyond the university. She has MA and PhD degrees in English and cultural studies and a master of social work in community development.

KAREN ROSENBERG directs the Writing and Communication Center at the University of Washington Bothell. She helps students become stronger, more confident writers and advises faculty on how to best use writing to enhance student learning. She also designs and delivers writing workshops for faculty, social service providers, survivors of domestic violence, people without homes, and general community members. She has a BA in comparative literature from Swarthmore College and a master's and PhD in feminist studies from the University of Washington.

CELESTE TƯỜNG VY SHARPE is faculty in the History and Political Science Department at Normandale Community College. Previously, she was the interim director of academic technology and the academic technologist for instructional technology at Carleton College, where she managed a team of academic support professionals and worked on digital pedagogy and projects with faculty, staff, and student partners. She has published and presented on digital humanities practice and pedagogy, history pedagogy, and the scholarship of teaching and learning. She received her PhD in history from George Mason University.

JENNIFER HODL SOLOMON is coeditor-in-chief of the *Journal of Librarianship and Scholarly Communication* and adjunct instructor at the University of North Carolina–Chapel Hill School of Information and Library Science. Her teaching and research interests include diversity, equity, and inclusion in scholarly communications, open-access sustainability, and building community for academy-owned publishing. Her work has been published in both traditional and emerging scholarly formats such as *Mid-American Review*, *Serials Review*, and *Peer Review Toolkit*. She received her MFA in creative writing from Indiana University–Bloomington and her MS in library science from UNC–Chapel Hill.

MATTHEW J. TRYBUS is an ever-evolving human being whose life is steeped in affective labor. He is also the coordinator of Peer Assisted Study Sessions and an instructor in disability studies at James Madison University. His writing has appeared in *New Directions for Teaching and Learning*. He holds a master's in education from the University of Vermont.

Index